Funny Business

An introduction to comedy with royalty-free plays and sketches

MARSH CASSADY

MERIWETHER PUBLISHING LTD.
Colorado Springs, Colorado

Meriwether Publishing Ltd., Publisher
PO Box 7710
Colorado Springs, CO 80933-7710

Editor: Theodore O. Zapel
Cover design: Tom Myers

Cassady, Marsh, 1936-
    Funny business : an introduction to comedy with royalty-free plays and sketches / Marsh Cassady. -- 1st ed.
        p.   cm.
    Summary: Uses twenty-two sketches and one-act plays to explore the major devices of comedy and various comedic genre.
    ISBN 13: 978-1-56608-037-8
    ISBN 10: 1-56608-037-1
    1. Young adult drama, American. 2. Comedy. [1. Comedy.
2. Plays.]   I. Title.
PS3553.A79526F86   1997
812'.54--dc21   97-45060
                                         CIP
                                         AC

To E. Anne and Bob Pennington

CONTENTS

PREFACE

Funny Business is more than simply a book of comedy sketches and comic one-act plays. What makes it unique is that I have included examples of as many different forms of comedy and humor as possible, all with characters in their teens and twenties. I did this for several reasons. First, the wide choice of plays and sketches should, I hope, provide enjoyment and entertainment, as well as introduce readers to a greater range of comedy than they are likely to find in most anthologies. Second, such a range of comedy in one volume should make it easier to find material that suits individual needs both for acting practice and live performances. Third, the book defines the various types of comedy, comparing and contrasting each form to the others.

Because I didn't want to give away the endings of the sketches and plays before they are read, I have included only a brief introduction to each piece. In these introductions I discuss the type of comedy a piece illustrates and/or explain the comic devices it uses.

Knowing the style of a play can help to know how the playwright intended it to be seen and performed. This is important in that comedy has the widest range of any dramatic genre. Some comedy, of course, should be played broadly, some subtly.

Following each piece, I briefly discuss what should or can be considered in acting the roles and in preparing a total production. I also mention various themes touched upon in the pieces and the reasons for writing them in a particular way. I explain references to events, places, people and past or contemporary society and why each of these is important to the play or sketch.

I strongly believe in casting a play according to talent and ability, that is, without regard to race or ethnicity. I urge anyone presenting the plays to abide by this belief.

Performance rights to the drama sketches and plays included in this book are granted to amateur groups with the purchase of this book. Please refer to the copyright page of this book for additional information.

INTRODUCTION

The first goal of comedy is to create laughter. Because of this, some comedy exists only for entertainment. Much of it, however, has other goals, as well. Many writers want to teach us not to take ourselves too seriously. Some want us to change our behavior. Often, playwrights want either to point up or point out something they see as socially unacceptable, such as prejudice or injustice, or they may want to present their viewpoints and beliefs. Because of this we can see and read sketches and plays on women's or minority rights, war, political parties and politicians, and so on. Writers often show the ridiculousness of a part of life in an attempt to sway audience members to their point of view.

In most comedy, writers exaggerate characters, situations, feelings, and personality traits to emphasize them. Usually, this is to show that things we sometimes consider important don't matter much. A driver impatiently honks a horn, cuts in front of another car, or makes rude gestures, and the second driver reacts in kind — leading, in extreme cases, to violence. Behavior of this sort is a result of making something that is of little importance a major problem.

Playwright Neil Simon is a master at pointing up such small irritations. In *The Odd Couple*, Felix Unger constantly overreacts to Oscar's sloppiness. On the other hand, Oscar becomes so angry at Felix's pettiness that he slams a plate of linguine into the wall. In the play, this is funny. If we had to live with an overly neat person like Felix or a sloppy housekeeper like Oscar, we might not consider it funny. The humor comes from the exaggerated actions and reactions.

Any subject can be used for comedy if it can be treated humorously. However, it would be cruel to make fun of physical problems or illnesses. The only way this might be acceptable is if a character is laughing at his or her own limitations.

However, "black humor" does continue to exist. Medical students make bizarre jokes about cadavers. People often joke about others' deaths. This often is a way of fighting depression or despair. In part, it shows a person's relief at triumphing over death, at least for the time being, while the victim was not so lucky. After major tragedies, such as airplane crashes or bombings, there are jokes relating to these disasters. These stem from the same reactions. Years back, when a public figure was decapitated by the blades of a heli-

1

copter, jokes sprang up about this man's being the latest person to join the Rotary Club. On television, "Saturday Night Live" has mocked actress Katherine Hepburn's shaking as a result of Parkinson's disease. Though in bad taste, this sort of humor also is the result of rejoicing or maybe even feeling smug about our own good fortune.

More often, comedy deals with the things over which we can or should have control. Examples are egotism, greed, laziness, hypocrisy, lying, or cheating.

Comic protagonists often become involved in situations outside their knowledge or experience — a truck driver's posing as a psychoanalyst, for instance. The Peter Sellers film *Being There* (1980 and based on Jerzy Kosinski's book of the same name) is funny because everyone comes to view the central character as profound rather than as the slow-witted person he is. The film is not a satire of the character but rather pokes fun at people who need to attribute symbolic meaning to simple statements, or who feel that they need a guru to provide advice on how to live, instead of being self-reliant.

In other words, comedy makes fun of our wishing to be what we are not, on placing too much importance on achieving our goals. It begins with an idea in which normalcy is somehow reversed. Comedy always ends happily. The protagonist wins the battle against the opposition, as you see in the one-act plays in *Funny Business,* as well as in some of the shorter sketches. Otherwise, the audience might feel uncomfortable for having laughed. Thus it's important for the writer to establish a comic frame of reference (an atmosphere that is comic), so the audience learns how they are supposed to react. There should be no doubt that what the audience is about to see is being treated in a humorous way. For instance, plays and sketches in the book deal in a satiric way with such problems as drugs ("Users") and prejudice ("The Eyes of the World").

In most types of comedy, the audience should know early on that they are not expected to identify strongly either with the character or the situation. (An exception is the audience's laughing with instead of at the character.) It's the stiff, unyielding characters who refuse to admit the error of their ways that provide the most laughter. An example is Harpagon in Moliére's *The Miser*. His most outstanding trait is his greed, which nothing else in his life can begin to approach in importance.

Although there are many exceptions throughout history,

2

comedy often does not hold up across the years so well as tragedy does. Many comic devices depend on the here and now, with allusions to present society, trends, and individuals. Occasionally, plays such as these are revived, but more as curiosities or pictures of bygone days.

Comic Devices

To provide laughter, comedy relies on several devices: **exaggeration, incongruity, automatism, character inconsistency, surprise,** and **derision.**

Exaggeration means overstatement. Most people are not as greedy as Harpagon in *The Miser,* nor as finicky as Felix in *The Odd Couple.* Nor are they usually as desperate to ask for a date as Paul in "Puce" (page 17), though each of these is based on human traits, needs, or desires.

Incongruity refers to conflicting elements that in some way deviate from the norm, such as a woman's wearing a formal gown along with running shoes, gym socks, and a sweatshirt.

Automatism is repetition, a person's acting without thought (like a robot), rather than rationally. It includes a visual or verbal gag repeated over and over, thus becoming funnier each time. In the English TV series, *Keeping Up Appearances,* the central character Hyacinth is extremely pretentious and hates visiting her sister who lives in a run-down area of town. A running gag is that every time she passes a broken-down car in her sister and brother-in-law's yard, a dog pokes its head out and barks. Hyacinth is startled and falls into a hedge. This sort of gag is even funnier when there is a variation. In one episode Hyacinth remembers the dog and asks her husband to pass the car first. He does, and the dog doesn't bark. Hyacinth then thinks it's safe to go on. The dog barks, and Hyacinth again falls into the hedge.

Character inconsistency, similar to incongruity, exposes a trait that doesn't seem to fit in with the rest of a character's personality. In Joseph Kesselring's *Arsenic and Old Lace,* Abby and Martha Brewster are known for their goodness and kindness. What nobody realizes is that they murder lonely, old men.

Surprise includes many of the other devices. It is the unexpected. We know each joke or comedy sketch will have a punch line, but don't know what it will be. The pun, the wisecrack, or the insult can surprise us. In "Somewhere in the Appellations" (page 241), the audience expects to hear each character's unusual name. The surprise comes in finding out exactly what that name is and why it's unusual.

Derision is laughing at both people and society. Writers often mock hypocrisy, pomposity, or ineptitude. Yet if the derision becomes too bitter, it defeats its purpose in making the audience feel sorry for the intended victim.

Satire, which is similar to derision, also ridicules but is gentler than derision or sarcasm. An example is "How Do You Spell Tree?" (Page 59), which pokes fun at the idea of changing the way words are spelled.

Types of Comedy

There is a great deal of overlapping among the types of comedy, so that a piece of writing is often difficult to categorize. The two extremes, however, are **high comedy** and **low comedy**. This doesn't mean that one is better than the other, but only that the appeal differs. High comedy uses verbal wit and so appeals more to the mind or intellect; low comedy is largely physical or slapstick. At times comedy even has been defined as any piece that ends happily.

The ultimate in high comedy is **comedy of manners**, which pokes fun at the excesses and shortcomings of a particular social group, most often the upper class. Its opposite is **slapstick**.

All types of comedy have common ground. First, the audience learns early on that the situations and characters are to be viewed in a comic light. Second, the humorous aspects are exaggerated, both in writing and performance. Third, comedy relies on timing; it involves pacing and pauses preceding a punch line. Fourth, the characters tend to be more stereotyped or less individualized than in tragedy (although there are many exceptions to this), because the writers often are more concerned with development of the plot rather than with characterization. In many cases, a comic plot is more complicated than a tragic one.

There also are other genres that have many of the characteristics of comedy. These are **absurdism, tragicomedy, farce**, and **melodrama.** The various types of comedy and the related genres will be discussed in the introductions to individual plays throughout the book.

The Structure of Plays

The most common structure is the play with a plot, sometimes called the story play. It involves a conflict of wills or forces, the protagonist against the antagonist. In many plays this means the "good guy" versus the "bad guy." Usually we root for the protagonist, the central character. Most often we identify with this person and want him or her to win the struggle.

Usually, the central character is an individual, while the antagonist can be another person, self, society, or the forces of nature or fate.

Plot involves an **inciting incident, rising action** (which usually involves a series of minor crises), a **turning point**, a **climax**, and the **denouement** or **falling action**.

Something happens to upset the evenness of the central character's life, something brought about by the antagonist. This is the inciting incident. The rising action is the actual struggle. Each incident in the play is a minor crisis. Each intensifies the action, which continues to build until it is apparent there will be a change that cannot be reversed. This is the turning point. The climax is when the change actually occurs. Sometimes the turning point and the climax are the same, sometimes not.

A play's climax begins to show what will happen as a result of the struggle. The falling action completes the answer by tying up the loose ends. It explains how and why a thing happened, or sometimes shows the effects of the struggle and climax on the characters. In a comedy, the audience wants to enjoy the protagonist's win over the antagonist.

Although plays with a plot are the most common, there are other structures, as well. One is thematic structure in which a variety of scenes deal with the same basic issues but are unrelated in continuity and sometimes even have a different set of characters.

Circular structure starts and ends with a similar set of circumstances. Although there appears to be action leading to the solution of a problem, there is not.

There are various other types of structures, but these are the most common.

Bits, Sketches, and Routines

A **bit** is any short piece of entertainment regularly presented. The term comes from vaudeville, which is a type of variety entertainment in which there were an assortment of acts from those including animals to comedy routines to singers. (Vaudeville was most popular near the end of the nineteenth and the beginning of the twentieth centuries.) Although the term "bit" more often refers to a performance by one or two actors, it can be any short type of entertainment no matter how many are involved. The word also refers to a particular performer doing a piece of business, usually improvised as a result of audience response.

Comedy, as you know, is satirical in nature. It pokes gentle fun at a problem. A **sketch,** which in vaudeville, variety shows or revues, is a short scene or playlet, is usually complete in itself. Vaudeville and variety shows comprise the same sort of things, while a revue usually has much more music and often a theme that ties the entire piece together. It may be songs, sketches, and blackouts all tied to a particular theme, such as governmental waste in spending, for instance, or any other subject. A sketch or playlet is not developed as fully as a one-act or full-length play, so far as plot and possibly even character. It usually deals with a single and simple set of circumstances with few complications.

Sometimes a piece is tied together through a series of **one-liners,** jokes that really are only one sentence long. Going along with the Shakespeare theme in the bit or series of **blackouts** that follows the "Introduction," we might use one liners instead. For example:

ACTOR: *(Holding up a bottle of bleach for the audience to see)* **Remember, for getting out those nasty food or grease stains, use "Out, Damned Spot," the bleach that really works.** *(Macbeth)*

ACTOR: So...if "all the world's a stage," just who on earth is the audience? *(As You Like It)*

Of course, a bit can be more than one line long. For example:

ACTOR: So there I was just finishing up my dinner when Caesar came in. "Et tu, Bruté?" he said in this pathetic voice. Man, I felt bad. I had no idea his wife was out of town and the poor guy didn't even know how to boil water. *(Julius Caesar)*

Another term for one sort of bit is a **routine,** which is what we usually call the **monolog** delivered by a standup comedian. Although it occasionally consists of a series of unrelated jokes, most routines are built around a particular theme, such as differences in pronunciation from one area to another as in "In Plain English" (page 67). A monolog, of course, does not have to be a routine or even comic. In fact, even though it is delivered by only one person, it can be a play in itself. An example is "The Monolog" (page 249).

Wild Willie's Bardic Blackouts

The following bits also can be called blackouts in that there should be a break between each of the segments. The lights actually can go to black, but other methods work as well. In *A Thurber Carnival,* for instance, a "Word Dance" opens and closes the show. Every few seconds during their dance, the actors freeze (stop and hold their positions) while one of them steps forward and delivers a one-liner. When each is finished, he or she rejoins the dance.

Each of the following segments begins with a line from Shakespeare, which then is given a totally different and usually contemporary meaning, something obviously not originally intended. The excerpts from plays and poetry then provide the focal point or theme around which the series is unified.

The humor is a result of the unexpected answers to the lines, the twisting of the original meaning. The footnotes show the sources for the Shakespearean lines.

MOTHER: *(Complaining)* **Boil and bubble, toil and trouble!**[1]

TEENAGER: Forget it, Mom. I just asked for a cup of hot chocolate.

(Scene Change)

BOY: *(Romantically)* **Shall I compare thee to a summer's day?**[2]

GIRL: Me?! You're the one who's all sweaty!

(Scene Change)

MOTHER: *(As if pushing in a thumbtack and then standing back to admire her work)* **And thereby hangs a tale.**[3]

TEENAGER: Uh, Mom. Can I break it to you gently? It's my sixteenth birthday. Don't you think that's a little old for pin the tail on the donkey?

(Scene Change)

BOY: But men are men; the best sometimes forget.[4]

TEACHER: That's the weakest excuse I've ever heard for someone's not doing his homework.

(Scene Change)

WOMAN: Bid them wash their faces,
    And keep their teeth clean.[5]

BABYSITTER: Their faces and teeth! I thought I was just going to babysit.

(Scene Change)

BOY 1: *(Complaining)* **The beast with many heads butts me away!**[6]

BOY 2: *(Showing no sympathy)* **Come on, man, that's what happens if you play football.**

(Scene Change)

(BOY and GIRL crossing stage holding hands)

BOY: *(Jerking a thumb over his shoulder)* **Look where it comes again.**[7]

GIRL: I know, Paul! But he *is* my kid brother, and Mom said I had to watch him.

(Scene Change)

[1]*Macbeth*
[2]"Sonnet 18"
[3]*As You Like It*
[4]*Othello*
[5]*Coriolanus*
[6]*Coriolanus*
[7]*Hamlet*

BOY: How weary, stale, flat, and unprofitable
Seem to me all the uses of this world.[8]

FATHER: That may be. But until you get those grades up, no new computer games!

(Scene Change)

TEENAGER 1: Brevity is the soul of wit![9]

TEENAGER 2: Yep.

(Scene Change)

TEENAGER 1: He will discredit our mystery.[10]

TEENAGER 2: Yeah! Sure wish I hadn't signed up for creative writing.

(Scene Change)

TEENAGER: *(Quoting from book)* There is nothing either good or bad, but thinking makes it so.[11]

PARENT: Really? Then think about what fun you can have cleaning up your room!

(Scene Change)

TEACHER: It is the disease of not listening, the malady of not marking, that I am troubled withal.[12]

STUDENT: I didn't hear the question, OK? Is that a reason to give me detention?!

(Scene Change)

THE STUDENT PRINCE: Uneasy lies the head that wears a crown.[13]

TEENAGE FRIEND: Wouldn't it work if you just didn't wear it to bed?

(Scene Change)

FATHER: You blocks, you stones, you worse than senseless things.[14]

TEENAGER 1: Don't overreact, Dad.

TEENAGER 2: A couple of C-minuses isn't that bad!

(Scene Change)

[8]*Hamlet*
[9]*Hamlet*
[10]*Measure for Measure*
[11]*Hamlet*
[12]*Henry IV, Part 2*
[13]*Henry IV, Part 2*
[14]*Julius Caesar*

FATHER: *(Sarcastically)* **Passion, I see, is catching.**[15]

GIRL: Daaaaddyyyy! All he did was kiss me goodnight. And I kissed him back.

(Scene Change)

FATHER: How sharper than a serpent's tooth it is
        To have a thankless child.[16]

TEENAGER: So thank me already.

(Scene Change)

BASKETBALL PLAYER 1: *(Bouncing basketball)* **Fair is foul, and foul is fair.**[17]

BASKETBALL PLAYER 2: Yeah, so what do you think? We should buy the ref new glasses?

(Scene Change)

MOTHER: *(Holding her arm out in front of her; gazing at the open palm)* **Is this a dagger I see before me?**[18]

SON: For gosh sake's, Mom, it's my Boy Scout knife.

(Scene Change)

TEACHER: Leave no rubs nor botches in the work.[19]

STUDENT: You mean if we mess up just once, we have to copy the whole thing over?

(Scene Change)

TEACHER: Bring me no more reports; let them fly all.[20]

TEENAGER: *(To audience)* **Seems to me the teachers are looking forward to summer vacation as much as we are.**

(Scene Change)

TEACHER: Here are a few of the unpleasant'st words that ever blotted paper![21]

STUDENT: *(Whining)* **So does that mean you're going to give me an "F"?!**

(Scene Change)

[15]*Julius Caesar*
[16]*King Lear*
[17]*Macbeth*
[18]*Macbeth*
[19]*Macbeth*
[20]*Macbeth*
[21]*Merchant of Venice*

STUDENT 1: A victory is twice itself when the achiever brings home full numbers.[22]

STUDENT 2: Keep rubbing it in. A hundred percent on your math test.

(Scene Change)

PARENT: Put money in thy purse.[23]

BOY: Purse! You gotta be kidding. No way am I carrying a purse.

(Scene Change)

BROTHER: *(Dejected; complaining)* O! this learning, what a thing it is.[24]

SISTER: For heaven's sake, Rick, just shut up and do your homework.

(Scene Change)

BOY: What say you to a piece of beef and mustard?[25]

GIRL: I've told you time and again, Tom. I'm a vegetarian. V-E-G-E-T-A-R-I...

(Scene Change)

STUDENT 1: O vile,
Intolerable, not to be endur'd![26]

STUDENT 2: Oh, come on. It's only five weeks till summer vacation.

(Scene Change)

MOTHER: A very ancient and fish-like smell.[27]

TEENAGER: OK, Mom, OK. I told you I'd clean out the cat's dish.

(Scene Change)

STUDENT: As an unperfect actor on the stage,
Who with his fear is put beside his part...[28]

MOTHER: Don't feel bad, honey. Out of the whole play, you messed up on only one line.

STUDENT: Mom, I had only one line!

(Scene Change)

[22]*Much Ado About Nothing*
[23]*Othello*
[24]*The Taming of the Shrew*
[25]*The Taming of the Shrew*
[26]*The Taming of the Shrew*
[27]*The Tempest*
[28]"Sonnet 23"

STUDENT 1: Full many a glorious morning have I seen
Flatter the mountain-tops with sovereign eye,
Kissing the golden face with meadows green,
Gilding pale streams with heavenly alchemy.[29]

STUDENT 2: *(Nodding; matter-of-factly)* Yeah, we went camping last summer too.

(Scene Change)

BOY: All men make faults.[30]

GIRL: Faults! Faults! You call it faults! Forgetting to pick me up for the prom!

(Scene Change)

BOY: Live with me and be my love,
And we will all the pleasures prove.
That hills and valleys, dales and fields,
And all the craggy mountains yields.[31]

GIRL: Don't be silly! We're only fifteen years old.

(Scene Change)

GIRL 1: *(Reading from a book)* Eye of newt and toe of frog[32]

GIRL 2: *(Making stirring motions)* Uh, Sara.

GIRL 1: *(Glances at GIRL 2)* Yes?

GIRL 2: Are you sure this is going to end up being brownies?

(Curtain)

---

[29]"Sonnet 33"
[30]"Sonnet 35"
[31]"Sonnets to Music"
[32]*Macbeth*

Production Notes and Considerations

You probably will want to deliver the Shakespearean lines in an exaggerated Elizabethan style. In preparation, you might want to read about different acting styles or even try to see a Shakespeare play on TV or film.

The responses, of course, can be delivered using a comic/realistic style in which the delivery can be exaggerated or heightened while suggesting everyday speech.

You may want to stage each blackout in a different area of the stage than the preceding, so that the entire sequence moves quickly. You can use different actors for each or simply rely on a group of eight or ten who go from one scene to another.

Where a generic name such as "Teenager" or "Parent" is used, the role can be played by either a male or a female.

A series of blackouts has to move quickly, which means it is important to pick up cues. It also is important to figure out the key words in the punch line and emphasize them through changes in tone, loudness, and/or by pausing slightly before saying them.

All in all, blackouts are one of the easier types of comedy to perform in that each goes fast, and there isn't the problem of memorizing a lot of lines or even of establishing a three-dimensional character. Of course, when delivering any of the non-Shakespearean lines, you can exaggerate sarcasm, protest, complaints, and so forth. An example is the word "Daddy" in the blackout that begins with "Passion, I see, is catching." The main thing is to have fun performing the piece.

15

Puce

In this sketch, the problem is the Boy wanting to ask the Girl for a date. He doesn't know how to go about it, so he takes a strong offensive approach, which he hopes will get her attention. Once he gets her to notice him, he can change tactics. At least that's his plan.

Obviously, since this is satire, it uses the device of exaggeration and incongruity in that we wouldn't expect someone to approach another so forcefully in this sort of situation.

There is surprise both in the Boy's approach and in the ending, which, at least for a time, seems to be moving in the opposite direction.

CAST: BOY, 16 or 17; GIRL, 16 or 17.

SETTING: The action takes place in the hall between classes. The GIRL wears a burnt-orange sweater; the BOY wears a puce-colored shirt and green running shoes. Otherwise, both are dressed casually for school.

AT RISE: The GIRL is taking her books from her locker Center Stage. As she looks up, the BOY enters Stage Left and crosses toward her. He stops a couple of feet away.

BOY: **That's the ugliest thing I've ever seen.**

GIRL: **What!**

BOY: **That orange thing.**

GIRL: **My sweater?**

BOY: **Makes me sick to my stomach.**

GIRL: **I can't believe this. Who do you think you are –**

BOY: **You don't have to be insulting!**

GIRL: **Me! You're out of your mind.**

BOY: **You don't have to get personal.**

GIRL: **Sheesh! Why am I even carrying on this stupid conversation? Just forget it. I'm going to be late for class.** *(She starts toward exit.)*

BOY: *(Grabbing her arm)* **I don't want to forget it. You said I was crazy.**

GIRL: **I'm sorry, OK? Just leave me alone.**

BOY: **Well, I don't think so.** *(Pause)* **I'm not, you know.**

GIRL: *(Furious)* **Not what!**

BOY: **Craz – Hey, why are you getting so angry?** *(Laughs.)*

GIRL: *(Annoyed, yet curious)* **Why are you laughing?**

BOY: **We meet in the hall, and out of nowhere we're having this argument.**

GIRL: **Let go of me.**

BOY: **I didn't mean anything. I was trying to help. You're...you're really a very attractive...woman. It's just that hideous sweater. Bet your mom picked it out, didn't she? I can't believe anyone our age –**

GIRL: **Not that it's any of your business, but I picked it out myself. I**

happen to like it. A lot.

BOY: Uh-huh. But you're not the one who has to look at it? Sure, if you happen to glance down. But it's people coming toward you. Or people behind you. Oh, well, I know we can't all have good taste.

GIRL: *(Incredulous)* Are you trying to tell me that you have good taste?

BOY: Yes. I suppose anyone can develop *some* sort of taste. But a sense of it is really something you're born with.

GIRL: *(Sarcastically)* Oh, really?

BOY: *(Shrugs.)* Yeah, like I said.

GIRL: You call that puce – that puce thing tasteful!

BOY: My shirt. *(Laughing)* Hu. Hu-hu-hu. Ho-ho-ho-ho. You really think – hu-hu – that greyish purple isn't tasteful? That it's ugly? *(Breaks up laughing.)*

GIRL: Ugly isn't the word!

BOY: *(Serious, attentive, short-tempered)* What!

GIRL: Anyone who wears a puce-colored shirt with those horrible green running shoes –

BOY: I paid a lot for these shoes.

GIRL: *(Sarcastically)* I am *sooo* impressed. *(A beat)* How much? A dollar ninety-eight? Four dollars tops?

BOY: Why are you making fun of me?

GIRL: Are you for real?

BOY: *(Acting hurt)* You know...it's possible my dad could be out of work. And Mom could be – Oh, man, why would you even care?

GIRL: *(Feeling sorry)* Look, I don't even know anything about you –

BOY: That's the problem.

GIRL: What do you mean?

BOY: You never even noticed I exist. Right?

GIRL: Well –

BOY: Isn't it?

GIRL: *(Biting her lower lip; trying to keep from smiling)* Not entirely, no.

BOY: Not entirely?

GIRL: You're in my American history class.

BOY: *(Shrugs.)* Yeah. I am.

GIRL: And you used to sit next to the wall, right by the door in Mrs. Drummond's art class. Last year, I mean.

BOY: You noticed me?

GIRL: Yes, why?

BOY: Actually, I think the sweater's attractive.

GIRL: What!

BOY: Why not?

GIRL: But you said –

BOY: Can I tell you the truth?

GIRL: What?

BOY: *(He closes his eyes for a moment, then opens them.)* Will you promise me something? *(GIRL shrugs.)* Promise you won't hate me?

GIRL: Hate you? *(Pause)* I have the impression that you may be a little...strange. But I don't hate you.

BOY: That's good; that's very good. So what I want to say is...I think the color's fantastic.

GIRL: Color?

BOY: Your sweater.

GIRL: You said it was the ugliest thing you've seen.

BOY: I lied.

GIRL: Why?

BOY: OK. Time for confessions. I wanted to ask you out.

GIRL: Then why the insults?

BOY: I didn't think you'd pay attention. I mean if I just came up and said, "Hey, Pam, let's go to a movie."

GIRL: You know my name?

BOY: I've known your name...for months now. For years.

GIRL: I know your name too, Paul. I always thought you were...

BOY: That I was what?

GIRL: Girls aren't supposed to say things like this. To boys, I mean. To other girls, it's OK. I think you're kinda...cute.

BOY: You – you think I'm –

GIRL: I do. Yes.

BOY: Then you'll...What I mean is...So *can* we go to a movie or something?

GIRL: No.

BOY: *(Shocked)* No? But you said you think I'm cute.

BOY: I do.

BOY: But you won't go out with me.

GIRL: *(Truly regretful)* I'm sorry, Paul. I really am.

BOY: I don't understand. You know what I did...was just a way to get you to notice me.

GIRL: I know, and it's OK.

BOY: It's OK? Then why won't you –

GIRL: Go out with you?

BOY: Yeah. Like maybe to the next home game?

GIRL: You want the truth?

BOY: I guess so.

GIRL: *(Walks by him and then turns back.)* I'll give it to you straight, Paul. I really can't stand puce!

(Curtain)

Production Notes and Considerations

If anyone were to try an approach like the Boy's, most likely it would be in a more joking manner. Therefore, when playing the role, you might want to project the over-assertiveness with an underlying hint of shyness. Keep in mind, though, that until near the end, the Boy lets go only briefly of his aggressive behavior. With the line, "You don't have to be insulting!" he is accusing the Girl, unjustly, of doing something that he obviously and deliberately is doing himself. He seems to be gambling on the idea that she will want to hear what he says because it is an unusual approach. His laughter at her anger is a slight change of tactics, also designed to keep her interest, which is waning since she tries to leave. Right after this he alters his approach once more by saying he finds the Girl attractive. Then he goes immediately back on the offense by saying she's not the one who has to look at the sweater.

The Boy then becomes extremely discourteous when he says that "we can't all have good taste." At this point, you probably could show a hint of uncertainty or else an overreaction or overcompensation in the use of laughter to show the audience that he realizes he is taking a chance here. This is a crucial point for him. Will the Girl stay, or will she leave immediately?

The Boy most certainly is delighted to know that the Girl has noticed him in class. You need to figure out how to show this feeling to the audience without having the Girl notice it.

The Girl most likely would be surprised and then disturbed or miffed by the Boy's approach. As the scene progresses, the emotion turns more toward amusement.

In playing the Girl's role, you need to decide why you think she stands and listens to all that the Boy says. Is it because she is too astounded to leave, or is it that she really does feel that he's "cute"? You need to analyze the character to figure out what sort of person she is and why she would reveal something like this to him. Besides projecting the emotions already mentioned, you may want to try to show a hint of regret that she has to turn him down. At the same time, you may want to provide a glimpse of her aversion to the Boy's shirt.

Since this sketch at least appears more realistic than "Wild Willie's Bardic Blackouts," you may want to deliver the lines in as realistic a manner as possible. The situation carries this scene, so the piece probably would fall flat if you over-exaggerated. As the last, this piece should move quickly.

You can have a simple set or none at all. There can be a locker or substitute for one, but it isn't necessary. The Girl can pantomime getting her books, or you can simply eliminate the business with the locker.

Ringside

The name "Ringside" refers to the fact that the two characters Beth and Paige, in being the friends of Susie and Oriana respectively, are at the "ringside" of their friend. But then in Scene iii, the term takes on a totally different meaning.

Although confrontations such as the one in "Ringside" do sometimes occur in everyday life, the situation is exaggerated and overblown. The real basis of the problem is the girls' explosive personalities, which makes this a satire since it involves something over which the characters should have better control.

The piece relies largely on the devices of exaggeration in the two situations getting out of hand, and surprise, particularly at the ending. Further, there is an incongruity in arguing over Shane since he really is free to date whomever he chooses, and there is no evidence that he even wants to date Oriana.

Although there is the potential for physical action, this piece would be classified as high comedy in that it is laughing at a situation and character traits — temper and stubbornness — which cause the girls to get themselves too deeply into a situation that shouldn't cause any problem at all.

"Ringside" is closer to being a play than either of the pieces so far, though it actually lies somewhere in between a sketch and a play. It is more fully developed than "Puce" in that there is a problem in which several people become involved. So there seems to be a plot that builds in intensity as Oriana and Susie argue. And the complications seem to build further when each tries to talk to and thus receive help from her friend in solving the problem of having to confront the other.

"Puce," on the other hand, presents a problem in one simple confrontation. However, both "Puce" and "Ringside" rely on a surprise or trick ending. Although there is humor in involving Beth and Paige in the last scene, this also keeps the piece from being a play with a plot in that Oriana and Susie do not solve the problems themselves, something characters in a story play always have to do. The piece does have a circular structure in that it ends as it begins, except with a different set of characters.

CAST: SUSIE, ORIANA, PAIGE, BETH. All are about 16.

SETTING: The action occurs on the sidewalk outside a high school, and in PAIGE's bedroom and in BETH's bedroom.

AT RISE: It is just after the end of the school day. SUSIE enters Stage Right and ORIANA enters Stage Left. They meet center.

Scene i

SUSIE: I hear you've been trying to get close to Shane.

ORIANA: So what?

SUSIE: I'm warning you to stay away.

ORIANA: That doesn't mean I'm going to.

SUSIE: He's my boyfriend, and I mean to keep him.

ORIANA: From what I can see, he's nobody's slave.

SUSIE: I'm gonna make you wish you never heard of anyone named Shane.

ORIANA: I don't think so.

SUSIE: I'm just telling you one more time.

ORIANA: I'm telling you I'll do as I please.

SUSIE: Get this through your head. He's my boyfriend.

ORIANA: *(Shrugs.)* If you were woman enough, you wouldn't have to worry.

SUSIE: If you were woman enough, you'd get your own boyfriend.

ORIANA: You telling me I can't get my own boyfriend?

SUSIE: If the shoe fits, girl...

ORIANA: I'm getting sick of you and your insinuations.

SUSIE: *My* insinuations?

ORIANA: *(Making a big show of looking all around her)* **Don't see anyone else around. At least anyone who's going to make me do something I don't want to do.**

SUSIE: Listen to her talk. Well, it doesn't worry me.

ORIANA: Isn't that something? Who was it who came up to me just now and told me to keep away from this person named Shane?

SUSIE: You know something? Nobody, and I mean nobody, in his or her right mind, wants to be around someone like you. A person would have to be crazy.

ORIANA: What's that you're saying?

SUSIE: I know the words for people like you. But my mama wouldn't want me saying those words out loud.

ORIANA: Your mama what!

SUSIE: You too dumb to know what I mean? Too stupid to find your own boyfriend? Gotta go off and steal someone else's?

ORIANA: I'm not stealing anything. Everyone knows you can't keep a boyfriend. Boys go out with you on a dare. Who's the stupidest girl? Susie. Who's the ugliest girl? Susie. Who's the –

SUSIE: Shane talks to you 'cause he pities you. I don't want him wasting his time.

ORIANA: What are you going to do about it?

SUSIE: I'm going to make you sorry you were ever born.

ORIANA: You saying what I think you're saying?

SUSIE: You got it!

ORIANA: Name the time.

SUSIE: Tomorrow. Right after school. Right here.

ORIANA: I'll be waiting. *(She crosses toward the Stage Right exit. SUSIE immediately crosses toward Stage Left. They deliberately bump each other. The lights fade to black.)*

Scene ii

(The lights come up to reveal two chairs Stage Left, and two chairs Stage Right. Immediately, ORIANA and PAIGE enter Stage Right while SUSIE and BETH enter Stage Left. Throughout the scene the actions and speeches on each side of the stage nearly match each other. The scenes are played simultaneously, although only one pair of characters speaks at the same time. ORIANA and PAIGE freeze while SUSIE and BETH speak and vice versa.)

ORIANA: How do I get myself into these things?

PAIGE: What things?

SUSIE: I got myself into it this time.

BETH: Into what?

ORIANA: I don't know what's wrong with me.

PAIGE: Sit here. I'll sit on my bed.
SUSIE: Sometimes I think I've lost it completely.
BETH: Sit down. Bed or chair. It doesn't matter.

ORIANA: Thanks.
PAIGE: Now what is it?
SUSIE: Chair's fine.
BETH: So what's this about?

ORIANA: You know I've been seeing Shane.
PAIGE: Shane McInnis?
SUSIE: Shane and I had a couple of dates. Nothing major. We saw a
movie. Then I went to this picnic with him and his folks.
BETH: Shane McInnis? Yeah, I know.

ORIANA: We've talked a few times. Sat by each other in the cafe-
teria.
PAIGE: And –
SUSIE: He usually stops by and walks me to school. After school he
has that job at the supermarket.
BETH: And –

ORIANA: OK. Susie Phillips was going with him.
PAIGE: Yeah?
SUSIE: Oriana started talking to him. Going around school with
him.
BETH: So what does that mean?

ORIANA: She thinks I'm taking him away from her.
PAIGE: Are you?
SUSIE: I think she's trying to take him away from me.
BETH: Couldn't they just be....friends?

ORIANA: Yes – No – I don't know.
PAIGE: *(Ironically)* Sure, I understand.
SUSIE: Yes – No – I don't know.

BETH: Have you asked him about it?

ORIANA: I like him, right?
PAIGE: If you say so.
SUSIE: He's the first guy I've been interested in. I mean really.
BETH: That's what I figured.

ORIANA: Maybe I shouldn't encourage him. He was with Susie.
PAIGE: He's a big boy. He can make up his mind.
SUSIE: I don't want to lose him. But if he prefers to be with Oriana...
    I don't know what to do.
BETH: He's a big boy. He can make up his mind.

ORIANA: I know.
PAIGE: So?
SUSIE: I know that.
BETH: So...I'm sure he likes you. I mean I can tell just by seeing you
    two together.

ORIANA: That's not the problem.
PAIGE: You're losing me, Oriana. Fact is, I'm already lost.
SUSIE: I hope so. But that's not the problem right now.
BETH: Did I miss something here?

ORIANA: It's Susie.
PAIGE: What about her? You don't feel sorry for her?
SUSIE: It's Oriana.
BETH: Oriana? Are you afraid if she finds out you're the one Shane
    likes...

ORIANA: For Susie? You gotta be kidding?
PAIGE: Then what's going on?
SUSIE: You gotta be kidding.
BETH: Then what's this about?

ORIANA: I met Susie after school. Maybe she was waiting for me. I

29

don't know.

PAIGE: I think I'm beginning to see the light.

SUSIE: After school I saw Oriana. Maybe she was waiting for me. I don't know.

BETH: Think I'm finally beginning to understand.

ORIANA: She told me to leave him alone.

PAIGE: And knowing you, I bet I can predict what happened.

SUSIE: I told her to leave Shane alone.

BETH: And knowing you, I have a pretty good idea what happened.

ORIANA: Yeah.

PAIGE: So what did happen?

SUSIE: Right.

BETH: So what did happen?

ORIANA: We got into this fight...argument. You know what? I hardly even know Shane McInnis. He's good-looking. Seems nice enough –

PAIGE: But once Susie called you on it.

SUSIE: We started to fight...to argue. It got worse. I was being silly. They haven't gone out. Shane's with me except sometimes at school and when he has to work.

BETH: But I'll bet Oriana wasn't about to admit that.

ORIANA: I always have to get so defensive...

PAIGE: By going on the offense.

SUSIE: I have this temper that gets me into trouble.

BETH: You're telling me.

ORIANA: You know me, all right.

PAIGE: So what happened? You argued and then what –

SUSIE: You know me, all right.

BETH: What happened? You two argued and –

ORIANA: I can't believe this. She said all kinds of things, implied a lot more.

PAIGE: And all the time you just stood there, huh?

SUSIE: I can't believe it. She said a lot of stuff about me, called
me –

BETH: And you just let her say all those things?

ORIANA: *(Chuckles.)* Sure, you know me.

PAIGE: So she said things, and you said things, and then...

SUSIE: *(Chuckles.)* Sure. You know the kind of person I am.

BETH: So she said things to you, and you said things to her. And
then...

ORIANA: I'm scared. I got a big mouth, I know that. Always getting
me into trouble.

PAIGE: Go on.

SUSIE: I'm scared. I'm always mouthing off. And it gets me into
trouble.

PAIGE: Go on.

ORIANA: We're supposed to meet tomorrow after school. I can't
believe this, I really can't. We're going to have it out.

PAIGE: Fight? Fists and fingernails? That kind of fight?

SUSIE: We're going to have it out with each other. I can't believe
this. I haven't had a fight since kindergarten.

BETH: You mean like a real fight? Punching and gouging? That
kind of fight?

ORIANA: What am I going to do?

PAIGE: I don't suppose you'd want to pick up my phone and –

SUSIE: What am I going to do?

BETH: You wouldn't consider just picking up the phone and –

ORIANA: And what!

PAIGE: OK, OK.

SUSIE: And what!

Beth: All right, all right.

31

ORIANA: Call her? I couldn't do that. You know me. And what's everyone going to think?
PAIGE: Everyone?
SUSIE: I couldn't call her. You know me better than that. And if I did, what would everyone think?
BETH: Everyone? Who, for instance?

ORIANA: I don't know who all she told. I just know I don't want to do this.

SUSIE: I don't know how many people she told. I just don't want to go through with it.

Scene iii

(We are back in front of the campus just after the close of school the following day. At Stage Right SUSIE and BETH are peering around the corner of a tree or maybe the edge of the school building. At Stage Left ORIANA and PAIGE are doing the same thing. Until BETH and PAIGE meet center, the two sets of characters nearly mirror each other as they did in the previous scene.)
SUSIE: Can you see? Is she there yet?
BETH: There's no one there. Believe me.
ORIANA: Is she out there? Can you see her?
PAIGE: I don't see anybody.

SUSIE: Maybe she won't show up.
BETH: We can always hope.
ORIANA: Maybe she isn't going to show.
PAIGE: I hope you're right.

SUSIE: But I don't believe it.
BETH: Knowing her, I wouldn't either.
ORIANA: I'm sure she will though.
PAIGE: I bet she does too.

SUSIE: It's past time.

BETH: *(Glancing at her watch)* **Just a little.**

ORIANA: She's late.

PAIGE: *(Glancing at her watch)* **A couple of minutes.**

SUSIE: Are you sure you can see?

BETH: I can see.

ORIANA: Are you sure she's not hidden. Maybe something's blocking our view.

PAIGE: What? There's nothing there to block any view.

SUSIE: Do me a favor?

BETH: What?

ORIANA: Will you do something for me?

PAIGE: What is it?

SUSIE: Will you go out and look?

BETH: Why not?

ORIANA: Will you walk out to the sidewalk and see if she's there?

PAIGE: Be glad to, even though she's not.

(BETH and PAIGE cross a few steps toward center.)

PAIGE: Beth, what are you doing here?

BETH: What about you?

PAIGE: Bet you're checking up to see if Oriana chickened out.

BETH: She did too, didn't she?

PAIGE: I don't see Susie around anywhere.

BETH: She's here, all right, which is more than I can say for Oriana.

PAIGE: Oh, yeah?

BETH: You better believe it.

PAIGE: You know what I believe, girl? You don't know what you're talking about.

BETH: Says who?

PAIGE: I say. So what are you going to do about it?

BETH: I'm not afraid of you.

PAIGE: Well, I'm not afraid of you either!

BETH: Oh, yeah?

PAIGE: Yeah. I can beat you anytime.

BETH: Well, I guess that now's your chance. *(PAIGE and BETH lunge for each other as the lights fade to black.)*

(Curtain)

Production Notes and Considerations

You may notice that the way Oriana and Susie speak in the first scene is different from the way they talk in Scene ii and even in Scene iii. In the first scene, each is trying to appear "tough" or unbeatable to the other. They try to come across as much more sure of themselves than they really are. The humor relies on their going too far and then agreeing to face each other the following day.

Further humor occurs when the audience is led to believe that because Paige and Susie are sympathetic, they may help.

Although arguments obviously occur in real life, they usually spring up for stronger reasons. It's silly and illogical for the two girls to fight over Shane since he and Susie have had only two real dates, and so far as we know, he and Oriana are merely talking with each other.

The last scene is exaggerated and condensed in that it is conceivable, though probably not anticipated until close to the end, that Beth and Paige would also confront each other. The scene also would lose humor or punch if it were as long as the first scene between Susie and Oriana.

There is a touch of automatism in the last scene because Paige and Beth, the supposed peacemakers, react to each other just as Oriana and Susie did.

In performing the roles of Oriana and Susie in the first scene and the roles of Paige and Beth in the last scene, the actors should use a realistic style, while still exaggerating their actions and reactions to show that their feelings and their need to "win" are getting out of hand. The scenes between Paige and Oriana and between Susie and Beth should be realistic, though played at a lower emotional pitch than in the scenes for confrontation.

The break between each nearly matching pair of lines in Scene ii should help to point out the similarities between the two sets of speeches and so make it easier to see the similarities and differences of each set.

The piece can be presented without any setting. All that is really necessary is to have two seats of some sort Stage Left and two Stage Right. Everything else can be imaginary.

Users

The idea for "Users" was developed from a *turnabout*, a situation where something is given a 180-degree twist, so that it's exactly opposite of reality, yet with a little bit of truth.

The piece seems to start out on a serious note, though the reader or audience member soon discovers that this is a cover-up. The play is not serious at all. It is a satire, poking fun at people in general, rather than at anyone specifically. It pokes fun both at what our bodies consume and at how truth over the years can become twisted and distorted. It's highly unlikely that a situation such as this ever would exist, which means the subject matter is highly exaggerated.

Although "Users" is a satire, its main purpose is to entertain.

CAST: The Pushers: LARRY, 14-17; RODNEY, 14-17; WENDY, 14-17; JEN, 14-17. The Pushees: TYSON, 14-17; MICHELLE, 14-17.

SETTING: The action occurs on the campus of a high school. It is early morning some time in the future.

AT RISE: LARRY, RODNEY, WENDY, and JEN, dressed all in black, each wearing jeans, running shoes, baseball caps, and windbreakers or warm-up jackets, sneak in from Stage Right. They are hunched over, obviously hiding various objects under the jackets.

LARRY: Now remember, I'm counting on you. You need the stuff yourself, you gotta sell it. It's a fair deal, remember that. Pure stuff, all of it. I don't go in for cutting it. An ear is a full ear. Same with the other stuff. Be careful, that's all, but when you got someone hooked, make sure you show what you're selling. But you still got to keep it hidden from anyone else.

RODNEY: Hey, man, why we gotta go through this same thing all the time? Every morning, the same speech.

WENDY: It's OK by me to have a little bit of reminding. Keeps us on our toes, right?

RODNEY: You sound like my old lady. I been doin' this for what – a couple of months already.

WENDY: Yeah, which means you could start to get careless.

RODNEY: Who made Larry the ruler of the world?

JEN: Well, I'm with Wendy. I'm glad to be reminded. I'm scared enough, as it is.

RODNEY: Yeah, well, OK, that I can understand. I remember how it was my first week too. Just gotta be careful who you approach. That's the main thing. You'll find there are some people who are gonna turn you in just for the fun of it.

LARRY: It's the radicals you have to watch out for. That's been my experience.

JEN: You mean you've been busted?

LARRY: Yeah...I have. Got off with a warning. *(Laughs.)* 'Cause I had no priors. What a laugh!

RODNEY: Like you ain't been doing this for no two, three years now.

LARRY: Proves my point. You gotta be careful. *(Pause)* Now look,

38

kids are gonna be coming along any time now, OK? Here's what I want you to do. Rod, you go –

RODNEY: My name's Rodney, man. Got that?

LARRY: All right...*Rodney*. Teamwork, that's the key to it.

RODNEY: I ain't takin' no rap for nobody else. Ain't no teamwork. Every man for himself.

WENDY: Man?

RODNEY: OK, OK. It's a figure of speech.

WENDY: "Woman" would do just as well. And in case you don't know that's spelled: W-O-M-Y-N! 'Cause I ain't no part of you, *man*! And you ain't no part of me.

LARRY: All right, all right. I think we just need to consider each other here, and what we're trying to do.

RODNEY: What we're trying to do is spread the word. Show the advantage of using. What we're trying to do is get 'em hooked, whether you say so or not.

JEN: I suppose that's true, but...

WENDY: Don't back out, Jen. It's important.

JEN: Well, what if I do?! I'm not so sure about this.

LARRY: It's a hard, cruel world, Jen. You'll get your own supply cut off. Understand?

RODNEY: Better heed what he says, little girl, or you're gonna be going through agony. Right?

LARRY: That's the rules, Jen. Sorry.

JEN: You wouldn't...You couldn't! *(Cries.)* I never thought...I've always been the kid who never got into trouble.

WENDY: Nothing's going to happen. Just remember what you've been told. It's a big school. You see kids you know, steer the other direction.

JEN: Dressed like this? They take one look at me, they're gonna know.

RODNEY: Gotta protect ourselves, Jen.

JEN: Yeah, but aren't you taking a chance. What if I tol – Never mind.

WENDY: Don't even think about it.

RODNEY: Am I missing something here?

39

LARRY: Forget it, Rodney.

RODNEY: No, I wanta know what I missed.

WENDY: Don't blame her. We all had doubts, didn't we? Didn't we all think of quitting? Ratting on each other? Be honest now.

LARRY: Sure, we did. Right, Rodney?

RODNEY: Long time back, I expect. Wouldn't do nothin' like that now. Wouldn't even enter my head.

LARRY: Hey, we gotta get in position. *(As LARRY speaks to each of the others, he sends them to various areas of the stage. By the time they're finished, all four are evenly spaced from him and from each other. Their movements are furtive. All except RODNEY appear worried. He exudes a swaggering confidence that merely shows his basic insecurity and the danger of the situation.)* Jen, the safest place, I think, is right over there. *(He points.)* See? By the bench. Close to the street. If you sense trouble, you can always run. Rodney, you stand next to Jen, between her and Wendy. Since this is her first day, she probably could use a boost to her confidence. *(He smiles at JEN.)* If there's trouble, divert attention away from her.

RODNEY: *(A touch of derision in his voice)* Sure thing. Rodney is always willing to do his civic duty.

LARRY: OK, let's go. Once you're rid of all your stuff, you can quit. If there's time and you want to, Jen, you can change clothes before school starts.

JEN: Good. I really don't want my friends seeing me. Can I ask a question?

LARRY: Go ahead.

JEN: How come we have to dress like this?

RODNEY: Should be obvious, baby. It sets us apart; shows who we are. Anyone who is wanting or needing, all the person has to do is look up and see us.

JEN: Pretty dumb of me, huh?

WENDY: Hey, you're going to do all right. *(All take up their positions. TYSON and MICHELLE enter Stage Right, crossing slowly and talking.)*

MICHELLE: Did you get the third question on the algebra homework?

TYSON: Yeah, why? Didn't you get it?

MICHELLE: No, I – My God!

TYSON: What!

MICHELLE: I don't believe this. Jen, is that you?

JEN: Oh, no. *(Tries to turn away.)*

MICHELLE: Jen?

JEN: *(Turning slowly to face them. Miserably)* It's me.

TYSON: Not you! Of all people. You joined them?

MICHELLE: Why?

JEN: To be able...I'm a user, all right? Yeah, I know. Not Jen; she'd never do a thing like that.

MICHELLE: How long?

JEN: Last summer. We visited my grandparents. I stayed there a week. One day I found these plants.

MICHELLE: There on the farm?

JEN: Don't look so shocked.

MICHELLE: Why did you do that?

JEN: There's nothing wrong with it. Look, I'll show you.

MICHELLE: I don't want to see this. If I don't see it, I won't have to say for sure that you were...You know what I mean.

JEN: Trying to push these? *(She yanks open the jacket and draws out a bunch of carrots.)* Yeah, I use 'em. Nothing wrong with it either.

TYSON: Carrots! Yeah, well, I guess I have heard things –

MICHELLE: *(In disbelief)* Tyson? What are you saying?

TYSON: All I'm saying is what I heard.

MICHELLE: I'm listening.

TYSON: At this lab they've tested them. Just on rabbits so far.

JEN: It's true, what you heard.

MICHELLE: Not you, Jen. I can't accept it.

JEN: Look at me, will you?

TYSON: Something's different! *(Peering closely at her)* Yeah, I see it. You're not wearing –

MICHELLE: What! You used the money you made to buy contact lenses!

JEN: I can't wear contacts, you know that.

MICHELLE: Your allergies. Yeah, I forgot. They irritate your eyes.

TYSON: It's true then, what I read? Carrots improve eyesight.

JEN: Maybe. I don't know.

MICHELLE: But the glasses. You used to wear thick glasses.

JEN: I still don't see as well as I should, but I think I'm improving.

MICHELLE: Maybe...so long as it's only carrots. You haven't –

JEN: I have. I really have. *(She turns toward the others.)* **Wendy? Guys?** *(LARRY, WENDY, and RODNEY all look toward her.)* **Come here, OK?**

MICHELLE: I don't think this is such a good idea. Anyhow, I heard that carrots can be a hallucinogen.

TYSON: I've heard rumors, but I doubt it. Kids thinking they can fly and jumping off roofs. Just on carrots. Nah, I don't think so.

MICHELLE: Why are you so sure? You haven't –

TYSON: Once. I mean, I had to find out. *(LARRY, WENDY, and RODNEY come up to the others.)*

LARRY: Problems, Jen?

JEN: No, it's just...This is Michelle, my best friend. And Tyson. He's a good friend too.

WENDY: Bad luck, Jen. Your friends.

TYSON: No, it's OK. I kind of side with you. I can't see anything wrong with carrots. Sure, I wouldn't eat the tops. But the rest of the plant is darned good.

RODNEY: Lots of vitamins.

MICHELLE: Vitamins? I heard they were dangerous –

LARRY: Dangerous. No way. I was reading up on this. People used to take vitamins every day. Helped the body in all kinds of ways.

MICHELLE: You can't get me to believe something like that.

RODNEY: He's right.

WENDY: I don't mean to butt in where I don't belong, but... *(Shrugs)* well, it's even said they help prevent the common cold.

MICHELLE: *(Sniffing)* Cold! I always have a cold.

RODNEY: Maybe if you tried –

MICHELLE: No!

RODNEY: Look, baby, OK, all right. I'm backing off.

JEN: I heard that too. Did you know that there was this famous man...Dr. Linus Paul – whatever.

TYSON: Linus Pauling. Yeah, I heard of him. Didn't he win a Nobel Prize or something?

WENDY: Two Nobel Prizes, actually.

MICHELLE: You're kidding!

WENDY: No, really.

RODNEY: And this dude said that by taking lots of vitamin C – Wasn't it C? *(Looks to Larry who nods.)* Yeah, vitamin C, you could prevent a lot of colds.

MICHELLE: So...do carrots...Do they have this vitamin C thing?

WENDY: A lot of fresh vegetables do.

MICHELLE: You've...tried other kinds?

JEN: Come on, guys, show her.

RODNEY: Naw. It isn't a good idea.

MICHELLE: Hey, now you got me curious. I really want to see.

RODNEY: *(Removes a couple of ears of corn from inside his jacket.)* Corn. You eat it right off the cob.

TYSON: Off the what?

RODNEY: Cob, man, this cylindrical-like thing they grow on.

TYSON: Hmmm. I see.

LARRY: Or you can cut it off and cook it separately.

MICHELLE: Jen. You've tried this too?

JEN: *(Biting her lip)* I admit it.

TYSON: *(To WENDY)* So what are you hiding?

WENDY: *(Pulls out two ripe tomatoes.)* Vine-ripened tomatoes.

TYSON: I heard of them too. Centuries back people used to think they were poison.

MICHELLE: But they are!

TYSON: No, they're not.

MICHELLE: I don't believe this. You sound like – It's like you believe in all this stuff. In legalizing it.

TYSON: Well, maybe...

LARRY: Didn't seem to bother our ancestors. There are old records of people living on nothing but vegetables and fruits.

MICHELLE: Vegetarians! Yeah, I know. We read about them in history. How could they be so –

43

TYSON: Healthy?

MICHELLE: That isn't the word I was going to use.

JEN: Michelle? Are you all right? You don't look so good.

MICHELLE: Oh, God. I've never been around this sort of thing. For the family and me it's basic stuff like candy bars, burgers, steak, a slice or two of white bread.

WENDY: Bread comes from a vegetable.

MICHELLE: What?

TYSON: Wheat that makes flour.

MICHELLE: But that flour was – I don't know. Fixed. Changed somehow. Made OK to eat.

TYSON: *(To LARRY)* So what are you hiding under your jacket?

LARRY: I'm not sure I should tell you that. It's the hard stuff, OK?

TYSON: Like what?

LARRY: You sure?

TYSON: *(To MICHELLE)* Michelle?

MICHELLE: What the heck! How could I be more shocked?

LARRY: *(Pulling out a couple of stalks of broccoli)* OK, here it is.

MICHELLE: What...is it?

WENDY: Broccoli!

MICHELLE: Broccoli. But didn't some president say that that was the worst of all. I mean, other – ugh – vegetables are bad enough. But broccoli!

RODNEY: The president's name was Bush. George Bush. Things got twisted around a bit though, I think.

MICHELLE: What do you mean? That's where the whole thing started, right? This president – Bush?

RODNEY: Yeah.

MICHELLE: He said that anyone possessing even a kilo of broccoli would have his right to cook removed.

LARRY: No, not quite.

WENDY: I've studied this a bit too. It was a sort of snowball effect.

JEN: What do you mean?

WENDY: That's what started it. This happened around the end of the twentieth century. People started thinking that maybe broccoli really was bad for you.

RODNEY: And pretty soon, legislators were making the whole shebang illegal. Possession of nearly any vegetable.

MICHELLE: And the world has become a much better place because of it.

JEN: You can't believe that, Michelle, you really can't. I mean if you'd only try —

MICHELLE: No, no! I'm willing to be a little open-minded here, but that's as far as I'll go.

WENDY: *(Takes a paring knife from her jacket pocket and cuts off a piece of the tomato.)* **Here, just smell it.** *(She thrusts it under MICHELLE's nose.)* **See!**

MICHELLE: Oh, God, I'm so hungry. I want it. I want that tomato.

TYSON: What about your candy bars, your cola, a piece of steak or a sausage patty? Butter, grease, fat!

MICHELLE: No, no. I gotta have it. I need it. I don't care how much it costs. I don't care. *(She grabs a carrot in one hand and a tomato in the other. She takes a bite from the carrot and then the tomato.)* **Heavenly.** *(Pause)* **Oh, God, what will my mom say? My dad? My grandmother? Everyone? I'm in trouble. I'm really in trouble.**

RODNEY: What you have to do is convince them. Subtly at first, a hint or two.

WENDY: Maybe leave a slice of tomato lying around where they can smell it.

MICHELLE: Do you think it will work? Do you think it really will work?

LARRY: Can't tell you, Michelle. It's a choice you have to make. A choice we all have to make for ourselves.

MICHELLE: I'm going to try it. I really am. Tyson?

TYSON: Yeah?

MICHELLE: What about you?

TYSON: OK, the cat's out of the bag. I didn't just try carrots once. Eat 'em all the time. Peppers and beans and corn and peas. That's about all we ever have anymore at my house. Why do you think I never invited you over? I couldn't tell you. I was scared, Michelle. Afraid you wouldn't —

MICHELLE: *(Shakes her head in disbelief.)* **To think...this time**

yesterday, it would have mattered. It would have mattered a lot!

LARRY: So what do you say?

MICHELLE: What do you mean?

JEN: Will you join us?

MICHELLE: Join you?

RODNEY: The movement to legalize vegetables.

MICHELLE: I say...let's go for it.

TYSON: That's my girl. *(The others all gather around hugging, laughing, crying, cheering as the lights fade to black.)*

(Curtain)

Production Notes and Considerations

What if "angel dust" or "crack" or "grass" had nothing to do with illegal drugs? What if they didn't exist? What then would be illegal? What would drug dealers push? Since this is a turnabout, it has to be something healthful, not something dangerous or deadly. Well, what's one of the most healthful things there is? Vegetables. How could this be funny? Well, there's always been a battle between parents and kids — especially young kids — about eating vegetables. But what if this were turned around? What if parents didn't allow their kids to eat vegetables? Or what if things, at least, became so twisted that laws were passed banning the eating of vegetables? Americans, as a whole are overweight. Why? Because of junk food, lots of good old red meat, and cholesterol!

And what if a United States president named George Bush publicly denounced the eating of broccoli — or at least said he wouldn't eat it. (He did, in fact, say this.) And what if, as years passed, this statement became all twisted around so that it was the germ of a movement that led to the banning of all vegetables, except those that were highly processed, changed, and de-vitaminized. And what if the general public didn't even know anymore what vitamins were? Then we'd have the basis of a turnabout play.

"Users" is a satire of the American way of eating, taking it to the extreme where people have to become criminals to sell, buy, and eat vegetables. The piece in no way is meant to condone the use of drugs. Rather, it completely reverses the fact that parents often try without success to get their families to eat vegetables so that now vegetables have come to be thought of as dangerous.

In playing any of the roles, it's okay to exaggerate but not so much that the play becomes completely melodramatic in acting style. Since there are more roles in "Users" than in any of the preceding, you need to do a thorough job of analyzing your character, figuring out why the person feels, talks, and reacts as he or she does. Much about the characters is only implied, so you have to build on these implications to make the role come alive.

Rodney, for instance, talks tough. Why do you suppose that is? Is he really tough, or is he overcompensating in some way? (A hint may be provided in the stage directions that say, "He exudes a swaggering confidence that merely shows his basic insecurity," etc.)

What sort of backgrounds do you think these characters have?

What do you suppose their parents think about the subject of illegal vegetables?

You need to figure out why Michelle is so much against eating vegetables and then why she gives in so quickly. Much of the humor, of course, comes from the idea that once she smells a tomato she's hooked.

There is a feminist statement in the play, as well. Why do you think Wendy feels as she does? Is this logical? Why do you suppose she mentions it when she does? Do you agree with her sentiments or not? Why?

You need to figure out the most humorous lines and why they are humorous. Once you do this, you can more easily determine how to present these to an audience. For instance, it's an extreme over-statement to suggest that "carrots can be a hallucinogen." How do you think Michelle ever got such an idea? Do you think she really believes it? She makes other outrageous statements such as the one about the "kilo of broccoli." Do you think it logical that the truth can become distorted? Can you think of any real life examples where, over time, a distortion of truth has occurred?

"Users," as the other pieces so far, requires no specific set. In fact, it can be performed on an empty stage. There is reference to a bench, but it can be imaginary. You will need special costuming for the "Pushers" so they can be set apart from Michelle and Tyson. It can be black or any other color or color combination, just so they dress alike for easy identification and to suggest that they may be members of a street gang — but a gang with a difference. They are united only to push the idea of legalizing vegetables.

Father Knows Better

"Father Knows Better" is a parody of the old television series, "Father Knows Best," a situation comedy. Like the characters on the series, Father and Mother simply are too naive and perfect, seeing the world through a rosy haze. The "Father Knows Best" family was romanticized in the same way, and all the problems were fairly minor — like having two dates for the same school function, and so on.

The piece deals with a subject that is universal, existing from the first time a parent ever bumbled into doing something really dumb for a child, but all with the best of intentions. The play is simply for fun, deriving much of its humor from the fact that nearly everyone, young or elderly, can recognize themselves and their parents in it. The piece is a character comedy, which means that it deals with the eccentricities of a particular individual. It carries characters' personality traits to extremes. It also is a situation comedy, which means that the characters are involved in unusual situations. This sort of comedy more often than not is associated with television. Each segment, much like an episode of a television series, revolves around a particular situation, all either entirely created or else intensified by the father. The entire play revolves around Father's being proud of his three teenagers and wanting to help them out in as many ways as he can. Yet he doesn't stop to think things through.

Rather than having a plot, the play is a series of connected scenes and monologs unified around the theme: If Father would only stop to think, he would know better. The piece has a circular structure in that nothing really changes, and nothing is solved. So far as we know, Father will continue to behave as he has throughout the play, despite being told over and over again that he knows better. The title is a play on words, implying that Father knows better than anyone else how to handle a situation versus his knowing better than to do something to humiliate his children.

CHARACTERS: FATHER; MOTHER; HEIDI, 14; DIANE, 17; SEAN, 16; RESTAURANT MANAGER, 20s; MRS. HIGGINS.

SETTING: Various locations including a fast-food restaurant, the Thompson family dining room, and an office at a high school.

AT RISE: As the lights come up, HEIDI enters and crosses Down Right to the edge of the stage. SEAN and DIANE enter and cross Down Left to the edge of the stage. They listen as HEIDI addresses the audience.

HEIDI: My dad's a nice man. Nobody could possibly believe that he isn't. Yet he's...well, I suppose you could say socially challenged. He's always doing these stupid things that end up really embarrassing one or more of us kids. One time, see, my brother wanted to buy this guitar. Been saving money for it for a long time. Then he got a job at this fast-food place, OK? Bussing tables. It was Sean's first actual job, and he was real happy about it. He figured in two or three months he'd have enough money to buy exactly the kind of guitar he wanted. Mom and Dad were proud of him, and well, OK, he's my big brother, and he's always pulling these dumb things on me. But, well, I was proud of him too. You know what happened? I hate to tell you because:

SEAN, DIANE and HEIDI: *(In unison)* **Father knows better!**

(The lights come Up Left on the fast-food restaurant where SEAN works. It consists of a counter and a couple of small tables. The MANAGER stands behind the counter. SEAN is busily cleaning the tables when FATHER walks in.)

MANAGER: Good evening, sir. May I help you?

FATHER: Good evening.

SEAN: *(To himself)* **Oh, no!** *(He squats behind one of the tables trying to hide from FATHER.)*

FATHER: I'm looking for the manager.

MANAGER: That would be me, sir.

FATHER: I'm Sam Thompson. My son works here.

MANAGER: Oh, you're Sean's father.

FATHER: Yes. It's his first job, you know. I just wanted to check that

he's doing OK.

MANAGER: Oh, fine. No problem.

SEAN: *(Spreading his hands, palms up, speaking to himself)* **What did I do to deserve this? Tell me what?**

FATHER: Hiring him was a good thing then?

MANAGER: Well, yeah, I suppose so.

SEAN: *(Still to himself; exasperated)* **Go home, Dad. Go home. Go home.**

FATHER: I'm sure he's a good worker but a typical teenager, if you know what I mean.

MANAGER: *(Losing interest)* **I wouldn't know.**

FATHER: He's a good boy. And I assure you that if there are any subjects that need to be addressed, Sean and I will have a man-to-man talk.

MANAGER: I don't think that will be necess –

FATHER: Oh, no problem. I'm proud of my son. Very, very proud. And I just wanted you to know that I'll do anything I can to help him through life's perilous sea.

SEAN: *(Standing up and screaming)* **Aaaargh! Aaaargh! Aaaaaaargh!**

FATHER: Son, I didn't know you were here.

SEAN: It's where I work, Dad.

FATHER: Of course. I mean, I didn't see you.

SEAN: I can't imagine why.

FATHER: Your manager and I were just having a nice chat. *(DIANE enters Down Left just as HEIDI enters Down Right. They look at SEAN and FATHER.)*

SEAN, DIANE, HEIDI: *(In Unison)* **Father, you know better than that.** *(The lights quickly fade to black and then come up a second or two later. SEAN stands alone at the Down Right edge of the stage. HEIDI and DIANE cross to Down Left edge of the stage.)*

SEAN: If that sort of thing happened only once in awhile, it wouldn't be so bad. Overall, I wouldn't want to trade my dad for anyone else's. He loves us kids and Mom too. But I think that's sometimes the problem. He wants to do things for us, things he thinks are good. But he needs to give them more thought because:

SEAN, HEIDI and DIANE: *(In unison)* **Father knows better!**

(The lights fade to black and come up on the Center Stage area where FATHER and the three children are seated around the dining room table. MOTHER enters carrying a casserole dish, which she sets on the table. FATHER quickly rises and pulls out her chair. She sits. Throughout the scene, when appropriate, the family pantomimes eating dinner.)

FATHER: I have a surprise for you, Diane.

DIANE: *(Knows it can't be good.)* You have...a surprise?

MOTHER: Well, whatever it is, dear, don't keep us in suspense.

FATHER: Well, you know, Dan Lucas and I work together?

DIANE: Kyle's father?

MOTHER: Don't interrupt, dear, you father is trying to tell you something.

HEIDI: *(Stage whisper to SEAN)* Something Diane won't want to know, I'll bet.

SEAN: *(Whispering to HEIDI, sarcastically)* Whatever would make you think that?

MOTHER: Sean, dear. Heidi, sweetheart, don't distract your father.

SEAN and HEIDI: *(Simultaneously)* Sorry, Mom.

FATHER: Now then. As I was saying, I know how much you like young Kyle.

DIANE: Father!

FATHER: It's true, isn't it? Didn't I hear you tell your mother that you wish Kyle would ask you to the senior prom?

SEAN: Uh-oh!

HEIDI: Oops!

MOTHER: Please, children, please. Your father is trying to speak.

DIANE: *(Through gritted teeth, the words are in a monotone and evenly spaced.)* Yes-I-said-that-why-are-you-asking?

FATHER: Well then.

DIANE: *(Becoming hysterical)* "Well then" what?!

FATHER: What did I say? Did I say something wrong?

HEIDI: *(To SEAN)* Not yet, he didn't.

SEAN: *(To HEIDI)* But you know it's coming.

MOTHER: Children, please. Do give your father the respect he deserves.

HEIDI and SEAN: *(Rolling their eyes)* **Yes, Mother.**

FATHER: **Well, today I saw Dan and asked if he'd like to go to lunch at that French restaurant on Third Street. You know the one, Mother.**

MOTHER: **Well, yes, I believe I do.**

FATHER: **My treat, I told him. And, of course, he was glad to accept.**

MOTHER: **Why wouldn't he be?**

FATHER: *(Somewhat surprised)* **Well, yes.**

DIANE: **What-has-this-to-do-with** *me?!*

MOTHER: **Diane, sometimes I just don't understand your behavior. I try my best.**

DIANE: *(Very short with her)* **I'm sorry.**

MOTHER: **Thank you, Diane.** *(To FATHER)* **Please do go on, dear.**

FATHER: **As I said –**

HEIDI: **We know what you said, Daddy?**

FATHER: **Er...uh, what's that?**

SEAN: **She said, "We know what you said, Daddy."**

FATHER: **Yes, yes, of course.**

MOTHER: **Do get on with it, dear. I've made the most glorious dessert. An old recipe handed down to me by my great Aunt Hilda –**

DIANE: **Mother, please!**

MOTHER: **Yes, dear?** *(DIANE shakes her head and lets her body fall against the back of the chair.)*

FATHER: **At any rate, Dan's a nice guy. Never knew him well. Found we have a lot of the same interests. Our families, our community, global peace, human welfare.**

HEIDI: *(Mumbling to herself)* **That narrows it down, all right.**

SEAN: **Father?**

FATHER: **Yes, son?**

SEAN: **I do believe Diane would like to know the surprise.**

DIANE: *(Breathing hard as if exhausted, she turns to SEAN, nodding her head up and down repeatedly.)* **Thank you, Sean. I owe you one.**

FATHER: **Well, yes. Here it is then. I told Dan of your interest in his son.**

DIANE: *You what?!*

MOTHER: Diane, what has come over you? I just don't understand the younger generation. Why back in my day –

DIANE: *Mother, please!*

MOTHER: What, what? What?

HEIDI: Mother, I believe she wants Father to continue.

SEAN: *(To himself)* Get this over with, more likely.

DIANE: Daddy, please, tell me. Now. Right away. What did you say, Daddy? Please. Tell me, what did you tell Mr. Lucas? Tell me, please. Please, tell me.

FATHER: Well, now, isn't this nice. It looks like my little scheme is a success. You're so eager to find out...makes a man feel as if it's all worthwhile.

HEIDI: *(To SEAN)* Can you believe this?

SEAN: *(To HEIDI)* Oh, sure. Can't you?

FATHER: Yes, well, I told him how much you liked young Kyle, and how you'd been wishing he'd ask you to the prom.

DIANE: You didn't! Tell me you didn't!

FATHER: Oh, yes. Anything for my children.

DIANE: *(Swallowing hard)* And...and –

MOTHER: Diane, are you all right?

DIANE: *(She juts out her chin at MOTHER and quickly jerks her head around to face FATHER.)* Well...what did he say?!

FATHER: Well, of course, being the sort of man he is – forthright, understanding, he said he'd speak to the young man, insist he give you a call.

DIANE: *(Angry scream!)* *Whaaaaaat!*

SEAN and HEIDI: *(In Unison)* Father, you know better than that.

FATHER: I do? Yes, yes, I guess I do. I've...done it again, haven't I?

(The lights quickly fade to black and then come up a second or two later. DIANE stands alone at the Down Right edge of the stage. HEIDI and SEAN enter Down Left and cross to the edge of the stage.)

DIANE: Can you imagine how humiliated I was? An honor student, homecoming queen, class president. And Father was out asking people to have their sons call and ask me to the prom.

But that's dear old dad. Actually, he is a dear. He just doesn't stop to think. And it's not just one of us who've felt the heavy hand of interference. Oh, no, all three of us live in constant dread knowing that at any time disaster can strike because:

DIANE, HEIDI and SEAN: *(Shouting in unison)* **Father knows better.** *(The lights fade to black and quickly come up again Stage Left where there is an executive-type desk and chair and two other chairs. Behind the desk sits MRS. HIGGINS, in charge of admitting new students to Benjamin Harrison High School. HEIDI and FATHER sit in the other chairs.)*

MRS. HIGGINS: So this is our new student, is it?

FATHER: That's right.

MRS. HIGGINS: What's your name, young lady?

HEIDI: Heidi Thompson.

MRS. HIGGINS: I'm sure you'll find the students friendly. And the teachers more than willing to answer questions.

FATHER: She is an exceptional young woman, you know.

HEIDI: Daddy!

FATHER: Very, very bright.

MRS. HIGGINS: Yes, now if we can get you to fill out –

FATHER: Don't know where she got her brains. Her mother, I suppose. Oh, I was bright enough. But nothing like Heidi. All her teachers have told Mrs. Thompson – that's her mother – and me that she was just about the brightest –

MRS. HIGGINS: *(Losing her patience, though trying to be pleasant)* **As** I said, if you have proof of vaccinations –

FATHER: Besides being bright, she's very, very talented.

HEIDI: *(Grimacing in agony, she twists her hands over and over in front of her chest.)* **Please, Daddy, don't do this.**

FATHER: Well, of course I will, darling. I'm proud of you. Your mother and I are proud of you. *(Turns back to MRS. HIGGINS.)* Why just last year, in her last year of junior high school, before we moved, Heidi placed first in the county in the annual spelling bee! Isn't that wonderful? And she plays the piano like an angel. An absolute angel.

HEIDI: Daddy, please. Please, please. Daddy, I have to go to class. I want to go to class. Please let me go to class.

FATHER: See what I mean? Such an eager learner. I can't imagine anyone's being more eager for knowledge than my Heidi. My little girl.

MRS. HIGGINS: Yes, well, be that as it m –

HEIDI: Aaargh! Aaaaargh! Aaaargh! *(Panting)* Ah, ah, ah, ah.

(DIANE and SEAN enter Down Right. They look at HEIDI, FATHER, and MRS. HIGGINS.)

HEIDI, DIANE and SEAN: *(Shouting in unison)* Daddy, you know better than that!

FATHER: Er, uh, I do?

(FATHER and MRS. HIGGINS exit as the lights fade on the desk and simultaneously come up Downstage. The three children cross Down Center where they talk among themselves and occasionally address the audience.)

DIANE: Father knows better. He really does. Sometimes he gets so carried away because he cares about us. I understand that, but still it's embarrassing. You guys remember my telling you about the time Daddy dropped me off at school because Mom had a cold or something. It made him late for work, so it was a really nice thing to do, right? I was in eighth or ninth grade, and Dad let me out in front of all these other kids, which was fine. But then he rolled down the window on the passenger side and yelled at the top of his lungs, "OK, honey, you have a nice day. You know your father loves you." I wished this big hole would open in the ground in front of me and swallow me up.

SEAN: I know what you mean. There was that time I brought Kathy Ronson to the house. I didn't have my driver's license yet. Anyhow, Stewart Abrams was picking up his girlfriend and to save time was going to pick both Kathy and me up at our house; we were going to a movie. Anyhow, Dad walks in and you'd have thought Kathy was on trial. He asked her her whole life's history. That was bad enough, but then he has to say, *(Makes his voice deeper)* "I hope you don't mind all the questions. I'm simply interested in my son's friends because he's such a good boy, and I want only what's best for him." I wanted to drop dead on the spot.

HEIDI: You remember the trip my class was going to take? We all had to earn a certain amount of money or we couldn't go. Some of it we raised through car washes and things like that, but then each of us had to raise a hundred on our own. Well, I baby-sat and pulled weeds and helped the old lady next door carry in her groceries. I needed about fifteen dollars more. Dad knows this, and he comes in all enthusiastic and tells me he's arranged with his boss that I baby-sit their three kids for a day. Great idea, right? Except it was the day of the class trip, and it was Dad's boss.

(MOTHER and FATHER enter Stage Left and cross to the children, so there are two groups facing each other.)

DIANE: We want to ask you something, Mom.

SEAN: Why do you always let Father do the things he does?

HEIDI: What he means is, why do you always think that Father always knows better than any –

MOTHER: Your father's a fine, fine man. And the three of you know better than to question that!

DIANE, HEIDI, and SEAN: *(Simultaneously staggering backwards)* Er, uh, yes.

MOTHER: Now! What if I make us some nice brownies? I have just the recipe. Handed down to me from Grandma Hopkins. *(To FATHER)* You go into the living room, dear, and make yourself comfortable. *(FATHER exits.)*

MOTHER: *(To SEAN)* Sean, run get your father's slippers. *(SEAN exits. To HEIDI)* Heidi, go lift your father's feet up onto the footstool. *(HEIDI exits. To DIANE)* Diane, untie your father's shoes and take them off. *(DIANE exits. To the audience)* What a wonderful family I have. Isn't life just grand? Well, I'd better go now and get started on those brownies.

(Curtain)

Production Notes and Considerations

Although all the roles are exaggerated, the characters are simply too good to be true. Besides a parody of the television series, the piece also pokes fun at what has been viewed as the "ideal" American family where the mother and father are wrapped up in their families and where each plays a specific role. The father is the breadwinner and head of the family; the mother presumably stays home happily cooking old recipes, and supporting and looking up to her husband, no matter what he does. Nobody could be as totally unaware of the friction and undercurrents around the dinner table as she is.

The mother and father, in other words, are inane caricatures, who apparently have no aspirations of their own and live only for their children — except that the mother sees only what she wants to see, and the father is too well-intentioned in a clumsy way to do the children any good.

The children say they care for Father, but actually he's the sort of person who can't make much of an impact on anyone's life. Although seemingly realistic, they also are idealized in that they protest what Father does, but they don't do much of anything about it, except to yell at him a little bit. Real sons and daughters would have more feelings of resentment. They wouldn't stand around reminiscing about all the dumb things poor Father has done.

At times, the children speak in unison, which is also unrealistic. They sometimes overreact as characters often do in television sitcoms. Nobody in real life would breathe "hard as if exhausted" and then turn to someone else "nodding her head up and down repeatedly." That's sitcom acting, not stage acting. Here, of course, it's satirizing this sort of thing which occurs time after time on television.

There really are two different styles of acting required, the children's "sitcom" acting of television and the highly romanticized and idealized acting of the mother and father.

For this play, only set pieces are necessary — that is, the various pieces of furniture.

Since the characters are two-dimensional, most of the time you spend analyzing the piece should go on line delivery and humor. If you try to play the characters as real people, you will defeat the play's purpose.

How Do You Spell Tree?

(For Sue Schumer)

The monolog "How Do You Spell Tree?" can be delivered either by a male or female. The piece pokes fun at dictionaries' changing the way words are spelled, going against the way most have been spelled for years. Yet, of course, this sort of thing is tradition in that many of the words we use today previously were either two words or hyphenated, or sometimes evolved through all three stages. Our word *tonight* used to be *to night*. Then in the nineteenth century it became *to-night* and finally the word we know.

"How Do You Spell Tree?" also pokes fun at lexicographers' (dictionary compilers') seeming tendency to determine how words are spelled, rather than following standard usage. A lexicographer's job traditionally has been to compile, not to make new rules. However, *The American Heritage Dictionary* says that in the twentieth century lexicographers did begin "to adopt criteria of use rather than of etymological purity," which implies that they tended to set the rules rather than simply to describe them.

Another of the monolog's targets is dictionaries that call themselves Webster when they have no relationship whatsoever to the Noah Webster family and have not continued on with a business begun by anyone named Webster. The piece overstates or exaggerates in that obviously there are such as *The American Heritage Dictionary of the English Language*, and *The Random House Dictionary of the English Language*, which have entirely different names.

The man for whom so many dictionaries are named *is* Noah Webster whose most important book was *An American Dictionary of the English Language,* published in its first edition in 1828. He also published other books such as his 1783 *Spelling Book*, which was a big factor in the standardization of American spelling.

STUDENT: How long since you learned to spell? A long time, huh?
Almost since the time you started to read. And so maybe you're
pretty good at it, and maybe you aren't. No matter which, I got
news for you. You're going to have to start all over at the beginning. You think I'm kidding? Well, I'm not.

Let me ask you something? Did you know the Japanese
have Noh theatre? "What?" you say, "no theatre?" "No," I
answer, "they have Noh theatre." "But that's what I said," you
tell me. "No, I didn't," I say. "They have Noh theatre. That's N-
O-H."

But all that's changed now. No theatre really is absolutely
no theatre. You don't believe me? Look in the tenth edition of
Merriam Webster's Collegiate Dictionary. It says the Japanese
have No theatre. And it's spelled N-O.

So what is this, I ask you, some sort of plot to destroy the
world's theatrical heritage? What are these little people who
sit on their little behinds at their little desks trying to tell us?
No theatre indeed!

Or do you know what a greenroom is? *(The monologist
says the word quickly, running it all together, almost like "grnrm.")*
Me neither. Or I didn't until recently. I did know what a green
(Beat) room is – a place for actors to wait very calmly before
they go on-stage. A place to leisurely go over lines. A place to sit
and contemplate the universe. The fly speck on the wall. What
a great body the person has who plays opposite you.

But "grnrm!" All run together in one word sounds about
as relaxing as dodging cars out on the interstate.

And since we're on the subject of acting, let's take the
word for finding the meaning behind a play. What is that
word? If you're familiar with Konstantin Stanislavski, the guy
who developed the system of acting called the System...of
acting. Clever idea there, Connie! Anyhow, while working at
the Moscow Art Theatre, Stanislavski brought together all
these things that tell you how to analyze a play to figure out its
meaning. And what is that called, boys and girls? Right! The
super-objective.

Sorry, that's what it used to be called. Now it's something like suprbjctv! All one word! Can you imagine looking for your suprbjctv? Far as I'm concerned, the darn thing can just stay lost.

Or let's take Eugene O'Neill. One of the greatest of American playwrights — *Strange Interlude, Mourning Becomes Electra, The Great God Brown, Where the Cross Is Made, Long Day's Journey Into Night.* Lots of plays in lots of styles.

Some of his plays are semi-autobiographical. Oops. Did I say "semi-autobiographical"? Darn, that's not right. It's really smotabigrpahcl! That's right. I'll say it one more time, just so you're sure you've got it right. Smotabigrpahcl. One word, no hyphen.

What's going to happen if this sort of thing continues? I'll tell you what's going to happen. Consider the last play I mentioned, *Long Day's Journey Into Night,* a play about O'Neill's father and mother and brother and himself. A long, long play. Depressing too.

But it has some beautiful scenes. If you don't believe me take a look at Jamie's speech about the sea, about the beauty of sailing. Just listen to the words in your mind when he talks about the *Squarehead* square rigger headed for Buenos Aires. You feel like you're right there with him.

What's this *Squarehead* square rigger, you may ask? I don't know. I'm not a sailor. But it sounds nice. But what if the *Collegiate Dictionary* continues on its way. Right! Sqrhdsqarggr! Now isn't that a beautiful sound? Just listen. Sqrhdsqarggr! Ugly! Harsh! But it sure saves time. Squeezing up all those words together. And we all know how important it is to save time. So what are you going to do with this time you save?

Well, if you're smart, you'll scoop it right up and stash it away somewhere. Like maybe in that old Barney Rubble lunch box you haven't taken out since third grade. And, OK, like when you need more time to study for an exam, you're just gonna go to the old lunch box and take out a little extra time. Like going to the bank? I don't think it works quite that way.

So what's the big hurry? What is this about pinching up all these words? Pretty soon *Long Day's Journey Into Night* is going to be *Lngdysjurntanght*. And this play, this four- to five-hour play. It's gonna become a one-act. A short one at that. Speech and scenes all scrunched up together.

And acting isn't ever going to be the same. Besides memorizing things like Sqrhdsqarggr, which is going to be a big job in itself, to be an actor, you're going to have a whole different kind of training. You know what it's going to be like? You don't? Well, I'll tell you. Every acting course is going to consist of watching a lot of silent movies. Have you ever watched those old silent movies? Things like the Keystone Kops? Everyone rushing and scurrying around like a wind-up toy with the springs wound too tight. I mean, you're going to have to move fast. Everyone who becomes an actor automatically makes the Olympic team. Olympics and the theatre will be nearly synonymous. Scrunch, scrunch, scrunch! Run, run, run.

What's the point of all this? Let's look at the downside first. Like I said at the beginning, you're going to have to learn to spell all over again. Now let me ask you something else. All of you who use a computer to write your essays for English or your term papers for social studies, will you please raise your hands? Uh-huh, I see, well just forget it. You want to know why? You're going to be in big trouble, particularly if you don't know how to spell. And who knows how to spell with the way they keep scrunching up words?

Remember in seventh grade English when your teacher told you a lexicographer's job is simply to gather words and stick them in a book? The lexicographer goes around listening to people talk and reading their writing and then records what he or she finds to be the most common way of doing things. Look it up if you don't believe me. Lexicology. L-E-X-I-C-O-L-O-G-Y. Right there in your dictionary. You know what? It's still going to tell you that this means studying how words are formed and what they mean. And some other stuff dealing with the idiomatic combination of words. Slang like "the cat's pajamas" or "hubba, hubba, ding, ding."

That's what they're supposed to do. All these millions of people named Webster. OK, I'm going on a little side trip here. But what is this? Do all the lexicographers in the world think if they change their names to Webster, they'll do a better job or something? Like does that mean if I change my name to Will Shakespeare, I'm going to write all these plays that high school students will have to study for centuries to come? Like all those idiom-compiling lexicographers used to write in their dictionaries, "Get real. Get a life. Get on to the point of this monolog." I don't think they said that last part, but there are so danged many Websters, how can you know for sure?

Well, not really, there aren't. It's just that everyone seemed to figure that old Webster, the original old Webster – his name was Noah – did so well they're going steal his name and fool the public.

You know what? Your seventh grade teacher was wrong. I mean if these old lexicographers really looked at how people spelled words, there'd be things like K-A-T and S-K-U-L. So right away they aren't doing their job. They aren't interested in how common people spell. They've been interested only in how really bright people spell. Geniuses. Those with the big IQs. But now they're not even listening to them. Think of the brightest people in your class. Your theatre class. Your psychology class. Are they going to spell semi- *(Pause)* autobiographical as just one great long word? Not unless they're misled by someone named Webster!

So we know then that these lexicographers are too impatient anymore to be followers. They've got to be leaders. Trendsetters. And what's the best way to do that? Get together and decide how everyone else is going to learn this new way of spelling.

And what is that way? Yeah, you know, by jamming all the

words together. OK, then, I ask you, if *Merriam Webster's Collegiate Dictionary* wants to do that, why don't they really be bold and call themselves *Mrmbntrclegtdicshnry*? Ah-hah! You won't find them ever doing that, I'll bet. Does have a nice ring to it, doesn't it? *Mrmbntrclegtdicshnry*. The new lexicographers' newest resource book.

What's good for the goose isn't good for the gander, not according to *Mrmwbntrclegtdicshnry*. Oh, no. With them it's "do as I say, not as I do. My name isn't Mrmwbntrclegtdicshnry; it's *(Very slowly)* **Merriam Webster's Collegiate Dictionary.**

I wonder about people's names though. You know how some people hyphenate their names. Will *(Speaking slowly)* Mr. and Mrs. Morris Fillmore-Morrison fast become known among their friends and family as *(Pronounces the name very quickly)* **Mrandmrsmorrisfilemoremorrison.** Or worse yet. **Mrndmrmrsfmrmrsn.** Imagine. Like an old record player stuck in the grove. **Mrndmrmrsfmrmrsn.** Makes you want to slap your face right in the middle. **Mrndmrmrs** *(Slaps self on the cheek)* **fmrmrsn.**

As I started to say a while back, if you use a computer, try this on your spell checker and see what happens. I'll tell you what happens. That poor old computer is going to start spitting sparks and smoke. And right before it blows itself up right in your face, it's gonna turn its screen right at you and say, "nvrdidlrntaspllenethngrghtdmbnynowdidja." Once more, it's going to say "nvrdidlrntaspllenethngrghtdmbnynowdidja." Hey, I'm used to this by now. Just let me translate. *(Slowly)* "Never did learn to spell anything right, dumb bunny, now did you?" And then it's going to burst into flames and die. I'm telling you it's the truth.

OK, that's the downside. What's the upside? More jobs. Many more jobs. If you learn the new way of spelling, you're going to be in such demand – your next job could be holding classes in the summer program at the park teaching first and second graders how to spell.

But the big thing is the nature people. The Save-a-Tree

Foundation. Just think, all those words scrunched up together, you're going to get much more on a page. And the more you get on a page, the less pages you use. The less pages you use, the more trees you spare. The more trees you spare, the more oxygen to breathe. And so come next summer, you and your girlfriend or boyfriend want to go strolling among the trees in the park. You stop and give a moment of silent thanks to all the world's lexicographers. If it weren't for them, maybe you wouldn't have trees to walk amidst. Or air to breathe. But...on the other hand, maybe you would know how to spell.

(The End)

Production Notes and Considerations

"How Do You Spell Tree?" is an example of a standup comedy routine built around a particular theme, the changes in the way words are spelled. A secondary theme is how these changes in spelling relate to theatre. Of course, no set is required. You may want to present this sitting on a stool or standing Center Stage, or you may prefer having a speaker's stand. Do whatever you think will make you feel most comfortable.

The main thing to be aware of when memorizing and presenting the routine is where the comedy occurs and what makes it funny. The material is highly exaggerated, which is at the base of the humor. Also contributing to the comic effect are the scrunched up words. Of course, it will be funnier if you learn to say these easily and in exactly the same way each time.

In Plain English

"In Plain English" is meant only as a gentle satire, not to be offensive but to poke fun at the idea that there is really any such thing as standard English spoken in the United States.

In the early days of television, there were many predictions that with the spread of the new medium, the entire country would be speaking in precisely the same way. There were two sides to the issue. Some felt it was good to eliminate regionalisms so that everyone would have an equal chance to achieve success in their careers. Those who felt this way supported the idea that people with regional accents come across as less educated or less intelligent than those who follow what these experts felt should be the standard and called Mid-American Standard English.

The other side felt that differences in pronunciation or dialect should be preserved, much as we try to keep species of plants and animals from becoming extinct.

So the monolog satirizes the differences in pronunciation from one area to another, without singling out any specific region of the country. It also pokes fun at those who predicted that within two or three decades from the time most homes contained television sets, that there would be no regional accents left.

STUDENT: Did you ever realize that when someone mentions the English language, there's no way of knowing what the person means? I'm serious. We've lived all over the United States, even in Canada. And it's all different. When we moved to Missouri, I asked the kid next door where the school was, and he says, "It's a fur piece." "No," I tell him, "I asked you where the school is." Again he says, "A fur piece." And I say, "Well, you know, I'm glad you told me that, though my family's always believed in animal rights —"

He looks at me really funny and says, "I best go now. I think I hear my mama calling." "Please wait," I say. "We just moved in, and I want to find out where the school is." "I tole you, it's a fur piece." "Like a stole?" I ask, and he says, "Nobody stole it." He points down the road. "See that far down there." "I can see pretty far," I told him, and again he looks at me real strange. "A pretty far! What are you, a pyromaniac?" And then it sinks in. He was pointing to a pile a burning leaves. Ah-hah, I figure, if far is fire, maybe fur is far!

So I say to him, "What you're telling me is the school's a long way from here." He peers real close at me. "You from a furrin' country that you don't understand plain English?" "Well," I says, "this country does seem pretty foreign to me."

Anyhow, Frankie offered to show me the way to school. It was the end of August, still hot. The school was a couple of miles. Just before we get there, Frankie says, "A fur piece, all right. Bet you're tarred." "Tarred?" I looked down at my shoes. "No, I'm not tarred. Why should I be? We were walking on the sidewalk, not in the tar melting on the road."

Well, 'bout the time I was gettin' the hang of Ozark English, my family ups and moves to Maryland. I meet another kid, name of Don. We were outside when a storm came up. "Might've known," he said, "the weather's unpredictable this time of year. But overall I like Balmer."

"Balmier?" I ask. "Well, so do I, though sometimes the farmers can use the rain."

"That isn't what I said," Don tells me. "I was talking

about Balmer." "Bomber?" I cower and cover my head with my arms. Then I started to think, Why would a bomber be flying over Baltimore? Yeah, Don was using the Baltimore version of English.

Speaking of which, bet you didn't know the favorite musical instrument in Minnesota. It's da lute. Like strolling minstrels used to play. Not many people play it today, except in Minnesota. At least that's what I thought when we moved to Duluth. You guessed it. Minnesota English.

Next we moved to Luvel. Luvel? And here I thought we were moving to Louisville. From there we went to Texas. As usual, I had to find my new school. I see this kid walking along, and I ask, "Is this the way to school?" And he calls me a rat. By now I'm getting onto this sort of thing, and I figured this had something to do with Texas English. So I ask once more, trying to be extra polite, "Is this the way to school?" "I tole you. Raht." So I finally say, "Why are you calling me a rat?" He says, "I didn't call you a rat. I said it was the raht way to school."

Then we moved to Joja, and I ask some kid why everyone was always talking about boats there. "What do you mean?" he asks. And I tell him that though anyone can plainly see we aren't near any big body of water, everyone keeps mentioning their yawls. "I mighta known you wooden undastand, bein' a damyankee." Still trying to be polite, I said, "I'm sorry you think I'm a damyankee. But I don't know what that is. If you tell me, I'll try to change." It was like studying a whole new language. Then I figured it out. Like when you're a little kid and it suddenly comes to you that your parents are using this way of talking you later find is pig Latin. Well, in Joja, if a word is one syllable, you can't go far wrong by making it into two. If it's two syllables, you make it three or four. There are exceptions, like the word Joja, which Northerners know quite well is Georgia. So in this case, you cut the number of syllables, but you draw them out. Jooooojaa.

In the Ozarks, you remember, when you burn something

you have a far. In Jooooja you have a fiyah.[33] There are a few words that change many times over depending on where you are. One that is very important is the word "fire." Suppose your visiting a friend and you notice a big fire creeping up one wall of the house. If you're in the Ozarks, remember, you have to yell "Far!" In Georgia, you have to yell "fiyah," and in New England, it's "fi-uh." If you get confused, and start yelling fire or far or fiyah, when you really mean fi-uh, by the time you get to fi-uh, the house could be nothing but ashes.

Remember the yawls that sail through the South? I got news for you. Around Bayonne or Brooklyn, the boat becomes a man. People in these places are always saying things like, "Hugh's comin' wit me?" For a long time I thought this Hugh was really a popular guy. In parts of Western Pennsylvania, it's not a boat or a man. It's a yunz. Or you'uns if its South PA. You know how southerners drawl out their words.

Speaking of Pennsylvania, when we lived there, I'm visiting this new friend. He asks if I'd like a pop. Well, I got a pop and I got a mom, and I wonder why he's asking me that. "I'm going to get one," he says. And I think, well, fine, I'll stick with the one I got. He moves us around a heck of a lot, but other than that he's just fine. "No, thanks," I say, and wish I hadn't when I see him come back with a soft drink. By the way, did you know that in some parts of the south a Coke isn't necessarily a Coke. It's a soda or a pop. You can go into a store there and order a root beer coke, a Pepsi coke, or a Nehi orange coke.

But the real question is, would you ever drink wuter? Some people do in New Jersey. But sometimes instead they drink cohafee that comes from an aluminum keyan. Strange place, New Jersey. Speaking of drinking things, you know how some people take a tonic when they're ill. In New England they drink whole bottles – root-beer flavored, orange-flavored, Coca Cola-flavored. Isn't that a fine eye-dear? So what's an eye-

[33]Fiyah — soft final syllable; Fi-uh — hard final syllable.

dear? A person of the opposite sex who looks attractive? A strange animal with a big rack of antlers and a gigantic eye in the middle of its forehead?

Let me ask you something? Did you ever know that in some houses from Pennsylvania on out through the Ozarks, you can wrench your hair and it doesn't even hurt? And in all those places you've got to make sure you keep this guy named Earl in your car. I mean, what is he, a bodyguard? Or did you know wry cheer is a synonym of raht heyah. Or that farther west, in Southern California, fur shur, fur shur means yes?

But talk about being confused. Do you know that in Canada cars wear boots instead of tires. And they also wear hats? Sunbonnets, Easter bonnets, stuff like that. Well, that's what I thought when we moved there. Had me puzzled, too, till I figured out a boot is a trunk, and a bonnet is a hood. A hood? You mean like Little Red Riding wore?

I'll just leave you with these final words. Listen, y'all, the bonfar's too fur since da cah's boot uz fillin' with wuter. Hits all raht though, we'ull jes' stay ta home 'n eat ow-uh keaydy bahs.

(The End)

Production Notes and Considerations

This monolog is similar to "How Do You Spell Tree?" in that it is a standup comedy routine built around a particular theme.

It also can be delivered either by a male or a female, and the staging arrangements can be similar. That is, you can stand, sit on a stool, or use a speaker's stand. The reason for a stool, rather than a chair, is psychological. You are higher up, and therefore the audience will look "up" to you.

The names of the friends can be of either sex. Frankie can be a nickname for Franklin (or Frank) or for Frances or Francis. Don can become Dawn. It's then easy to change such pronouns as "he," "his," and "him" to "she" and "her."

In preparing the routine, keep in mind that you need to be able to say the same word with ease in all the different ways. If you stumble over words in your delivery, you most likely will destroy the humor.

Some of the comedy in the routine comes from exaggeration, but it's from exaggerated incidents, rather than facts since these pronunciations actually are used by at least some of the residents of the various localities mentioned. In other words, there is more literal truth to this piece than to "How Do You Spell Tree?" Yet, it is unlikely that a person would move so often from one locality or extreme of pronunciation to another.

Because the piece is factual in talking about the differences in pronunciation, the delivery probably would be more realistic than for the previous piece, which is more exaggerated. Here it's as if you're telling a funny story that progresses from one point in time to another than that you're presenting a series of outrageous incidents and predictions like those in "How Do You Spell Tree?"

Mix and Match

"Mix and Match" is a farce, which is considered a separate genre from comedy though it is meant to be funny. It is also similar to melodrama (see "A Tale of the Bog," page 109) in that coincidence or fate usually plays a large part in the outcome. The primary purpose of farce is entertainment; usually there is little or no deeper meaning whereas most plays in other genres have some sort of message for the audience.

It takes little effort or imagination to follow the plot, and the characters are types or *stock characters* rather than individuals. Each usually has one outstanding trait that is exaggerated. If any other traits are mentioned, it's just in passing. The plot has slapstick or physical humor and devious twists. It shows only how the major characters manage to release themselves from entanglements.

The success of a farce relies heavily on the actor and director's uninhibited presentation of outlandish actions and speeches. Farce uses many of the devices of comedy: automatism, incongruity, derision, and physical violence. Many farces deal with unfaithfulness.

The plot usually relies on misunderstanding, mistaken identity, deception, and unfamiliar surroundings. The characters are the victims of their vices, and when caught, appear ridiculous.

Nearly any subject can be treated in a farce, though often this type of play involves romantic triangles, or, as in "Mix and Match," a "quadrangle." "Mix and Match" is typical in several respects — the characters having something to hide from the others, their frenetic scurrying about, and their interchangeability. None is well-rounded, and it's difficult to remember which character is which.

Generally, a farce that involves romantic adventures or misadventures has characters that are amoral. That is, they see life as neither good nor bad. They simply set their sights on a goal, usually a romantic interlude, and do not allow scruples or moral considerations of right and wrong to get in the way of achieving the goal. The characters in "Mix and Match" are close to this, though they do have some genuine feelings for each other and at least a tinge of conscience about how their actions may affect their current girlfriends or boyfriends. They do not want to hurt each other, whereas in a pure farce, the characters have no true compunctions about how they treat others.

In other types of farce, particularly the kind that involves even more frenzied activity than this one, there may be too much racing around and mock beatings to acknowledge the audience as is sometimes done. However, there certainly is physical activity in the constant scurrying around to hide in "Mix and Match." This is also evident in Maggie's trying both to remember who is where and how to keep the characters apart.

The title is a play on the idea of mix-and-match clothing, where various combinations are possible and with only a limited number of pieces. As mix-and-match clothing, the couples are interchangeable, except that at the end things "look" a little different but are substantially the same.

CAST: MAGGIE JOHNS, 16-17; WILL RASMUSSAN, 16-17; JOAN
HANSEN, 16-17; SETH CORELLI; 16-17.

SETTING: The action occurs in and around the Johns' household. A rug
or piece of carpeting can define the edge of the "house." The
Downstage area represents the sidewalk and lawn.

AT RISE: MAGGIE and WILL enter Stage Left, holding hands. They
cross nearly to Center Stage and stop.

MAGGIE: Wish I could ask you in, but my folks aren't home. And I
have strict orders.

WILL: It's OK. I understand.

MAGGIE: You sure?

WILL: You wouldn't lie to me.

MAGGIE: I'm glad you feel that way.

WILL: Would you?

MAGGIE: Gotta go, Will. I'm sure Mom wants me to start dinner
before she and Dad get home.

WILL: They're together?

MAGGIE: Went to my aunt's. In Denver.

WILL: Your dad had the day off?

MAGGIE: Yeah. But they'll soon be back. I really have to go.

WILL: Sure. See you tomorrow. I'll stop by on the way to school.

MAGGIE: Well...OK, if you want to.

WILL: What do you mean if I want to?

MAGGIE: I didn't mean anything. It's just –

WILL: *(Kidding)* You'd better not. You are my girlfriend, you know.

MAGGIE: Of course, I know.

WILL: OK then. *(Squeezes her hand.)* I'll call you. *(He hurries Off
Right.)*

MAGGIE: Boy, do I ever know.

SETH: *(Appears Up Right and obviously tries to stay out of sight as he
sees WILL exit.)* **Whew! Close one.** *(SETH hurries around behind
the house and to extreme Stage Left and runs lightly Downstage.
He turns and crosses to just behind MAGGIE. He grabs her around
the waist, and she screams.)* **Gotcha!**

MAGGIE: Oh, Seth! You scared the heck out of me.

SETH: *(Mocking)* **Sorry.**

MAGGIE: Uh-huh. Sure, you are.

SETH: So did you tell him?

MAGGIE: Who?

SETH: You know who.

MAGGIE: No, I don't.

SETH: Will.

MAGGIE: Tell him what?

SETH: You're such a kidder.

MAGGIE: What do you mean?

SETH: You have to tell him.

MAGGIE: *(Teasing)* **Why is that?**

SETH: I said I'd go along with this till you had a chance.

MAGGIE: Want to come inside?

SETH: What's the matter? You afraid Will's going to come back?

MAGGIE: I don't think so.

SETH: You don't think so, huh?

MAGGIE: Come on. *(They step to the edge of the carpet where MAGGIE pantomimes opening a door. SETH makes a mock bow and follows her inside.)*

SETH: So where are your folks?

MAGGIE: Gone for the night.

SETH: Where?

MAGGIE: To my aunt's house. In Denver.

SETH: How'd you manage that? *(He plops down on the sofa.)*

MAGGIE: Manage what?

SETH: My mom and dad would never leave me alone all night.

MAGGIE: You're a big boy.

SETH: Yeah. *(He stands up, grabs MAGGIE and tries to kiss her.)*

MAGGIE: *(Pushing him away)* **Like a Coke?**

SETH: Yeah, maybe.

MAGGIE: Maybe?

SETH: Depends on what goes with it.

MAGGIE: What's that supposed to mean?

SETH: We are alone.

MAGGIE: I think maybe Will's going to stop by later.

SETH: *(Letting go of her)* **You're not serious.**

MAGGIE: Maybe I am, and maybe I'm not.

SETH: Why would you let a creep like that –

MAGGIE: I thought you and Will were friends. Best friends. *(As MAGGIE and SETH talk, JOAN enters Stage Left, crosses to the imaginary front door.)*

SETH: What's that got to do with it?

MAGGIE: I don't –

JOAN: Maggie! *(She pantomimes knocking on the door.)* **Maggie, are you home?**

SETH: Oh, no, it's Joan.

MAGGIE: So what?

SETH: You don't understand. She can't see me here.

MAGGIE: What is this, Seth?

SETH: *(Panicking)* **Where can I hide? Just tell me where I can hide.**

MAGGIE: Why do you want to –

SETH: *(Frantic)* **Tell me, will you?!**

MAGGIE: The bathroom, I guess. *(SETH glances around frantically, and MAGGIE points to a doorway Up Left, real or imaginary. SETH rushes toward it, hurries inside and closes the door behind him. MAGGIE opens the front door.)* **Hi, Joan. What are –**

JOAN: Have you seen Seth?

MAGGIE: Seth? Well...why?

JOAN: I'm going to kill him, that's why.

MAGGIE: What did he do?

JOAN: It's not what he did; it's what he didn't do.

MAGGIE: I don't quite see –

JOAN: He said he'd meet me after school. We were going to study together. We're in the same biology class. And anyhow...

MAGGIE: *(Suspicious)* **Yes?**

JOAN: I think he's kind of cute, don't you? *(SETH is listening through a crack in the bathroom door. He reacts egotistically to what JOAN says.)*

MAGGIE: I never...never thought about it. I mean –

JOAN: Come on now. Isn't he just about the cutest guy? And you know what? He asked me – *(SETH grabs his forehead in the palm* *of his hand.)*

MAGGIE: Yes?

JOAN: See, he asked if I'd like to go to the con – *(SETH coughs very loudly to try to interrupt, though he can't reveal himself.)* **What was that?**

MAGGIE: I don't quite know what it was.

JOAN: Sounded like someone coughing. Or a dog barking. Do you have a dog in your bathroom?

MAGGIE: No, er, uh...Why are you asking me all these questions? *(Suddenly, WILL runs in from Stage Right. He knocks on the imaginary door.)*

WILL: Maggie. Are you in there, Maggie? I thought maybe you could use some help making din –

JOAN: Oh, God, it's Will. He can't see me here. Can I hide somewhere?

MAGGIE: Why? What is this?

JOAN: He asked me – Oh, no, he's your boyfriend, isn't he?

MAGGIE: Well...yeah, we've had a few dates.

JOAN: A few!

MAGGIE: OK, we've had a lot of dates.

WILL: Maggie, are you there? *(In the meantime, SETH rolls his eyes and throws his hands in the air.)*

JOAN: Can I hide somewhere?

MAGGIE: What?

JOAN: The bathroom maybe.

MAGGIE: Sure, I guess. But I don't see –

JOAN: Good! Thanks. You're a friend. A real true friend. I'll try to explain it all later. *(She hurries toward the bathroom.)* **Oh, someone's in there. I forgot.**

MAGGIE: My dog. Just my dog. He isn't housebroken yet, and –

SETH: *(To himself)* Well, thanks a whole bunch.

MAGGIE: Tell you what, you wait in the kitchen –

JOAN: In the kitchen? Why do you want me to go into the kitchen?

MAGGIE: The dog. He's – he's dangerous. I don't have him trained yet.

JOAN: Dangerous?

MAGGIE: Police dog. Former police dog. With the police, I mean. He's really a collie. But trained to attack.

JOAN: I never heard of a collie being an attack dog.

MAGGIE: Collie? Did I say collie?

JOAN: That's what you said.

MAGGIE: I meant a dachshund. Yes, that's exactly what I meant.

WILL: Maggie, come on. I can hear you. And I hear other voices. Do you have the TV on?

MAGGIE: I've got to go to the door.

JOAN: You don't understand.

MAGGIE: We've got to get you –

JOAN: Out of here!

MAGGIE: OK, OK, I'll get the dog. Put him outside or something. *(Pushing her toward the Upstage Center door)* Go to the kitchen and wait. As soon as I get the dog outside.

SETH: *(To himself)* Dog! Well, I like that.

WILL: Maggie. Turn down the TV set. Hey, can you hear me?

JOAN: Why are you so anxious to get me into the kitchen?

MAGGIE: The dog, I told you. The dog. I'll take him out the side door and –

JOAN: OK, but you don't have to shove me around.

MAGGIE: Sorry, I'm sorry. Now hurry up.

JOAN: All right, all right, I'm going. *(She exits to just behind the upper door, her back to MAGGIE. MAGGIE hurries to the bathroom door and is about to knock when the door bursts open.)*

SETH: *(Loud stage whisper)* Why did you let her in?

MAGGIE: What?

WILL: Maggie, I mean it, open up. This isn't funny anymore.

SETH: Joan. Did you have to let Joan in?

MAGGIE: Why wouldn't I let her in? Come on. You can hide in the closet. *(She grabs his arm and drags him quickly across the stage. She opens a door Right Center and shoves him inside, slamming it behind him.)* Whew! *(She sticks her head out the Upstage entrance.)* Now, Joan, now!

JOAN: All right, OK. *(She enters Upstage and hurries to the bathroom.)*

WILL: Maggie!

MAGGIE: OK, OK, I'm coming! *(She crosses to the front door and opens it.)*

WILL: Maggie, there's something I have to tell you.

MAGGIE: Tell me? What do you mean?

WILL: I wasn't being...exactly honest.

MAGGIE: About what?

WILL: It's just that I don't want to go with you any –

MAGGIE: *(Shocked)* **What?!**

WILL: What I mean is that I don't want to go with you anywhere but to the concert. *(It's obvious that this isn't at all what he meant to say.)* **I mean, I'm really looking forward to it, aren't you?**

MAGGIE: I'm looking forward to it. Why wouldn't I be?

WILL: Me too. I'm really, really looking forward to it.

MAGGIE: Are you all right?

WILL: Not really. I don't feel so good. May I use your –

MAGGIE: *(Almost shrieking)* **Bathroom? You want to use the bathroom. Well, er, uh...of course, you can use the bathroom. But first...**

WILL: What? What is it? I just want to... My head hurts. Yes, that's it. I was going to get an aspirin tablet.

MAGGIE: I see. Well, I'll get it for you. And then maybe if you're not feeling well, you'd better go home.

WILL: No, there's something I have to say first!

MAGGIE: For heaven's sake, what is it?

WILL: Well, you see, it's...it's about the concert.

MAGGIE: The concert?

WILL: Saturday night. The concert in the amphitheatre.

MAGGIE: I know perfectly well where the concert is.

WILL: I know you know where the concert is. I want to go to the concert with – *(Pause)* **I've got to get the aspirin.** *(He turns and starts to cross to the bathroom.)*

MAGGIE: *(Screaming)* **No!** *(WILL turns to her startled. As he does, JOAN sneaks out of the bathroom and tiptoes to the closet. MAGGIE sees her.)*

MAGGIE: No, no, no.

WILL: Well, for heaven's sake, if you feel that way about it, I guess

I'll just go.

MAGGIE: *(Very forceful)* **Go get your aspirin, Will! Will, go get it now.**
(WILL rushes to the bathroom and slams the door. He makes a play of looking in the imaginary mirror, breathing hard and shaking his head. In the meantime, MAGGIE rushes toward JOAN.) **No, Joan, no, I wouldn't do that if I were you!** *(MAGGIE is too late. JOAN opens the closet door and we hear a fierce barking. JOAN screams and runs toward the front door, as MAGGIE slams the closet door.)* **I tried to tell you. I put the dog in the closet.**

JOAN: *(At the front door, she turns. She's puzzled.)* **In the closet? Why would you put the dog in the closet?**

MAGGIE: **He's dangerous.**

JOAN: **You said you were going to put him outside.**

MAGGIE: **Obviously, I didn't.**

JOAN: **I can see that.** *(WILL comes out of the bathroom.)*

WILL: **I thought I heard screaming and barking? Is there a dog in here?** *(Spying JOAN)* **Joan! What are you doing here?**

JOAN: **I might ask you the same question.**

WILL: **I came to talk – to talk to Maggie.**

JOAN: **Well, isn't that interesting? I find that very interesting.**

MAGGIE: **Am I missing something here?**

WILL: **You're not missing anything. What makes you think you're missing something?**

MAGGIE: **You two are acting really strangely, that's all.** *(In the closet, SETH suddenly sneezes.)*

SETH: **Mothballs! I'm allergic to mothballs.**

JOAN: **Is someone in your closet?**

MAGGIE: **In my closet?**

WILL: **A very good question. Is there someone in your closet?**

JOAN: **You were going to take your dog outside.**

WILL: **Dog? What dog? Do you have a dog?**

MAGGIE: **I give up!**

WILL: **You never told me you had a dog? What kind of dog is it?**

MAGGIE: **I don't care what kind of dog it is. I don't know what kind of dog it is. I don't like dogs. I don't care about dogs.**

JOAN: **What is it, Maggie? What's wrong?**

MAGGIE: OK, OK. I've had it. It's silly. It's childish. It's dumb. *(She crosses to the closet door and yanks it open. SETH steps out, raises his right hand up beside his head and wiggles his fingers in greeting.)*

JOAN: Seth!

WILL: Seth, what are you doing here?!

SETH: *(Taking the offensive)* I might ask you the very same question.

WILL: All right. OK. I came to tell Maggie I want to break up. That's it. It's over. I'm sorry.

MAGGIE: Break up!

WILL: I know. It hurts. And I wanted to avoid that. That's why I waited so long.

MAGGIE: Hurts? You think it hurts?

SETH: OK, OK. Since we're being honest.

JOAN: Yes, we are being honest. You know what I said about Seth?

MAGGIE: That he was cute? One of the cutest boys –

JOAN: Something like that.

MAGGIE: I remember, and I can't say I like –

JOAN: He is cute, I admit it. And we were going to study. And we were going to go to the concert.

WILL: What she's trying to say is that –

SETH: Before you go on, I owe you an apology, Will. I'm sorry. I'm really sorry. You're my best friend and –

MAGGIE: What he means is that we planned to spend the evening together.

WILL: Without your parents.

MAGGIE: Oh, they'll be back. Actually, any time.

SETH: But you said –

MAGGIE: I was kidding. My folks would never trust me to take care of myself, let alone take care of the house.

WILL: What's going on here?

SETH: You mean you were just leading me on?

MAGGIE: Of course not, Seth. I was pretending. Thinking how nice it would be if we could be together.

WILL: What?

MAGGIE: I'm sorry, Will.

JOAN: But that's perfect.

MAGGIE: What's perfect?

JOAN: Will and I...How can I say this?

WILL: What she means is we like each other.

JOAN: A lot.

SETH: You do!

JOAN: Sorry, Seth.

SETH: Oh, no. That's fine. That's fine. Maggie and I –

WILL: What?

SETH: It was something – something that just kind of happened. I didn't mean to steal your girlfriend, Will.

WILL: Nor I yours.

SETH: You're kidding.

WILL: No, I'm not kidding. *(He goes to JOAN and puts his arm around her waist.)* **What do you say?**

SETH: About what?

WILL: The concert?

MAGGIE: What about the concert?

WILL: Joan and me. You and Seth.

JOAN: Go together, you mean?

WILL: Sure.

MAGGIE: *(Laughing)* I can't believe this.

JOAN: That we'd like to go to the concert together?

MAGGIE: No, that's not what I mean. Just that we were fooling each other. And we didn't need to.

SETH: Yeah, so what do you say? I think it's a good idea. Dad already said I could use the car.

WILL: Hey, that's great. We are all friends, after all.

JOAN: Uh-huh. Girlfriends and boyfriends. *(WILL puts his arm around JOAN'S waist. All laugh as the lights dim to black.)*

(Curtain)

Production Notes and Considerations

The acting style for "Mix and Match" or this sort of farce in general can be somewhat different from that used for most types of humor. In performing the play, you can present it with a "tongue-in-cheek" attitude. You can stand apart from the character and project to the audience the idea that this is all in fun and not to be taken seriously.

Occasionally, in farces, a character will go so far as to wink at the audience or perform other actions showing that what they are about to do isn't to be taken seriously. This, of course, depends somewhat on what would be comfortable for you in performance and on how the director interprets the play.

Pace is probably even more important in farce than in most forms of comedy in that the success of a farce depends so much on the action moving quickly. The audience should have the feeling that it is caught up in a whirlwind that keeps on spinning from one incident to the next without ever letting up.

As suggested earlier, farce is often amoral in outlook. "Mix and Match" is a little bit atypical in that the characters are friends. Still there are many hints here that they are not being quite truthful or honest. An example is Maggie's third speech, "I'm glad you feel that way." She doesn't exactly lie here, but she isn't telling the truth either. Throughout there are examples of dishonesty of one sort or another. It's important that the audience understand these.

The fast pace can keep the audience entertained, but it is much better if they can follow what the characters actually are doing and their changing relationships with each other. This is more difficult in a farce like "Mix and Match" than in other types of plays since there really is little characterization. If the characters in "Father Knows Better" were cardboard, those in "Mix and Match" are paper thin. They have no distinguishing characteristics and really are interchangeable in the eyes of the audience. This means you do not need to try to individualize your character. For this sort of piece, it's better if you don't.

You can have as elaborate or as simple a set as you wish. The stage directions suggest that much of the set is imaginary — the front wall and door, for instance. However, you can completely rearrange things and have the front entrance at the side. Then an existing set can be used, just so there are enough doorways and entrances. If a real set is used, you will, of course, have to figure out a way for the audience to see Seth hiding in the bathroom.

Pails by Comparison

The humor in "Pails by Comparison" comes from the unexpected situation in which the audience finds the two familiar characters. Now, however, they are not so familiar. In fact, they are drastically changed from the two children of the nursery rhyme. Partly, the fun is in the unexpected changes that Jill has undergone, while Jack has remained much more faithful to the more pervasive beliefs of his time.

Although the sketch is largely for fun, it does make a statement about past versus present and about the changing role of women in Western society.

CHARACTERS: JACK, 21; JILL, 21

SETTING: An empty stage.

AT RISE: JACK and JILL stand Center Stage facing each other. JILL carries an umbrella; JACK carries a pail.

JILL: What are you doing, Jack?

JACK: I'm getting a pail of water.

JILL: A pail of water? What on earth for?

JACK: Nothing on earth. Rather for the spirit.

JILL: The spirit.

JACK: I stick with the old values, Jill. A little of all this newfangled stuff goes a long way.

JILL: Newfangled stuff?

JACK: Faucets. Running water.

JILL: For heaven's sake, Jack. The ancient Romans had running water. The Aztecs of Mexico had running water.

JACK: Perhaps that's true. But some of us weren't so lucky.

JILL: That was long ago, Jack.

JACK: The old values are the ones that last.

JILL: I suppose you think women should marry at twelve or fourteen and by the time they're thirty, look sixty from caring for a brood of useless brats.

JACK: Jill!

JILL: Come into the present, man!

JACK: Man? I'm just a boy.

JILL: Boy, schmoy. You must be at least in your twenties by now.

JACK: I'm twenty-one, as you very well know.

JILL: Age is of little importance. It's not how we mark our years that count. It's how we live them.

JACK: I see we have some fundamental differences here. I suppose you haven't carried a pail of water in –

JILL: No, Jack, I haven't. I have better things to occupy my time.

JACK: What things?

JILL: Women received the right to vote decades back, true?

JACK: Is this a history lesson?

JILL: But no woman has ever been president of the United States.

Nor even vice president.

JACK: A woman's place is in the —

JILL: Yes, well let me finish that statement. A woman's place is in the House *(Pause)* and the Senate and wherever else she'd like to be.

JACK: Poppycock!

JILL: I might have expected that from you.

JACK: Oh, really, and why is that?

JILL: Your so-called values.

JACK: They're what keep families together. They contribute to the moral fiber —

JILL: That keeps them together in the dark ages. Tell me, how does carrying buckets of water help anything?

JACK: Have you ever heard of bucket brigades? People passing buckets to save their neighbors' homes from burning to the ground!

JILL: Fire hydrants, Jack, for heaven's sake. Running water. Much more effective. Those with special training should handle such things.

JACK: You mean you'd let your neighbor's house burn to the ground?!

JILL: Get a life, Jack!

JACK: *(Deeply hurt)* I would like to, Jill. But you know that's impossible. We're not real peo —

JILL: Oh, Jack, I'm sorry. I shouldn't have said it.

JACK: So then, will you go with me to fetch a pail of water?

JILL: Why would you want it?

JACK: To drink, to bathe, to scrub the floors and wash the dishes.

JILL: You know what, Jack?

JACK: What?

JILL: You're not even going to have to fall this time.

JACK: What...are you talking about?

JILL: Your crown, Jack, your crown. *(Clutching the closed umbrella in both hands, she raises it high over her head.)*

JACK: *Aiieeeee. (He races Off-stage, screaming.)*

JILL: *(Yelling)* **And Jill came running after.** *(Which, indeed, she does.)*

(Curtain)

Production Notes and Considerations

Since the play is simply for fun, the characters are two-dimensional and need not be developed further. The incongruity of the situation and the contrast between the characters, at opposite poles, is humor enough. To develop the two further would be a distraction for the audience.

Besides the incongruity of nursery rhyme figures growing older and appearing outside their world or frame of reference, the humor comes from the fact that each seems to believe so strongly in her or his side of the argument over new ideas versus old ideas.

You not only don't need a set for this piece, you actually don't even need a stage. The piece can be performed in front of the curtain or almost anywhere else.

The Eyes Have It

"The Eyes Have It" is a parody of racial prejudice. More than that, however, it is an example of derision in that the humor, particularly in the last two scenes, beginning with the entrance of the Coo Coo Policeman, becomes very heavy-handed. As you've learned, there can be danger in using derision in that if the ridicule becomes too extreme, the audience may begin to sympathize with the intended target. In this instance, however, the derision is not directed at a specific target but rather at an attitude. Of course, a secondary target is specific. It is hate groups that try to poison people's minds about those of different races, ethnic groups or religions. The Grand Dragon of the Coo Coo Kooks is symbolic of hate groups as is Roberta's goose step exit.

Although the location is Dold Souf, or, in other words, the Old South, the play is not meant to point out any specific area of the country or the world as a target for racial prejudice. In many ways, in fact, the South has come a lot further in the area of race relations than other sections of the country. The reason for choosing Dold Souf as the location is that the South is the area of the United States in which slavery was practiced, despite the fact that there were many sympathizers living elsewhere.

The play turns into total burlesque and slapstick, another type of farce than that in "Mix and Match," to point up the silliness of the sort of prejudice ridiculed in the play. This is a definite way of saying that this sort of feeling is wrong. The idea that the characters can wear colored contact lenses to disguise their true "race," pokes fun at the idea that any one race is different in any significant way from any other.

The silliness should be apparent in the highly exaggerated southern accent, two thick and drawling to be believable. A word about this: In certain places the same "word" is spelled differently. An example is "yo" and "yo-ah" for your. This is deliberate in that the flow of the language, and the words following often determine how a word is pronounced. It would be impractical and confusing to write every word in dialect. Thus, the dialect is suggested through the spelling variations, but, in performing the play, feel free to take whatever liberties you wish.

The idea that both the Smiths and the Joneses help those wishing to "escape" or "pass" is symbolic of the Underground

Railroad, the people who helped Jews escape to freedom during the Holocaust, and all others who have helped entire groups escape persecution.

CHARACTERS: CONSTANCE and ROBERTA, 16-17; JEROME and
EDMUND, 16-17; MR. and MRS. SMITH, 40s; a COO COO
POLICEMAN, any age; the MAJESTIC GRAND DRAGON of the
High Order of the Coo-Coo Kooks, any age.

    The characters, except for the POLICEMAN and the DRAGON,
are dressed in old-fashioned clothing, fairly plain in looks. The
COO COO POLICEMAN wears a blue suit, a shirt, and a dark blue
tie and has a cap similar to those worn by the Keystone Kops of
silent films. He has a clown's face with red circles on his cheeks
and a cherry-like fake nose. He also wears a bright red wig under
his hat. The DRAGON wears a white mask. Around his body are
wrapped white sheets trimmed in gold. A white dunce cap perches
on his head.

SETTING: The action takes place in the mythical land of Dold Souf. It is
the present, barely. A pair of flats Up Right represent the exterior
of the Smith household. A similar pair Up Left represent the exterior of the Jones' house. Up Center are a table and chairs which at
times represent the dining room of the Smiths and later the Grand
Council Chamber of The Grand Dragon of the Coo Coo Kooks.

AT RISE: CONSTANCE and ROBERTA enter Stage Right and stop in
front of the Smith home.

CONSTANCE: **I have a secret, Roberta. I'm jus' dyin' to tell ya. I will
if ya promise not to reveal it to another livin' soul.**

ROBERTA: **Why, Constance, honey, you know I wouldn't tell anyone
what passes between us.**

CONSTANCE: *(Giggling)* **I met a boy!**

ROBERTA: **A boy?**

CONSTANCE: **He's the cutest little old thing you evah did see.**

ROBERTA: **Oh, Constance. I'm so happy fo you. What's his name?**

CONSTANCE: **Edmund. Edmund Jones.**

ROBERTA: **Don't know as I've evah heard a name like that. Does he
go ta owah school?**

CONSTANCE: **No. And this is the part you promise you will nevah
reveal.**

ROBERTA: **You know I'd nevah.**

91

CONSTANCE: All right then. He doesn't go to owah school. He's a blue!

ROBERTA: *(Gasps and grabs the base of her throat.)* **Why Constance Marie Smith, I don't believe I want to be entrusted with that sort of news.**

CONSTANCE: Roberta, I've known you all my life, and I nevah would have believed –

ROBERTA: There's a place for the greens like us, and a place for the blues. If God had meant us to mix, he would have put us in the verra same school. I do declaah, Constance Marie, I am shocked. Shocked, do you heah?

CONSTANCE: Yes, I do. I do heah, and I'm mightily disappointed. Since owah births, haven't we practically shared the same cradle? The same *(Sobbing)* homes almost.

ROBERTA: There is somethin' in what you say, Constance. So I will considah caahfully. Befoah I climb between my satin sheets, I will contemplate the mattah and come to a conclusion. But I have to tell you, the verra idea is so alien to my bein' that I can't even imagine it.

CONSTANCE: If you met this boy of whom I'm speakin', maybe, just maybe, you would not have to do any contemplatin'.

ROBERTA: Constance, honey, have I hurt you? I nevah intended such a thing a'tall. I jus' need time to sort through what you told me. I best be goin' on home now. You know my daddy doesn't like me lingerin' on the street too long in case one of them blues comes into the wrong part of town. Why you nevah know – Oh, Constance, honey, I wasn't thinkin'. I jus' wasn't thinkin'. Fohgive me, say you'll fohgive me.

CONSTANCE: I fohgive you! Ah you happy now?

ROBERTA: *(Sobbing)* **I didn't mean it. I didn't.** *(ROBERTA runs straight across to Stage Left and exits. CONSTANCE watches for a moment and then exits Stage Right.)*

  (JEROME and EDMUND enter Stage Left and stop in front of the JONES' home.)

EDMUND: I met a girl, the most wondaful woman I have evah seen in my entiah life. But you have to promise you won't tell anyone about this.

92

JEROME: I don't undastand.

EDMUND: You've been muh friend fo a long time now, isn't that correct, Jerome?

JEROME: It surely is. We been as close as flies and molasses practically since the day we wuh boan.

EDMUND: I've always trusted you, and you've always trusted me, isn't that true?

JEROME: 'Cept that time in second grade when you stole that ripe peach I was gonna give to my teacher and gave it to huh yoahself.

EDMUND: That's long time past now. *(Pause)* You promise you won't tell anybody what I'm gonna reveal to you? Will you promise me that?

JEROME: What is it?

EDMUND: She's the most beautiful creacha I evah saw.

JEROME: Wheah did you see huh?

EDMUND: I was walkin' along and owah eyes jus' happened to meet.

JEROME: Wheah did this occuh?

EDMUND: Outside the school.

JEROME: I must have seen huh too then if she goes to owah school.

EDMUND: I didn't say it was owah school.

JEROME: Edmund, what do you mean?

EDMUND: She's a green.

JEROME: What? Can it be? You know verra well theah should be no mixin' of the eyes. If God had meant there to be a mixin' of the eyes he wouldn't have allowed two school buildin's to be erected heah.

EDMUND: I'm not so shuah, Jerome.

JEROME: This is a great responsibility yo ah givin' me. I don't know if ah want that responsibility.

EDMUND: You promise you won't tell anyone?

JEROME: I have to contemplate what you have revealed.

EDMUND: Jerome, please. You ah a true-blue friend.

JEROME: I won't be a green one!

EDMUND: I undastand.

JEROME: I'm sorry. I truly am.

EDMUND: She's glorious, Jerome. The most wondahful, the most beautiful –

JEROME: I'll see you at school tomorrow. *(JEROME hurriedly exits Stage Right, followed a second or two later by EDMUND.)*

(CONSTANCE and MR. and MRS. SMITH enter and sit at the table Center Stage. As they talk they pantomime eating dinner.)

CONSTANCE: Mama, Daddy?

MR. and MRS. SMITH: *(Simultaneously)* **Yes?**

CONSTANCE: Theah's somethin' I jus gotta tell ya. I can't keep it a secret any longah. I jus' can't.

MR. SMITH: What is troublin' you, Constance, honey?

CONSTANCE: I don't know how to tell you. I'm sorry about it, and yet I'm not. *(Nervous)* I know that's verra confusin', and I don't like to be confusin'. But I can't help it.

MRS. SMITH: Oh, muh little magnolia blossom, muh little honey-suckle vine, I hate ta see you so upset.

CONSTANCE: Oh, Mama!

MR. SMITH: Perhaps it would be bettah if you told us what's troublin' you, sweetheart.

CONSTANCE: I met...I met a boay. The most wondahful boay I've evah, evah met.

MR. SMITH: Well, darlin', theah's nothin' wrong with that. Why you awah in high school now, and this is ta be expected. Ah hate the thought of losin' muh little bitty peach petal, but I've known it was comin'. So don't you worry, sweetie, yo mama and I undastand.

MRS. SMITH: Look at it this way, Constance. It is a pawt a' the natural coase of events in a human lifetime. So don't you worry none.

CONSTANCE: You don't undastand. You can't undastand.

MR. SMITH: Whatevah it is, honey, we'ull try owah verra best.

MRS. SMITH: Ah've nevah seen you so worked up. It's about this boay, you say?

MR. SMITH: He hasn't...I mean he didn't try to take advantage of my poor little darlin'.

CONSTANCE: *Daddyyyyy!*

MR. SMITH: Sorry. But I love you, darlin'.

MRS. SMITH: Look at me, sweetie.

CONSTANCE: Yes?

MRS. SMITH: Don't blame yo fathah. We all jus' want ta make shuah owah baby gull is happy. That everthin' is all right.

CONSTANCE: Oh, Mama. Oh, Daddy. It isn't. It truly isn't.

MR. SMITH: You mean he did try to – Wheah ah my pistols, Jennifah Joy? I want my pistols.

MRS. SMITH: Why Henry Winfield Smith, owah daughtah already told you it wasn't like that.

MR. SMITH: Well, when it comes to muh little gull –

CONSTANCE: He's a blue!

MR. SMITH: I don't believe it. I surely don't.

MRS. SMITH: *(Fanning her face with her hand, looking as if she might faint)* I'm shocked. I surely am shocked.

CONSTANCE: I love you, Mama. I love you Daddy. I didn't deliberately try. I mean – *(MR. and MRS. SMITH exchange glances. MRS. SMITH nods.)*

MR. SMITH: Honey, there's somethin' you ought to know.

MRS. SMITH: It's not that we wanted to deceive you. It's jus' that we love you too much evah to want to bring you hahm.

MR. SMITH: *(He pantomimes popping out a pair of contact lenses.)* Look at me, Constance, honey. Look at me. Now you know the awful truth.

CONSTANCE: Daddy! Oh, my goodness. Oh, my! Oh, my! Daddy, yoah eyes are *blue!*

MR. SMITH: I surely cannot deny that, can I?

CONSTANCE: All these years...you've passed.

MRS. SMITH: Maybe someday, someday in the far distant future, maybe in our great-great-grandchildren's time or in our great-great-great-great-great-great-great-great –

MR. SMITH: It's all right, Jennifah Joy, we get the idea.

CONSTANCE: But how – When –

MRS. SMITH: It's a long, long story. Theah ah those who would considah it a sordid tale.

MR. SMITH: What yoah mama means is that we both grew up in

anothah city in a fah fah cornah of Dold Souf. But it was –
Well, it was –

MRS. SMITH: Love...at first sight.

MR. SMITH: And a close friend of your mama's told huh about an illegal dealah in colahed contact lenses.

MRS. SMITH: We were jus' young then. Eighteen and nineteen. But we both worked hard and saved evrah penny we could scrape up. And when we had enough, we bought those lenses, and we left. Nevah to retuhn.

CONSTANCE: I always wondad why I didn't have any cousins or aunts or uncles or grandmamas or granddaddys or great-great uncles, and cousins twice removed. I always wondered why –

MR. SMITH: We get the idea!

CONSTANCE: I'm sorry. I'm just so suprised. I think it's wondaful. The most wandaful thing I evah huud in my whole life. I really do. *(Crying, she jumps up and runs to MR. SMITH, leans over and kisses him on the cheek. Then she runs to MRS. SMITH and does the same.)* How did you know?

MR. SMITH: What's that, darlin?

CONSTANCE: How'd you know, I wouldn't turn out ta be a blue, like you, Daddy?

MRS. SMITH: We wanted to do the right thing. All the time we were savin' up those pennies, we resuched the subject of genetics. And we found that most likely a child of a green and a blue would turn out to be a green.

CONSTANCE: Then you don't object to muh seenin' Edmund?

MR. SMITH: That's the boy's name then, is it?

CONSTANCE: Edmund Randolph Jones. Isn't that just the purtiest name you evah heard?

MR. SMITH: That's exactly what I said about youah mama's name. Jennifer Joy.

MRS. SMITH: You ah shuah he's a nice boy now?

CONSTANCE: Oh, I'm shuah, I'm shuah, I'm shuah.

MR. SMITH: If you decided to go on seein' this boy, you could be in verra great dangah.

MRS. SMITH: The Coo Coo police.

96

CONSTANCE: I know.

MR. SMITH: You haven't told anyone, have you?

CONSTANCE: Roberta, that's all.

MRS. SMITH: Seein' as how you've been such good friends all your life, I 'spect that's all right.

MR. SMITH: Now then, Constance, you know there ah bound to be problems if you puhsist in this.

CONSTANCE: I know. I surely do.

MR. SMITH: I want you to considah this verra carefully. But your mama and I —

MRS. SMITH: She needs to know.

MR. SMITH: All right. We help people just like youahself. Make arrangements for them.

MRS. SMITH: Help them have happy lives togethah.

CONSTANCE: I don't undastand.

MR. SMITH: If this boy is really impotant to you, we can help you out buh showin' one of you how ta pass. Not that I'm suggestin' that this has reached the stage of complete seriousness now. But it would be easier for a blue to pass as a green.

MRS. SMITH: Because the green-eyed gene is dominant.

MR. SMITH: But if you wish, we have sets of both blue and green-colored contact lenses.

CONSTANCE: What?

MR. SMITH: *(Smiles.)* I suppose it is always a shock to find out yo parents are people with theah own secrets, theah own lives.

MRS. SMITH: If you and this boy do want to —

MR. SMITH: See each other?

CONSTANCE: Of coase. Oh, Mama, Daddy, you don't know what a relief it is that you undastand.

MRS. SMITH: Oh, but we do honey, we suhtainly do.

CONSTANCE: *(Giggling as she looks from one to the other)* I suppose you do.

MR. SMITH: You think about it, darlin'. And if you want a pair of blue-colored contacts, we're pretty good at fittin' 'em to anyone's eyes.

CONSTANCE: Oh, Mama, Daddy. I am so happy. So verra, verra happy.

(The SMITH FAMILY rises and exits Stage Right.)

(EDMUND enters from behind the flats Up Left and crosses Down Left. At the same time JEROME enters Stage Left and the two of them meet.)

JEROME: All right if I walk with you to school?

EDMUND: Why wouldn't it be?

JERMONE: I though maybe you'd still be angry at me?

EDMUND: Ovah yo reaction when I told you about Constance?

JEROME: Is that her name then?

EDMUND: Constance Marie Smith. Isn't that the most beautiful name you ever heard?

JEROME: Listen, Edmund, there's somethin' I have to tell you.

EDMUND: *(On the defensive)* **I'm listenin'.**

JEROME: This time I'm the one who's gonna have ta ask that you make a promise.

EDMUND: What promise is it?

JEROME: I wasn't angry yestaday. That's the fust thing.

EDMUND: Could have fooled me.

JEROME: I was startled.

EDMUND: Would you caah to explain that remock?

JEROME: If you promise nevah to tell another living soul what I'm gonna reveal to you.

EDMUND: All right, Jerome. I promise, though I don't see –

JEROME: My daddy's a green.

EDMUND: What? What is this youah tellin' me?

JEROME: It's true. My daddy's a green. Mama's the only one who's a blue.

EDMUND: The only one?

JEROME: You sure you won't tell anyone, will you?

EDMUND: You have my word.

JEROME: *(Pantomimes popping out contact lenses.)* **Theah! What do you think?**

EDMUND: I – I don't undastand. Theah's no use denyin' it.

JEROME: I nevah told anyone else.

EDMUND: Why *do* you weah those lenses?

JEROME: My daddy always wore blue-colored contact lenses. How

do you think it would look to have a green for a son? My
daddy's life would be in jeopady. My life would be in jeopady.

EDMUND: I nevah knew.

JEROME: Nobody knows, 'cepting muh mama and muh daddy and
me. But if you can't trust youah best friend, who can you trust?

EDMUND: Why did you tell me this, Jerome?

JEROME: My mama and my daddy, they help people like you.

EDMUND: What do you mean?

JEROME: Colored contact lenses is what I mean. That's why I have
to be so cahful. *(Pause)* Well, what do you say?

EDMUND: Say? I guess I don't follow yo meanin'.

JEROME: We just get you a pair of green-colored contact lenses, and
a lot of yo problems will be solved.

EDMUND: You awah indeed a true blue...Sorry. *(JEROME laughs.*
EDMUND and JEROME exit Stage Left.)

   (The lights fade momentarily to show the passage of time. They
   come up to show CONSTANCE and her PARENTS entering from
   behind the two flats Up Right.)

CONSTANCE: Well, now that I'm a blue, isn't Edmund gonna be
mightily suhprised?

MR. SMITH: You be cahful now, honey. You know this is not a game,
and it can be verra dangerous.

MRS. SMITH: Remembah, no mattah what, youah mama and daddy
love our little honeysuckle vine.

CONSTANCE: And I love you, and I thank you evah so much.

MR. SMITH: It's what we do. We jus' didn't expect to do it fo owah
own daughtah.

CONSTANCE: Ah you shuah it's all arranged at the school? Nobody's
gonna suspect anything?

MR. SMITH: Don't you worry, honey, everthin' is goin' ta be fahn.
   (CONSTANCE continues to talk quietly with her folks, though the
   audience cannot hear any more of what they say.)

   (EDMUND and JEROME enter Stage Left and pause for a
   moment before crossing the stage.)

EDMUND: You shuah it's all arranged now? Goin' ta the new school
and everthing?

JEROME: I told you my folks have been doin' this for yeahs.

EDMUND: Thank you, Jerome. It's a wondahful thing youah family has done. *(JEROME turns from EDMUND and exits Stage Left. From opposite sides of the stage, EDMUND and CONSTANCE cross toward Center Stage. They nearly collide. They look at each other. They react simultaneously.)*

CONSTANCE: Edmund!

EDMUND: Constance!

CONSTANCE: What have you done?

EDMUND: I got fitted for green-colored contacts, and I'm goin' to your school.

CONSTANCE: But I – I did the verra same thing.

(As CONSTANCE and EDMUND continue to talk, unheard by the audience, ROBERTA and the COO COO POLICEMAN sneak in Up Center. ROBERTA grabs the POLICEMAN's arm and points to CONSTANCE and EDMUND.)

ROBERTA: *(In a stage whisper)* What did I tell you? Theah they awah.

POLICEMAN: You awah a fine and propah citizen. I shall see that you receive a commendation.

ROBERTA: I jus' hate to see it, don't you? *(She says the word blue as if it is utterly revolting.)* A green and a blue together.

POLICEMAN: Thank you, Miss. You best run along now.

ROBERTA: It is awah duty to put a stop to –

POLICEMAN: Yes, yes. *(He pulls a water pistol from his holster and turns toward CONSTANCE and EDMUND.)* You theah! *(ROBERTA, very stiffly and militarily erect, puts one heel behind the other and executes a perfect about face. She goose steps through the Up Center exit.)*

EDMUND: Run, Constance, run.

CONSTANCE: I can't leave you, I can't.

EDMUND: *(Grabbing her arm)* Come on then. *(They start to run.)*

POLICEMAN: Halt! *(He grabs his whistle and continues to blow sharp blasts on it as he runs around hither and yon like a Keystone Kop of silent films.)* Halt, I tell you, or I shall – What is it I shall do? Oh, yes. I shall shoot. That's what I'll do. I'll shoot. *(He fires long arcs of water at CONSTANCE and EDMUND, barely missing*

them. *CONSTANCE and EDMUND freeze. The POLICEMAN is a
totally ridiculous person, and he behaves and talks like a clown.)*
What have we heah? What have we heah? I say, what –
CONSTANCE: **Suh, I can explain.**
POLICEMAN: **Not finished yet. Not finished yet. Not finished.** *(He
runs in circles around them.)* **I started to say, "I say what have we
heah? What have we heah?"**
EDMUND: **Offisuh, if I may be allowed –**
POLICEMAN: **A green – a green eyes, and a blue.**
> **A green, a blue.**
> **It really is green eyes and blue.**
> **I do not like them here, would you?**
> **Green eyes, blues eyes mixed, it's true!**
> **I do not like blue eyes with green.**
> **Blue eyes with green is quite obscene.**
> **Would I like them here or there?**
> **I would not like them anywhere.**
> **Green eyes and blue, blue eyes and green –**
CONSTANCE: **Offisuh, please!**
POLICEMAN: **Yes, yes, yes. What, what, what? What is it? What is it?**
CONSTANCE: **You are the one who is obscene.**
POLICEMAN: **I? Moi?**
EDMUND: **You're a poor excuse for a policeman.**
POLICEMAN: **And yet I'm the law; you must heed what I say;**
> **You will have to come with me; I'll lock you away.**
> **You'll be kept in a dark, gloomy dungeon all night.**
> **You'll never again see the sun's golden –**
EDMUND: **You are a ridiculous little man.**
POLICEMAN: **Ridiculous, ridiculous, oh, no. Oh, woe. Oh me, oh
my, don't make me cry. Oh my, oh me...oh me...oh...my.** *(He
pulls a sponge from a fanny pack and holds the sponge to his eyes,
squeezing out tears.)*
EDMUND: **Things ah not as they appeah.**
POLICEMAN: *(Stuffing the sponge back into his fanny pack)* **Not as
they seem? Is this a dream, a dream, a dream? Nightmare,
nightmare, I don't care.** *(He looks at them defiantly.)* **I'm a big**

101

boy now, and nightmares don't scare me. *(He pulls out a balloon from his pocket, quickly blows it up, ties a knot in the end, and holds it aloft threateningly.)* **If you don't come with me, I'll hit you with my billy club. I will, I will, I will.**

EDMUND: *(Takes out his contacts.)* **And what is the charge, officah?**

POLICEMAN: *(He puts his fingertips to his forehead, hunches over slightly and walks around and around CONSTANCE and EDMUND as he speaks.)* **What is the charge? I do not know? I do not know. It's truly so; I do not know. Your eyes, your eyes, a different hue. One set green, one set blue. I know it's true. I know it's true. What shall I do? What shall I do?** *(Stops abruptly; speaks in a taunting voice.)* **You awah tryin' to fool me, and that isn't especially nice.**

CONSTANCE: **All right!** *(She pops her contacts.)*

EDMUND: **Constance, no!**

POLICEMAN: *(Jumps in glee.)* **Ah ha, ah ha, it's true, it's true. One set green and one set blue. All right then. We're off to see the dragon, the majestic old dragon of Kook. He is a mighty dragon, yes, but sometimes he makes you...** *(Grabs his stomach and pantomimes throwing up. Suddenly, he points his water pistol at CONSTANCE and EDMUND.)* **Promise you won't tell him I said that. Or else I'll squirt you right in the eye.**

CONSTANCE: **All right! We promise.**

EDMUND: **I don't undastand. Why did you do this?**

CONSTANCE: *(Very sincere)* **A long time ago in a mythical land, there lived a woman named Rosa Parks.** *(Lights to black.)*

(In a few moments the lights come up on Center Stage. The Smith's table has become a judge's bench. The chairs have now been angled toward the bench. CONSTANCE and EDMUND occupy two of them. MRS. SMITH sits in the third. MR. SMITH stands behind her, one hand resting on the back of the chair. The COO COO POLICEMAN enters Up Center.)

POLICEMAN: **All rise, all rise, stand up, stand up, be erect, be erect. Rise, rise.** *(CONSTANCE, EDMUND, and MRS. SMITH stand. He points to MR. SMITH.)* **Up, up, up, up, up. I said rise. Get up. Get up. Get up.**

MR. SMITH: *(Slowly and forcefully)* **I already am up!**

POLICEMAN: **Yes, of coase. Of coase, yes. Forgive me, yes, do, please, yes. Forgive me.** *(He pauses and then actually repeats the word "ahem.")* **Ahem. Ahem. Ahem. Ladies and gentlemen of owah studio audience. No, no. Wrong, wrong, wrong.** *(Slaps his face.)* **Ladies and gentlemen of the jury, honored guests –** *(Slaps his face with his other hand.)* **Wrong, wrong, wrong, all wrong. Wrong, indeed yes, wrong.**

OFF-STAGE VOICE: *(It is the DRAGON, and he speaks in deep, sonorous, booming tones, as if to convince himself of his own importance.)* **Do....please. Get on...with it...Officah Coo Coo.**

POLICEMAN: **Yes, yes, well, ahem, yes, ahem.**

OFF-STAGE VOICE: **Officah!**

POLICEMAN: **Yes, well, then, the Majestic Grand Dragon of the High Order of the Coo-Coo Kooks.** *(Aside to the audience)* **Still, sometimes he makes me...** *(He grabs his belly and pantomimes throwing up.)*

(Slowly and regally, the MAJESTIC GRAND DRAGON of the High Order of the Coo-Coo Kooks enters. Just before he sits, he trips over his robe, and nearly falls on his face. He catches himself, but bumps into the POLICEMAN, who careens hither and yon all across the stage floor, finally coming to rest when he is able to clutch the edge of the judge's bench.)

DRAGON: **Yes, well...then...we shall proceed.**

POLICEMAN: **Yes, yes, let us proceed, go on, go on, let's go. The mighty dragon tells us so.**

DRAGON: **Shut up!**

POLICEMAN: **Yes, yes, yes. Shut** *(Draws an imaginary zipper closed over his lips and then tries to say the word "up" and then the words "shut up.")* **Umph! Guuu umph!**

DRAGON: *(Rotund tone)* **Now then...it is my...duty...and yes...my sacred trust...to enfoahce...the holy...laws of the...land...of...Dold Souf. If God had...evah...evah...meant for...blue eyes...and...green eyes...to mix...togethah...in...theeee...same classroom – he would... of coase...have allowed to be erected...only one...school ...building puh village. I shall now wait for the applause.**

(Gestures for applause. There is no applause.) **I see, then. Well.** *(He advances to CONSTANCE and EDMUND and speaks very swiftly.)* **I-am-the-judge; I-am-the-jury; I-am-the-prosecutor-and-the-defender. Yes, I am** *(He pauses for trumpet fanfare and resumes speaking very slowly)* **the Majestic Grand Dragon of the High Order of the Coo Coo Kooks. I shall hold for the applause.** *(There is no applause.)*

(During the following speech by the DRAGON, the COO COO POLICEMAN sneaks around behind the DRAGON and pantomimes both his actions and his speech.)

DRAGON: *(Continued)* **Well then, let's get on with it, shall we?** *(As if playing two parts, he hops one step to the left and turns to face the spot where he has been standing as the POLICEMAN does the same behind him.)* **Yes, we shall, of course, your very Majestic Grand Dragon of the High Order of the Coo Coo Kooks.** *(Quickly, he turns back to EDMUND and CONSTANCE. He gives them no time to answer his question and delivers the following lines quickly and without pause.)* **How do you plea? Guilty then; jury dismissed; you are sentenced to be chained to oars in galley ships never to be released till you die; thank you all and good-bye. I shall hold for applause.** *(There is no applause.)* **All right then. Sentence to be carried out immediately. I shall hold for ap –**

MR. SMITH: **Jus' a minute naow.**

DRAGON: *(Resuming his sonorous and deep tones)* **Do you know whom you are addressin'?**

MR. SMITH: **Of coase, I know.**

DRAGON: *(Normal voice)* **OK then. No problem. Just wondahed.**

MR. SMITH: **What gives you the raht to say that these ah the rules of the land of Dold Souf? Who appointed you judge, jury, and executionah?**

DRAGON: *(Coyly)* **Little ol' me?**

MRS. SMITH: *(Coming to stand behind her husband)* **Yes, you! And take off that silly mask.** *(Pause)* **Take it off, ah say.**

DRAGON: *(Parody of a little boy pleading)* **Promise not to hurt me.**

MR. SMITH: **No promises. Take it off.**

DRAGON: *(Taunting)* **You can't make me.**

MRS. SMITH: We shall see about that. *(She rushes up and yanks off his mask. She staggers backwards.)* **It cannot be. It cannot.**

MR. SMITH: Are those your real eyes, or are they colored contact lenses?

DRAGON: *(In a very small, childlike voice)* **They are my eyes. My verra own eyes. Don't you think I'm special?**

EDMUND: But – one is green.

CONSTANCE: One is blue.

POLICEMAN: *(Jumping up and down gleefully)* **And the one right in the middle of your forehead is brown!**

EDMUND: You know what this means, don't you?

MRS. SMITH: An end to puhsecution.

MR. SMITH: An end to hidin'. *(He pops his contacts.)*

CONSTANCE: It means –

POLICEMAN: *(Leaping about)* **It means, it means, it means, it means. Oh, yes, oh, yes, it means –** *(Stands still, puzzled.)* **What does it mean?**

EDMUND: It means –

   (The entire cast including ROBERTA and JEROME, who enter arm in arm, all turn and face the audience.) **At long last, we ah free.**

POLICEMAN: And as in all fairy tales, we lived happily ever after.

EDMUND: Well...

CONSTANCE: Actually... *(One by one the cast members shrug and walk Off-stage as the lights slowly dim to black.)*

   (Curtain)

Production Notes and Considerations

The tone of the piece changes drastically with the entrance of the Coo Coo Policeman in that it becomes burlesque or slapstick — completely divorced from any sane form of reality. The Coo Coo Policeman parodies the song from the film "The Wizard of Oz" simply because there is a parallel between the wizard, who turns out to be a mild human being, and the dragon who turns out to be meek and submissive. The policeman also uses rhyme schemes and meter reminiscent in places of Dr. Seuss's *Green Eggs and Ham* and *Sneetches,* both of which deal with prejudice. You might want to look them up to see how they treat the subject.

The Coo Coo Policeman's costume is meant to suggest the ridiculousness of racial or ethnic prejudice. The cap, incidentally, can be constructed out of cardboard and covered with fabric.

The Grand Dragon should also be ridiculously attired. Of course, he has to have a mask, and he needs to have a painted eye in the middle of his forehead.

Neither racial background nor eye color should matter so far as casting the scene. In playing the roles, you should keep in mind that although there is a lot of humor, "The Eyes Have It" is highly exaggerated, and in places is very heavy-handed in its derision of racial supremacists, such as Adolph Hitler, Tom Metzger, David Duke, and William Bradford Shockley, and hate groups such as the Nazis, Neo-Nazis and skinheads, and the Ku Klux Klan. An example of the exaggeration is the idea that the Grand Dragon sickens even the Coo Coo Policeman. Another example is the pomposity and posturing of the Dragon, who, without his costume, is childish and insecure.

Because it is heavy-handed in its derision, "The Eyes Have It" uses clichés and nonsensical arguments, such as the repeated gag about having two school buildings in the same locality. This, of course, is ridiculing racist arguments that have absolutely no basis in fact. "Southern" clichés include Mr. and Mrs. Smith calling Constance things like a "magnolia blossom" or "honeysuckle vine," and Mr. Smith's wanting to know where his pistols are.

The piece makes use of automatism or the running gag in such things as Mrs. Smith's and later Constance's reference to relatives — great-great-great grandchildren and absent cousins.

There also is a parody of people trying to "pass" or pose as one thing when they are another. This was much more prevalent in earlier years.

Although the piece deals with heavy issues, it generally is humorous. However, there are two serious notes. The first is the reference to Rosa Parks, a real person who one time while riding a Montgomery, Alabama, city bus refused to give up her seat to a white person, thus sparking a bus strike and advancing the civil rights movement. The second is the ending. The message here is that yes, the blues and the greens have more rights than previously, but they still have a long way to go.

Except for the Coo Coo Policeman and the Dragon, the characters are more individualized than those in "Mix and Match," so in playing any of the roles, you may want to try to figure out what makes them individuals — what motivates them; what gives them their individual traits.

The Policeman and the Dragon are stereotypes and highly exaggerated at that. You need to decide how to emphasize their silliness and stupidity.

A Tale From the Bog; *or* Whatever Happened to the Lost Lenore?

Melodrama is another genre that ends happily. Similar to tragedy, it treats a serious subject, and the audience identifies with the protagonist. Rather than exploring a character's inner being, pure melodrama presents one-dimensional characters, either all good or all bad. When it deals with anything painful or serious, the subject is pointed up only for its theatrical value much in the way popular tabloids exploit the real or imagined misfortunes of celebrities. Melodrama often appears to show three-dimensional characters in conflict, but the struggle usually is only surface, and the audience knows that good will win over bad at the end. Action generally is much more important than characterization.

Melodrama offers entertainment and an escape from everyday problems, but it can bring the plight of individuals and groups to the attention of the audience. Within recent years, melodrama has become more realistic than that of the nineteenth and early twentieth centuries. These earlier plays were filled with false sentiment that to us appears really hokey. The characters in today's melodrama are less stereotyped, and sometimes the play does not end happily. Yet even though melodrama has changed, in essence it has the same appeals: a virtuous hero or heroine, a despicable villain, and sensation.

A sub-genre of melodrama, often called "meller-drama," is a parody or spoof of nineteenth-century or early twentieth-century melodrama and novels. The best-known plot variation is the one in which the moustache-twirling villain attempts to repossess a farm on which live a penniless mother and/or father and an innocent young daughter.

To understand how ludicrous and far-fetched nineteenth-century melodramas are, you can try reading one, such as W. H. Smith's *The Drunkard* (1847). This might help you to understand the extreme silliness of "A Tale From the Bog," which makes fun of many of the conventions (practices or rules) of the genre. In addition to sentimentality, early melodramas often relied on great exaggeration of situation, detail, and character. The dangers were too extreme to be believed, the heroes too virtuous, and the heroines far too given to long-suffering martyrdom. Particularly in the popular novels of the period, there were supernatural elements.

"A Tale From the Bog" pokes fun at all these. It deliberately mixes everyday speech and slang with Shakespearean and Victorian phrasing and speech. Additionally, it has a lot of word play, including alliteration, a series of words in which the same sound is repeated.

You might see parodies of some familiar poetry, as well. But don't be surprised if the parody of one poet becomes completely tangled up with another. As you may be able to infer from the title, the major target of the spoofery is Edgar Allan Poe.

CAST: JERRY, 15-17; LIZ, 15-17; PETE, 15-17; LENORE, 20s. Although one is male and one is female, JERRY and LIZ are nearly identical "twins."

SETTING: It is a wintry day in the fens and swamps, and in the rest of the estate as well. But the rest of the estate is only the house. The weirdness occurs in the living room of said house.

AT RISE: JERRY is peering out a window Up Center. LIZ is standing nearby.

JERRY: The fog, Liz, do you see it?

LIZ: How can I see it, silly? You're the one at the window.

JERRY: The twin thing, I guess. Since you and I are nearly identical twins, I thought sometimes you could see what I see.

LIZ: Do you see what I see?

JERRY: That's a Christmas song, Liz, and it isn't Christmastide, though it is winter, and the fog is thick as angel hair smothering the life from an evergreen tree.

LIZ: I see.

JERRY: You really see? The fog, I mean?

LIZ: Yes.

JERRY: Then it's true! Though we are only nearly identical twins, you a few inches shorter than I, though much, much heavier!

LIZ: Jerry! Mama said we must be nice to each other.

JERRY: I was simply stating a fact.

LIZ: Shall I state one too?

JERRY: If you wish.

LIZ: Acne. Your cheeks, your chin, your forehead, your neck, your ears, your –

JERRY: All right, Liz, that's enough.

LIZ: I was simply going to say –

JERRY: That my head, my whole entire head is covered with horrible –

LIZ: *(Crossing to the window to stand beside him)* No! Merely how foggy it is. Thick as...as –

JERRY: Pea soup.

LIZ: Camphor-soaked blankets in a stuffy mummy's case.

JERRY: And the hounds are baying in the moor at the moon.

LIZ: Really? All this time I thought they were mooning at the bay.

JERRY: No more; no more.

LIZ: Of course, there's no moor; it's a bog. *(There is a crash of thunder and the sound of breaking glass. A figure in a black cloak stumbles on from Stage Right. He is covered in broken glass. LIZ gives a loud, piercing scream.)*

JERRY: And who are you, sir, that you dare come unannounced into our presence? We, who are the Guinness world record holders for being the world's most similar, almost identical twins... though we are male and female.

PETE: So sorry, old chap. Name's Pete. Nearly dragged down into the bog, I was.

LIZ: Pete? Bog? I don't understand.

PETE: Aye, and a pretty lass such as yourself so unaccustomed to the terrors of the lonely night in this rural area of boggery, this veil of mist, that contains these baying hounds of the moor.

JERRY: Really? Are they moored in the bog?

PETE: Nay, bogged down in the moor, more like.

LIZ: More like what? I thought they were ghostly dogs come straight from Dis.

JERRY: Liz, whatever are you going on about? From dis what?

LIZ: Just from Dis.

JERRY: Dis what, I asked you!

PETE: If I may interject here?

JERRY: Here? Exactly here.

PETE: Hear exactly...what I say, and then take warning.

JERRY: What say you?

PETE: Your sister, sir. The one who looks nearly like you. Take heed of her warning of the hounds of Dis.

JERRY: For the last and final time, Dis what?

PETE: Wow, you really don't have a clue!

JERRY: Clue? Clue? Is there some sort of mystery to be solved?

LIZ: The mystery of your missing brain cells, more like.

PETE: At least, brain cells bogged down in the moor.

LIZ: Or moored outside your head.

PETE: What your lovely, little lass of a sister means to say –

LIZ: Is dat Dis is de...I mean that Dis is the god of the underworld.

JERRY: The waters rage around us, threatening to bury our bodies in a bog by the bay. Under the world of raging water?

LIZ: Of course not, nutso! Dis is the Roman god of the underworld, Hades –

JERRY: What is?

PETE: Dis is.

JERRY: Dis is what?

LIZ and PETE: *(Simultaneously)* The god of the underworld.

JERRY: Ah, yes, and soon enough, since the muck and mire of the quicksand suck steadily at the very foundation of our home, shall we be joining Dis god. I've tried to tell Mumsy and Daddy: "We must move, or nevermore to move again."

PETE: Quoth the raven.

JERRY: Art thou mad, man, with your raving quotations. The mist is gathering.

LIZ: But if it's gathering, shall it be missed?

PETE: I, for one, shall not miss it. Begone, I say to the hellish place from which thou comest. *(A mighty bolt of thunder and a flash of lightning)*

LIZ: Aye, do not speak such words. Long have those of us who lived here known the hounds of Dis –

JERRY: Once and for all, Dis what?!

LIZ: You know the legend as well as I. They who curse the hounds shall suffer great peril.

JERRY: Say, you never have identified yourself.

PETE: As I did relate, there are some that know me as Pete. Others call me Mack.

LIZ: Mack?

PETE: *(Quickly)* Donald Mack. I once owned a farm...Nay, I shall not tell thee for 'tis but a long sad tale of cows.

JERRY: *(Insincere laughter; hammy)* Ha ha! The tail of a cow? Humorous? Hmmm.

PETE: Sir!

JERRY: Sorry. You were telling the tale of a cow. *(We hear the tolling of a bell.)*

LIZ: A tale best told as tolled the bell. Not the clamor and the clangor of the bells, bells, bells, bells, round the necks, necks, necks, necks of the cows, cows, cows, cows. Yet perhaps to tell the tale as the bell tolls, can cow the hounds of Hades.

PETE: What, say, signifies your telling of the tolling of the bell? And why would telling the tale of the cow on the farm during the tolling help you better tolerate the situation, as so you have implied?

LIZ: There is danger, great danger from sources unknown when the dogs be cursed by such as you *(Indicating Jerry)* or he or I. 'Tis said that when the bell tolls, it tolls for those who tell the baying hounds in the bog to begone to that place whence they once wildly wandered.

JERRY: And tales told, even long, sad tales of cows on a farm can divert our attention enough so that we not be taken in by the accursed tolling that foretells the trip that exerts the toll of our souls in crossing o'er the bog.

PETE: Let's see. Do I have this straight? You want me to tell you the tale of my cows on my farm when my name was Old Mack – Donald Mack.

LIZ: You look no older than Jerry or myself!

PETE: Yet creaked my bones as I followed the creek that crookedly crept to the bog. The cold and the muck and the mire and the mud were much more merciless than a mere man could credibly cope with in comfort.

JERRY: Get to it, man. Sis and I, we're pretty good listeners. Not that there's much to listen to stuck out here in the bogs, so to speak. Mired in the muck, as it were.

PETE: Well, then, I had this farm. A goodly farm, till the divils themselves stole it from me to make a fortune at a fast-food fill-up.

LIZ: Oh, you're that Mack, Donald!

PETE: Nay, lass, do not slander speak nor libel write. 'Twas not the hamburger joint of which you speak. It was a place that sold cow tails to the very imps of Satan's horde.

LIZ: Imps?

PETE: Aye. Love those cows' tails, they do. Slapped 'twixt the cows' hooves and slathered with slime from the slippery slopes of the slog... *(Vigorously shakes his head)* er, the slippery slopes of the bog.

LIZ: Ooooooo, ga-ross!

PETE: So thought I. And so thus slipped I away during noon's bright sun. And the farm was mine no more.

LIZ: You poor man.

PETE: Pity me not, for such is fate that some have farms and some have not. I am one of the fortunate ones for I always hated farming.

JERRY: Hated farming? I don't understand. Then why —

PETE: Working my way back home. You see, as a child, I was kidnapped by the very hellish hounds who moon over the bay in the bog. Mired down there they are, hoping to do as their mistress bids and capture me and take me back with her to these divils herself.

JERRY: Say, why the devil do you always say divil?

PETE: Because it would be a devil of a thing not to say divil, for a divil it is.

LIZ: But say, sir, prithee, answer me?

PETE: Aye, pretty maid.

LIZ: What the devil is a divil if a divil ain't a devil?

PETE: Ah, methinks I sees wherein there lies confusion. A devil, you see, is "evil" with a "d," which is live [pronounced as in "lift"] spelled backwards because that is a thing they never can do, you see. They can never live since they come not from natural life.

JERRY: And the "d" itself.

PETE: Stands for doggone, of course. There are two theories on the matter. First is simply that they use it as an oath. I discount that one. The other, the more likely of the two, is that the dogs themselves, as well you know, are gone from the place wherein they were meant to stay.

115

JERRY: From Dis, you mean.

PETE: Dat's right.

JERRY: Very, very interesting. And where, good sir, did you learn such lore?

PETE: The lore I learned from Lenore, who not so lately learned it from the one who wrote of raven lunatics and watery tombs for lasses named Lee.

LIZ: I perceive perhaps that you speak of the poet Poe.

JERRY: And perhaps most pointedly. Surely, Lenore lies lost as lost she has lain for many a long, lusty year.

LIZ: Lusty?

JERRY: I had to think of something that began with an "L."

LIZ: Do get on with your tale.

PETE: Nay, nay, the cows' tails be lost to the divils, I say.

LIZ: Tell us now, sir, what these divils are, if not devils they be.

PETE: So shall I proceed then, Jerry?

JERRY: Jerry! How knoweth you my name?

PETE: In good time. In good time. But first the matter of the divils. The divils aren't as bad as the devils, though close enough to scare the pants off a man.

LIZ: Sir!

PETE: Sorry, lass, if I offend.

LIZ: *(Radiant smile)* Thou art forgiven.

PETE: Shall I thus resume my recitation?

LIZ: With no reluctance, sir, with no reluctance.

PETE: How like thee lovely lass.

JERRY: Let *lon* lit lit – *(Shakes his head.)* I mean, get on with it.

PETE: Take off the "d" and spell divils backwards.

JERRY: Livy? Wasn't he a classical –

PETE: Nay, must keep the "s."

LIZ: Slivi.

PETE: Slivey, slithy, slivering, slippery, slimy slugs.

JERRY: Isn't that...stretching it just a bit far?

PETE: Wrote not I this script, though knoweth it I by rote.

LIZ: You mean by reading the writing scripted herein?

PETE: No! Memorization. Rote. Like learning the tables with which you multiply one number against another.

JERRY: Right! Now that everyone's thoroughly confused, I have a question to ask.

PETE: Right? I know not the subtleties of right or wrong. Multiplication tables? Calculators? Which be right? In one sense, if learned correctly, they both are right. Yet is it right to use them both in the same instance or one over the other, I cannot answer. Better to discuss such subtleties of morality with theologians or philosophers.

JERRY: I meant –

LIZ: *(Sounding bored)* All he means is he wants to ask you a question.

PETE: Hey, no problem.

JERRY: Thou toldeth us that thy name was Pete.

PETE: The divils be dumb, I tell ye. I changed my name to escape them.

LIZ: Dumb? *(There is a sound like squealing, scurrying rats. To JERRY)* Did you forget to set the mousetraps again?

PETE: Nay, he did not. That be the sound of angry divils, too dumb to know who I am though they suspect perhaps they knew me once in a different guise.

JERRY: Guys? How many guys were with you?

LIZ: Egad and merciful heavens, Jer. He means demeanor.

JERRY: Meaner than what? Who was mean?

LIZ: Persona then, if you wish.

JERRY: Pretending to be someone else!

PETE: Yes, when I was Old Mack – Donald Mack – and had my farm. I...oh... *(The bell tolls and the hounds bark, startling LIZ.)*

LIZ: Eeeeee!

PETE: I –

LIZ: Eeeeee!

PETE: I –

JERRY: Oh! Let's get on with it. You were Donald Mack, and you changed your name to Pete.

LIZ: Because you didn't want to remain bogged down with the divils.

PETE: **Indubitably.**

JERRY: **Why cometh you here?**

PETE: **Isn't it obvious?** *(He throws off his cape and hat and the scarf from across his mouth.)*

JERRY: **You**

LIZ: **Look**

PETE: **Just**

JERRY: **Like**

LIZ: **Us!**

Pete: *Yessss*, **I know. You are not identical twins. You are two-thirds of a set of identical triplets. And I am your long-lost brother.**

LIZ: **We never knew**

JERRY: **we had a**

PETE: **brother? Yes, I'm sure you didn't. I was taken, or so I was told by Lenore, in much the same manner as she relayed that she was. Snatched from my cradle.**

JERRY: **This Lenore of whom you speak. She was a wee child –**

PETE: **Precisely. In a poem by Poe, 'twas the narrator's kidnapped babe, not his affianced, nor his mate, as most scholars seem to think.**

JERRY: **Why were you taken?**

LIZ: **How did you meet –**

PETE: **The long lost Lenore?**

LIZ: **Of course.**

PETE: **Oh, well, just by tapping on her chamber door. Only that and nothing more. Startled the poor dear, I'm sure, for suddenly I came a-rapping, really very gently tapping.**

LIZ: **On her chamber door?**

PETE: **Yes.**

JERRY: **Surely then, there must be more.**

PETE: **'Twas as if she were entranced, enraptured, cast 'neath a mesmerizing spell.**

JERRY: **Surely then, this tale you'll tell.**

LIZ: **Enough with the rhymes already.**

JERRY: **Gosh!**

LIZ: **So what happened?**

PETE: It was many and many a year ago in a kingdom by the bog.

LIZ: Near here?

PETE: Yes.

LIZ: But you come here alone, Pete. Have you...have you then not...

PETE: Lost Lenore?

LIZ: What happened to the poor, dear thing?

PETE: Mired down in the bogs. Bogged down in the mire. Why do they call them quicksands, I've always wondered. For "quick," as you know, means live. But the lovely Lenore *(Starting to sob)* no longer lingers *(Crying so hard now he can barely get out the words)* in life. Lost, lost, all lost. Alone in a wide, wide bog. And not ever a frog in the deep, deep bog *(Again crying)* took pity on...

LIZ: Her soul in agony?

PETE: *(A sense of wonderment)* Yes, yes, how did you know?

LIZ: *(Hardly able to keep from crying)* We studied...the poem *(Sobs)* last year in English lit. *(Cries.)* "The Rime of the Ancient Lenore."

JERRY: Isn't that "The Rime of the Ancient Mariner"?

LIZ: You remember it your way; I'll remember it mine. *(The dogs begin a mighty howling.)*

PETE: That means –

LIZ: Yes, Pete? What does it mean?

PETE: It signifies that the hounds are baying their triumph at the finding of the lost Lenore.

JERRY: At least Lenore shall be lost nevermore.

LIZ: But tell us, Pete, how it came to be that you discovered –

PETE: That I am your brother? *(LIZ and JERRY nod.)* As you suspected, the bogs are bound by an ancient curse that causes suppression of certain selected memories.

JERRY: But if that's true...

LIZ: How did you know who you are?

PETE: Very simply, it was Lenore.

JERRY: Only that and nothing more?

LIZ: *(To JERRY)* *I* told you to stop it.

PETE: Never have I been one to interfere in family affairs, but since

119

these are the affairs of my own family, can you not but see how the curse is working its ways, attempting to wedge its wickedness 'twixt you?

LIZ: That's right. We've never quarreled.

JERRY: Mother often wondered why we didn't.

PETE: Ah, yes, mother. Where is the dear woman whose form has ne'er past afore my ocular orbs since I lay abed in the baby crib built for three?

LIZ: I've often wondered about that.

JERRY: About mother?

LIZ: No, about the crib built for three. You and I lay side by side by...

JERRY: Isn't that a musical?

LIZ: *(Gives them dirty looks.)* As I was saying: Side by side by...nothing. Yet now as I place my thoughts upon it, vaguely it is I seem to remember.

JERRY: Yes, just like now, a bleak December. And each dying ember –

LIZ: We don't have a fireplace, stupid!

JERRY: Of course, I don't know what I could have been thinking.
   (The thunder and lightning build to a crescendo. There is more breaking of glass. LIZ emits another long, piercing scream as a figure bound round and round with bolts of black silk battles her way into the room.)

PETE: Lenore! *(LENORE unwinds the long strands of silk, rather like unfurling a long, long party streamer. As she spins free, we see that she is a young and vibrant woman, perhaps a few years older than PETE.)*

LENORE: Peter, my love, my pretty, my darling, my child, my boy.

PETE: 'Tis I, sweet Lenore.

JERRY: I don't understand. It was many and many a year ago –

PETE: Remember the trance I mentioned. More it was like a life suspended.

JERRY: I've heard of such *things*.

LIZ: In science fiction books/
   and *magazines*.

JERRY: Now who's the one who's rhyming!

LIZ: Near rhyme only.

JERRY: You're right, and I apologize.

PETE: Thus explains why Lenore looks only a few years older than we.

LENORE: These, of course, are your birth mates.

PETE: My sister and brother. Lenore, may I present to you Elizabeth Allan and Jerry Allan –

LENORE: *(Swooning)* No, it cannot be.

PETE: Yes, I kept it from you all these years. The shock, I felt, would be too intense. Though you appear almost as our peer would appear, you, in fact, are *(Rolling his eyes, shrugging and spreading his hands, indicating he really doesn't want to say it)* our great-great *(Slight pause)* great-great grandmother.

LENORE: *(Gathering them all into her arms)* My darlings, my children, my loves. Elizabeth Allan, Gerald Allan, and Peter Allan Poe!

LIZ: Uh...

LENORE: What is it, child?

LIZ: I hate to tell you this...

LENORE: Yes?

JERRY: Our last name is...is...

PETE: *(Sarcastically)* What they mean to tell you, Grams, is that our last name is Longfellow.

LENORE: *(Sounding like a fishwife)* Longfellow! But I thought your name was Poe!

PETE: Ah-ha! I've always known. You thought you could fool me, but you couldn't. I fooled you instead.

JERRY: Fooled me too.

LENORE: I'll call my dogs.

JERRY: What – hey, what's comin' down here?

LIZ: I thought you loved the lovely lost Lenore.

PETER: No-no-no! Never then and nevermore! You see, it was Lenore's hellish hounds that guarded the bog all these years. Her divils that snatched me first, then later forced me from my farm. Hoping, you see, that I'd lead Lenore here to the family manse.

LENORE: *(Laughing like a witch)* And you did. *(Her voice cackles.)* You awakened me, my boy. And so you are mine.

PETE: Not yet. Not yet.

LENORE: I don't see why not. I'll simply call my hounds.

LIZ: You told us Lenore was Edgar Allan Poe's –

PETE: Child? Tiny, wee babe? Aye, that I did.

JERRY: Forsooth!

LIZ: What?

JERRY: It sounds good, OK? I don't know. I couldn't remember the line. It's no big deal.

LIZ: In the overall scheme of things, I suppose you're right. *(Clicks her tongue and turns her attention to PETE.)* **Yes, Peter, you were telling us...**

LENORE: That I am Poe's demon he thought he had put to rest once and for all.

JERRY: His...what?

PETE: All the stories about him. They were true. A poor, tortured soul of a man. Driven by demons. Living a hellish life. Driven insane by that which possessed him. That which possessed him was simply Lenore.

JERRY: Now she possesses him never – *(Glances at LIZ, swallows hard and turns back to PETE.)* **She stopped possessing him.**

LIZ: But how?

PETE: Simple. It was Annabelle Lee. She didn't drown. She had to pretend to, which was hard on him, of course. But she felt she had no choice. She was his guardian angel.

LENORE: And the kinsmen that came and bore her away were a – [pronounced with a long "a"] **Ain – Ainge –** *(Gasping)* **Ain – Rats! I never could say that word.**

PETE: Her family of angels. Then there was a battle. A battle of cosmic proportions.

LENORE: Not so cosmic, if you ask me. All those a – [long "a"] **Ain – Ainge –** *(Gasping)* **Ain – aaargh – whatever – to subdue one demon! I ask you now, is that fair?**

PETER: One demon? I don't think so. A demon, countless divils, the hounds of hell, and who knows what else.

LIZ: Then why did you awaken her?

PETE: I didn't know – Here I was in this...strange place, and somehow I knew it was Lenore. And because I have a poet's blood running in my veins –

LENORE: *(Overly sweet)* Anyone can make a mistake, sweetie, it's all right.

PETE: *(Sarcastically)* Yes, Lenore.

LENORE: Don't you "yes, Lenore" me!

PETE: *(Ignoring her)* When the divils put me into the room with her, she looked so beautiful.

LIZ: But you were just a baby.

PETE: In a situation such as that, I was forced to grow up fast.

LIZ: Of course, you were. Oh, Pete –

PETE: It's all right. Now that I've learned the truth and managed to escape, and especially now that I've found my birth mates, I regret it not.

LENORE: But have you escaped, my pretty one?

PETE: Ah, but do you hear your hounds?

LENORE: My hounds?

PETE: Well, do you?

LENORE: What have you done with my dogs?

PETE: Not I, Lenore. Annabelle Lee.

LENORE: Annabelle Lee! I don't –

PETE: How many dogs did you have, Lenore?

LENORE: Thirteen, of course.

PETE: Are you sure? Did you ever count them?

LENORE: What do you mean?

PETE: There were fourteen. Thirteen hounds from hell, *(Very hammy; overly melodramatic)* and one hound with wings as pale as a sunlit field of dandelions gone to seed. As soft as the breeze that spins in playful eddies along a sandy beach.

LENORE: All right, all right. I get your point. Now what has she done with my hellish hounds?

PETE: As you say...

LENORE: In Dis...

JERRY: Dis what?

LIZ: Jerry! *(She and JERRY exchange glances.)* Enough already.

JERRY: Right. Sure. No problem.

LENORE: My hounds are there, and what of your *(Her voice becomes venomous)* precious Annabelle!

PETE: Dancing on the head of a pin, I presume.

JERRY: What!

LIZ: Don't worry about it. I'll explain it later.

JERRY: What!

LIZ: I can't believe this. OK. For a long time, there's been this philosophical debate about how many angels can dance on the head of a pin. Now let's shut up and listen, OK?

JERRY: Why are you getting so...irritated?

PETE: It's Lenore.

LENORE: *(Melodramatically feigning innocence)* Me-ee?

PETE: Her influence. Why you quarrel. She likes it that way. But her little game is up. *(Suddenly the lights begin to flash on and off, and in one of the blackouts LENORE disappears.)*

JERRY: What happened?

PETE: All her minions were gone. She needed them to support her power as a demon. You wouldn't want to see her as she really is. Dreadful, really dreadful. Mottled skin, slimy hair. Have you ever smelled rotten meat on a grill?

LIZ: *(Shivers.)* Yuck!

PETE: Exactly.

JERRY: So now what happens?

PETE: We live happily ever after moored in the bay by the bogs. Or, if you like, Annabelle gave me the power to change our lives. Would you like that?

LIZ: Change?

JERRY: In what way?

PETE: Make them more...ordinary. More normal. More like the lives of other kids our age.

LIZ: I'd like that.

JERRY: Me too.

PETE: All right. We'll live in a small town, somewhere in a nice area of the country.

JERRY: *(With dread)* Near a bog?

LIZ: *(With dread)* **Or a bay?**

PETE: **Not if you don't want to.**

LIZ: **I don't.**

JERRY: **Me neither.**

PETE: **OK then.** *(He claps his hands once. Suddenly LENORE enters Stage Right.)*

LENORE: **Hi, kids. Your father's parking the car. He'll be right in. We've got a surprise for you.**

LIZ and Jerry: *Lenore!*

PETE: *(Whispering)* **Shh. Not...exactly. It's our mother.**

LIZ: *(Whispering)* **Mother! But it looks –**

JERRY: *(Whispering)* **Just like Lenore.**

PETE: *(Whispering)* **It isn't. Believe me, it isn't.** *(To LENORE)* **A surprise?**

LENORE: **Yes.**

PETE: **What is it, Mom?**

LENORE: **You kids have always begged for a puppy. We finally decided to get you one. Your father and I.**

LIZ: **A puppy?**

JERRY: **What kind of puppy is it?**

LENORE: *(Puzzled)* **Why, what did you expect? It's just what you wanted. A hound dog.** *(Lights quickly to black as the sound system plays Elvis Presley's "Hound Dog.")*

(Curtain)

Production Notes and Considerations

Try to figure out how many comic devices are used here, and how they are used. Actually, you can find at least a hint of every comic device mentioned in the opening section of the book. Of course, then, it's easy to see that the play exists simply for fun. It has no message whatsoever, and the characters have no depth. The situations and plot development, if indeed the progression of events can be called a plot, are highly unrealistic, and the ending unexplainable.

With this play, you can let go of any inhibitions of acting style. Be as overly dramatic or as sentimentally melodramatic as you like.

When playing Jerry and Liz, you might want to project the idea of innocence or naiveté and to make Lenore as stereotypically evil as possible. Pete, of course, is much more worldly or cynical.

The play can be produced using a simple set, though it would be fun to have an elaborate nineteenth-century setting suggestive of looming disaster.

The Boy With Nine Lives

"The Boy With Nine Lives" is a fantasy. It is also a melodrama. However, it differs from the classic definition in that there is no strict division between good and evil characters. Rather, the characters, due to circumstances and personality, are a combination. They are more true to life.

Although the play treats several serious themes, it meets the criteria of comedy in that it ends at least somewhat happily, and we can always hope completely happily despite the question left unanswered at the end.

Unlike "Mix and Match," for instance, it has substance. It touches on a number of problems or subjects including the unfairness of life and problems with drugs, illness, facing the unexpected, and moral values.

In large part, the play deals with how Ron will face the unexpected in the form of the gift he is given. The gift also poses moral problems. Will Ron throw it away, keep it only to benefit himself, or will he put it to good use?

CHARACTERS: RON, 15; Mer Heptaphanes (CAT), any age; BILLY, 15; MOM, late 30s to early 40s; MIKE, 17; FRANK, 17; CHERIE, 17; NATALIE, 17; FELINA, 15; YOUNG WOMAN, 20s; JEPSON, 30s; NURSE, 30s-40s; DOCTOR, 40s; BETSY, 21.

SETTING: An interstate highway and the fields on either side; the kitchen of the Pagliani's house; a hallway in Richmond High School; a parking lot outside Richmond High School; a television studio waiting room; a television studio; two separate wings of a hospital; outside the hospital.

AT RISE: The stage is dark; lights come slowly up to reveal a dim starry night. We hear the roar of an approaching semi. Two spotlights appear Upstage, a few feet apart, a few feet off the stage floor, and focused on the audience. They are the headlights of the truck. Directly in its path we see a tiny kitten huddled in fear. Suddenly, RON appears from Stage Right racing hard toward the kitten. He dives and skids on his stomach, scoops up the kitten, and stretches his hands to thrust it out off the highway. Almost simultaneously, there is a loud thud, the truck hitting RON's body, and the lights go immediately to black.

In two or three seconds the lights come up again. We hear meowing growing fainter and fainter to fade. The kitten has escaped. RON lies Center Stage in a crumpled, unmoving heap.

The stage is completely silent. Gradually, we hear the sounds of the night, crickets or perhaps an owl or the distant rumble of a train.

Suddenly, a spotlight focuses Up Right on a human-sized cat, a tabby or calico. She stands on her hind legs, cocks her head to one side, and stares at RON. Her facial expression is a mixture of pride, sadness, gratitude, and compassion. She crosses to just right of RON where she drops to all fours.

Scene i

CAT: Ron Pagliani. *(Her tone is musical, the soothing voice of a mother crooning to a fevered child.)* **You must awaken before another wheeled monster roars along this way, Ron Pagliani. I**

summon you to the world of the living. *(She gently touches a paw to his face.)*

RON: *(Opening his eyes, he shakes his head and grimaces.)* **Ohhh. What – I was –**

CAT: *(Giving his face a final caress)* **Arise now, Ron Pagliani. We must leave the roadway.**

RON: *(He sits up and glances around.)* **Roadway?** *(He begins to panic.)* **We're in the middle of the interstate highway! What am I...The kitten! I tried to save the kitten? Is it –**

CAT: **She has wandered off; she is fine.**

RON: *(For the first time he looks at the CAT.)* **Oh, God! Who are you? What are you?** *(Trying to rationalize)* **The truck. I must have been hit by the truck. I was trying to grab this little kitten –**

CAT: **I come to honor you.**

RON: **The truck hit my head. I had a concussion. Maybe I'm unconscious. Dreaming.** *(Nervous laugh)* **Wow, this is one wild dream.**

CAT: **It is no dream.** *(Again she touches her paw to his face. Raising her head, she stares into space in deep concentration. Once more she looks down at RON.)* **You are fine now. Is that not true?**

RON: **I guess so. That was weird. If I didn't know better, I think I'd taken –**

CAT: **You saved the life of a small one. One of my fine young children. Thus you are healed. And so you begin your second life.**

RON: **My what!**

CAT: **I am Mer Heptaphanes, mother of all children.**

RON: **Children?** *(RON is confused; he still thinks this is a dream or that he's been affected mentally by the accident.)* **The accident messed up my brain. This can't be happening.**

CAT: *(Laughing)* **No, child. Young...human man. Nothing is wrong with your mind. I saw your sacrifice. The disregard for your own life so that you could save...what you call the kitten.**

RON: **I – I remember the pain. Fireworks bursting inside my brain. My head ripping apart, exploding. I heard the snapping of – my arms like dry wood and terrible pain. And...I couldn't feel anything in the bottom half –** *(Breathing hard)* **I'm paralyzed!**

CAT: **You were, it is true. And the bones encasing your brain were**

shattered. *(She rises to her hind legs and reaches out.)* **Are you not whole?**

RON: **What!**

CAT: **You do not feel pain.**

RON: *(Running his hands over his arms and his legs)* **No.** *(A sense of wonderment)* **Not even a little. I don't understand.**

CAT: **Allow me to assist you to your back feet.**

RON: **Back feet?**

CAT: *(Laughing)* **For a moment I forgot. Human animals have feet... and hands.**

RON: *(Grasping her paw and allowing her to help him to his feet)* **Who are you?**

CAT: **I am the mother.**

RON: **Mother?**

CAT: *(Leading him to the side of the road)* **Perhaps a better word is...protector. Though still not precise. Forgiver, teacher. Yet rarely do I interfere in their lives. They must learn by themselves. To grow strong and become great stalkers.**

RON: **Are you sure I'm not...crazy?** *(Half sobs; half laughs.)* **Man! I can't believe this. I'm hallucinating. And then I'm asking the hallucination if it's real.**

CAT: **Rarely do I appear unto those of your race. I ask you a kindness. Never reveal my existence –**

RON: **Don't worry! I wouldn't tell anyone –**

CAT: **Except perhaps to your own mother.**

RON: **My mother?**

CAT: **For if you do, the healing may be affected.**

RON: **Healing?**

CAT: **Because you disregarded your own corporeal being in saving the life of my child, I grant you seven more lives.**

RON: **You brought me back to life?**

CAT: **I granted you lives; it is different. Your old life is lost. You have the life you now live. And you have seven more lives.**

RON: **Nine lives!** *(Frowning)* **Wait! I know what happened. I came home from the game. We beat Rockland High. I was tired and went to bed. I remember a headache, a terrible headache.**

**I...took an Advil. Or a Tylenol. Something. Then I went to bed.
That has to be it.** *(Pause)* **But the headache got worse, and I had
this dream.**

CAT: **Yet nowness is no dream nor vision.**

RON: **Nine lives! Like a cat?**

CAT: **So your myths would tell you.**

RON: **What do you mean, Mer Hepta – Mer Hepta –**

CAT: **"Mer" will do fine.**

RON: **An exaggeration?**

CAT: **My children are agile, able to care for themselves, to escape
the gravest danger. Except for the tiny ones such as you
rescued. My children have only one life.**

RON: **One? But –**

CAT: **Human animals seem to care little for those of other races.
They treat them as chattel. Not so with you. You have a loving
heart, a generous nature.** *(She sighs.)*

RON: **You don't know anything about me.**

CAT: **Your race eats of the flesh of other races. So too does mine. Yet
certain members of your race realize the sanctity of life. They
kill and eat others' flesh to fulfill basic needs. Many of what
you call Native Americans ask forgiveness of their prey. So
should the children of my race, and the children of yours.**

RON: **Why are you telling me –**

CAT: **Since the dissipation of the mist and the separation of races,
an indifference has taken hold. Fighting and the wasting of
precious lives. Coyotes attack human children. Gangs of
human males attack one another in the streets. Even my children howl and fight among themselves. Yet those such as you
give me the will to continue, to use my powers so that you and
others like you may live.**

RON: **You don't understand. I've done things. Things I'm ashamed
of. Drugs. Stealing money from my mother –**

CAT: **That is the past.***(She stares intensely at RON.)* **Would others you
know give up their lives for the life of one of my children?**

RON: **I – I don't – Maybe.**

CAT: *(She touches his cheek.)* **I must leave you. Remember, even in**

abundance, life is a precious thing. To your way of reckoning, Ron Pagliani, what is your age?

RON: *(Laughs.)* **Sixteen, in a week and a half.**

CAT: **At the end of each of your lives, then, you will return to the age you are now.** *(Teasing)* **Sixteen in a week and a half.** *(She steps back, reaches once more toward him, but her paw fails to touch his face.)* **I am honored to have met you. I wish you good fortune and good lives.** *(She turns and crosses gracefully to the Upstage entrance.)*

RON: **Wait! Mer! Please, wait!** *(RON rushes toward her.)*

　　(In a burst of brilliant light, Mer Heptaphanes [CAT] disappears. For a moment RON is stunned. He crosses to the highway, glances both ways for approaching vehicles, and then hurries to the spot where he was struck. He sees it is covered in a splotch of red. He moves off the highway, and in the starlight rips off his jacket and examines himself more closely. He touches his shoulders, his arms, his head. He finds no wound. He stretches his arms and legs but feels no hurt. He glances Upstage to where Mer Heptaphanes [CAT] has disappeared.)

BILLY: **Ron!** *(BILLY runs in Stage Right and crosses to RON.)* **I saw you. I saw what happened!**

RON: **Saw me?**

BILLY: **I told you I saw what happened.**

RON: **What did you see? That I saved a kitten from getting hit by a truck?**

BILLY: **That's not what I mean.**

RON: **I have to get home.** *(Starts to exit Stage Right.)*

BILLY: *(Grabbing RON'S arm)* **It was weird. I mean it, Ron.**

RON: *(Turning back, angry)* **What was? That I saved a cat's life? I like cats.**

BILLY: **There's a lot more to it than that!**

RON: **What do you mean?**

BILLY: **I saw the truck hit you!**

RON: **Mom's going to be angry enough that I'm late. This is the first time she's...trusted me.**

BILLY: **It ran over you, Ron! You were dead! You had to be.** *(Getting* *really worked up)* **I saw the blood. Then I got sick. Scared and sick. I couldn't stop throwing up.**

RON: **Can't you see I'm OK?**

BILLY: **No! You were thrown back and forth. Your body twisted. Weird angles. Your arms and legs. And I saw your head. The wheels ran over your head.**

RON: **Think what you're saying!**

BILLY: **The road was covered in blood. I wanted to see...see if you were alive. I knew you couldn't be!**

RON: **I gotta go. Mom's going to think the same thing happened as before.**

BILLY: **I know what I saw.** *(RON turns to leave.)* **Just one thing.**

RON: **Yeah?**

BILLY: **Road's empty, OK? No traffic. Never much this time of night.**

RON: **What are you saying?**

BILLY: **I could see the blood. Around your body. A puddle shining in the moonlight. Next thing I know, you're sitting up like nothing was wrong.**

RON: **There's no blood; nothing broken. You can see that.**

BILLY: **Look at your clothes.**

RON: **My clothes?**

BILLY: **Your windbreaker, and your jeans. Almost in shreds. I don't see blood, but I can smell it. Kind of...metallic. I should know how it smells, shouldn't I?**

RON: *(Looks at his clothes.)* **OK. So I scraped my arms and my legs.**

BILLY: **Then how come no blood? I told you I could smell it. I certainly know how blood smells.**

RON: **I don't know. My God, Billy, I really don't know.**

BILLY: **I saw you looking at your arms and legs. As if you were surprised. And you stood up, almost like someone was helping you.**

RON: **I'll walk you home.**

BILLY: **You go ahead.**

RON: *(Shrugs.)* **See you Monday then.** *(RON crosses to Stage Right and exits. BILLY watches him go. As soon as RON's out of sight, BILLY crosses to the highway. He looks both ways to make sure there's no* traffic. *He walks to the spot where RON was hit and kneels. In the glow from the moon, he sees a puddle of blood, still not dry. He stares at it.)*

BILLY: I knew it. *(He rises and steps off the highway and then looks back at the blood.)* **He was...dead.** *(Blackout)*

Scene ii

AT RISE: The action occurs at the Pagliani house just after RON has arrived home. It is about 10:30 p.m. A faint light glows in the kitchen.

(RON enters from Stage Left.)

MOM: Ron, is that you?

RON: Yeah, Mom.

MOM: *(Entering from Up Right)* **I've been worried sick. You'd better have a good reason.**

RON: Mom, I...

MOM: *(Angry)* **It's...** *(Glancing at her watch)* **Ten-thirty. The game —**

RON: You wouldn't believe me.

MOM: Try me?

RON: I tried to save this kitten.

MOM: Kitten?

RON: On the highway. There was a truck coming, and...Mom, you won't believe me.

MOM: You and cats? *(Laughs.)* **Well, I might have known it was some-thing like that.** *(Reaching for a cup)* **Would you like a cup of hot chocolate?**

RON: Thanks. *(RON sits at the table as MOM takes a packet of cocoa mix from the cupboard and tears it open.)*

MOM: You going to tell me about it? *(She dumps the cocoa into a cup and reaches for the teakettle. She continues to make the hot choco-late as she and RON talk.)*

RON: I'd — Mom, I'd rather not.

MOM: *(Suddenly aware of his clothes)* **Your clothes! Did you fight —**

RON: No! I'm sorry, Mom. I...can't explain.

MOM: *(She sits in the other chair. In a resigned voice)* **I thought you learned your lesson. Maybe I was wrong.**

RON: What do you mean?

MOM: No lies! Ah, Ronnie. They told me once you got hooked –

RON: It's nothing like that. I swear.

MOM: Please!

RON: I didn't get into a fight. I'm not – I'm not taking drugs. You have to believe me.

MOM: You put us through hell.

RON: *(Rubs a hand across his eyes.)* ***Mom*!** **I never would. After I got clean.**

MOM: I've never understood. It took all I had. Your money for college. A thousand times I've asked myself why. Because I'm a single parent? Because I have to work long hours? *(Stares into his eyes.)* **I can't go through it again, Ron.**

RON: That's not it. I'm telling you.

MOM: All right. What happened?

RON: I told you. I saved this kitten's life.

MOM: You didn't tell me how?

RON: The highway, the interstate. In the beams of these headlights. A semi. *(Shakes his head.)* **Remember old Fluff? I loved that cat.**

MOM: I did my best, Ron. You father and I – I guess we thought we were going to live forever.

RON: I don't mean we should get another cat.

MOM: *(She takes hold of the sleeve of RON's windbreaker. She lifts his arm.)* **Look at this! You aren't hurt?**

RON: No. That's what's so weird.

MOM: *(She lets go of the sleeve.)* **The jacket's ruined. The sleeves, the front. And your jeans.**

RON: I'm sorry.

MOM: *(Unsure whether to believe him)* **Tell me what happened.**

RON: I ran as fast as I could. The kitten was frozen in fear, staring at the headlights. *(Closes his eyes for a moment.)* **You won't believe me. Nobody would.**

MOM: *(Her hopes that he was telling the truth are fading.)* **Go on.**

RON: I'd rather not.

MOM: Was it...Did they send someone after you? Is that it? Is that why you're making this up?

RON: Mom!

MOM: What do you expect? *(Pause)* I'm sorry. *(Tears in her eyes)* I'm scared, Ronnie. I haven't been this scared since your dad died. I knew I had to go on, because of you. I didn't want to. Not at first. Can you understand? I wanted to be with your father. I wanted – *(RON stands and goes to her. He reaches as if to touch her hair. They stare at each other for a moment, and he drops his hand.)*

RON: I lost him too. *(Tears in his eyes)* Then you were gone. I'd come home from school, and no one was here. Sometimes I went to Billy's, so it wasn't like I was alone. But I was alone, Mom. *(Still in her chair, MOM grabs him tightly around the waist, her head on his shoulder.)*

MOM: I never meant it to be like this. I thought I was lucky to have found the job I did. After not working for nearly ten years. Skills outdated. *(Releases him and sits back.)* Tell me what happened?

RON: *(Trying to decide)* I...OK. I told you you won't believe me. Especially since...

MOM: The drugs?

RON: Yeah, the drugs. *(He pauses for two or three beats.)* I saved the kitten's life, Mom. That's what's important. I scooped it up and tossed it to the side of the road. And then – then – it's no use.

MOM: What are you afraid of, Ron?

RON: It's like...mythology. Or fantasy.

MOM: *(A moment of tenderness)* What do you mean, honey?

RON: I got hit by the truck.

MOM: Oh, my God! You're okay? You're not hurt?

RON: I was dead, Mom. It doesn't make sense.

MOM: Dead?

RON: *(Half laughs.)* You're going to think I'm nuts. Or I'm really back on crack or something.

MOM: Sometimes, Ron, people imagine things.

RON: Like when they're stoned! Why don't you say it, Mom? Go ahead.

MOM: No. I don't think – OK, I'll be honest. I hope you're not back on drugs.

RON: You don't trust me.

MOM: I'm trying.

RON: *(Dejected voice)* Guess I wouldn't trust me either.

MOM: I'm sorry.

RON: My arms. They were broken. Shattered. My skull was...I – I was paralyzed. But just for a moment, the pain was so bad – I can't describe it. *(A sense of wonder)* Then I stopped hurting.

MOM: That's enough, Ron.

RON: I said you wouldn't believe me.

MOM: *(Her voice stern, controlled)* OK, the benefit of the doubt. Tell me the rest, Ron. Tell me exactly what happened.

RON: I was lying there, and – Oh, man! I – There was this –

MOM: What? An angel with wings? An imp of Satan with a three-pointed tail? Who put you all back together? All the king's horses and all the king's men?

RON: *(Furious)* It was a cat! No matter what anyone says...it – was a cat. Her name is Mer Heptaphanes.

MOM: I'll say this for you. You've always been inventive.

RON: *(Furious)* Listen to me! You wanted to hear, and I didn't want to tell you. Now I'm going to tell you. And I don't care what you think. *(MOM gasps at the vehemence in his voice.)* I can prove it happened, Mom.

MOM: Finish your cocoa and go to bed.

RON: She came to me. A big cat. Big as a person. I must have been unconscious. No! I was dead. She touched my face, helped me sit up. She said...She said she was the...protector...of cats. And that most other races don't care about cats. Most races don't care about each other. She said I was good, Mom. Do you know what I told her? *(Pause)* Do you?

MOM: Of course not. How could I possibly know what...you supposedly told a figment of your imagination?

RON: I told her I wasn't good. That I'd used drugs. I used to use drugs. She said...she said she meant I was a person...who cares. *(He bites his lip to keep from crying.)* And so, she – she was

– she was going to give me nine lives, counting the one I have now and the one that I lost when I was hit by the truck.

MOM: For the moment, Ron, I'll accept you haven't gone back to using cocaine or...Why would you tell me something like this? People have one life, Ron. No more! One life each. Your father...didn't even – *(Crying)* No more, please. No more.

RON: *(He rises, rinses out his cup, and places it on the drainboard.)* **See you in the morning.** *(He exits Up Left as the lights fade to black.)*

Scene iii

AT RISE: The action occurs in the hallway and outside Fairmont High. It is lunchtime. RON is at his hall locker when MIKE comes up to him.

MIKE: Well, if it isn't the miracle boy himself.

RON: *(Stashing his books in the locker, taking out a sweater)* **What are you talking about?** *(Turns to MIKE.)*

MIKE: The dead shall rise again.

RON: I asked you what you're talking about! *(FRANK and CHERIE wander up.)*

MIKE: You hear about this guy? Flat as a pancake on the highway. Roadkill pizza, is that it, Ron?

RON: *(Angry and shaking)* **I don't know what you're talking about.**

MIKE: Come on, man, the whole school knows about your miraculous return from the jaws – or is that wheels – of death.

RON: I don't know where you heard anything –

MIKE: We heard. Right, Frank?

RON: I'd like to go eat lunch.

MIKE: *(Nudging FRANK)* **Right, Frank?**

FRANK: It's what I heard.

RON: Who told you whatever this is? *(BILLY enters Stage Left and rushes up to the group.)*

RON: *(To BILLY)* **It was you, wasn't it?**

BILLY: I'm sorry. I didn't mean –

RON: What didn't you mean?

FRANK: So what happened, kid? Is your friend here lying, or did you get hit by a truck?

MIKE: If we find out your friend's lying, he's in deep trouble.

FRANK: Can't stand kids who lie. How about you, Cherie?

CHERIE: Hey, Frank, I haven't got anything to do with this.

MIKE: Probably both on drugs. And this thing with the truck was... *(Thinks he's being really funny.)* **A bad trip.** *(To FRANK and CHERIE)* **Get it?**

CHERIE: You're funny, Mike. A barrel of laughs. *(Poking his stomach with an index finger)* **And I do mean barrel. That's funny too, right, Mike?**

MIKE: What's this about? It has nothing to do with you.

CHERIE: Why don't you pick on someone your own size, Mike? Or aren't there any more elephants in this school?

MIKE: I can't believe you. I thought we were friends.

CHERIE: I don't like you picking on younger kids.

MIKE: What's it to you?

CHERIE: I don't, that's all.

MIKE: OK, OK.

FRANK: Or are you supplying now, Ron?

RON: I don't do drugs.

CHERIE: That's not what I heard, Ron. I don't understand you. I've known you for years. We're in the same youth group at –

RON: I said I don't do drugs!

CHERIE: That's nice to know. *(NATALIE joins the group.)*

NATALIE: *(To CHERIE)* **What's up?**

MIKE: You mean you haven't heard about the miracle boy?

NATALIE: What miracle boy?

CHERIE: There's a story going around that Ron was hit by a truck.

NATALIE: That's you, Ron?

RON: I guess so.

BILLY: I shouldn't have said anything. I'm stupid.

RON: It doesn't matter.

FRANK: So what are you pushing? Crack? Heroin? Let's see. Since I never used, my vocabulary's a little limited. Grass, crystal –

RON: Stop it! OK, I did drugs. It was wrong. I went through a program, and I stopped using them.

MIKE: I heard that most times dopers start right back as soon as they can connect with a pusher.

BILLY: Let's go eat, Ron, come on.

RON: Yeah.

MIKE: *(Grabbing RON's arm.)* Just a minute.

RON: What!

FRANK: I think he wants to know if you got hit by a truck or you didn't.

RON: I got hit by a truck. *(To MIKE)* Now let go of my arm.

MIKE: What was it like to die? Angels with white wings? A tunnel of light? Your dad waiting?

RON: Leave my father out of this. It has nothing to do with my father.

MIKE: *(Sneering)* Except you both were dead.

CHERIE: What is wrong with you, Mike?

MIKE: Keep out of this Cherie! You don't know anything about it.

RON: Yes, my dad's dead. He's still dead, and sometimes I miss him.

NATALIE: What happened, Ron?

RON: I was trying to save this kitten. Right in the middle of the highway.

MIKE: Isn't that sweet? He tried to save the life of a cat.

BILLY: Something you would never do, right? *(Angry)* Not you. Even if it was your sister or your mother. You'd let them get killed. But you'd be alive. That's all that's important. Just you. Nothing else counts.

MIKE: Look, kid, if you're not careful, you're going to have a couple of broken arms.

RON: Billy, please. You know you can't get into a fight. Come on!

BILLY: *(Ignoring RON)* Speaking of your sister, why don't you tell us about her, Mike? Huh? *(To everyone)* A big dark secret! Anyone know Mike's older sister. Graduated three or four years ago?

NATALIE: I remember. Mom and Dad took me to the fall play that year. She had one of the main parts.

BILLY: Before you start yelling at Ron, tell us about your sister?

MIKE: I'll kill you, kid. Your life's not worth a nickel.

140

CHERIE: What is this, Mike?

MIKE: Nothing. It's nothing.

NATALIE: You told me your sister's in college.

BILLY: Was in college. *(MIKE rushes BILLY, but FRANK grabs him.)*

FRANK: Hey, Mike, settle down. This is not the place. You're going to get into trouble.

MIKE: Just you wait, kid. *(To RON)* And you. You aren't any more dead than...your stupid friend.

RON: I was dead.

BILLY: I saw it. There was blood everywhere. His body was twisted and smashed.

CHERIE: Why are you saying this, Billy? It only happens in cartoons.

BILLY: Never mind.

MIKE: So tell me, dopehead, is your friend lying or not?

RON: I told you I was hit. Then something happened.

MIKE: And I say you're a liar.

RON: I'm not lying.

MIKE: Then prove it.

BILLY: We can...I can show you the blood.

FRANK: You call that proof? Could be any dead animal. *(Nasty smile)* Maybe even a skunk.

NATALIE: I don't know how. But maybe it's true.

MIKE: You're kidding. You don't believe this...doper.

RON: Let's go, Billy.

MIKE: I said I want you to prove it.

RON: I don't have to prove anything.

MIKE: You're both liars.

RON: OK, what do you want me to do?

MIKE: There's a tree outside, right? A tall one. Overlooks the parking lot.

RON: So what?

MIKE: You can be dead, your body all smashed and come back to life? Isn't that what you're saying?

RON: Yeah, that's what I said. But I'm not going to do it again.

FRANK: *(Making chicken noises)* **Puuck, puuck, puuck.**

MIKE: You got it, Frank. He's not only a liar, he's a chicken. *(To RON)* Never heard of a dopehead chicken.

BILLY: How about just a plain dopehead? I know you've heard of more than one of those.

MIKE: *(Furious, to BILLY)* **Shut the** – *(Turns to RON.)* **Put up, or shut up.**

RON: I don't have to do anything you say.

FRANK: Right. Puuck, puuck, puuck.

RON: All right. OK. I'll make you a deal. I'll do it if you do it. And I'll go first.

MIKE: Hey, now, that's not part of the –

CHERIE: Scared, Mike?

MIKE: No, I'm not scared.

RON: Then you do it. We'll go outside. And we'll climb the tree. I'll jump first. I'll make sure I land on my head. The both of you do the same. But you'll have to wait. It may take two or three minutes –

FRANK: What? Are you crazy?

RON: I'm not the one who suggested this.

MIKE: If you think I'm going –

RON: All right, if you're such a chicken –

FRANK: This has gone a little too far.

RON: I understand. Puuck. Puuck.

FRANK: All right, it's a deal. *(FELINA rushes up to the group.)*

FELINA: Ron Pagliani?

RON: *(Turning to her, puzzled)* Yes, that's right.

FELINA: The boy who died.

RON: What is this? I don't even know you.

FELINA: I...I just transferred to this school. But I heard –

RON: What did you hear?

FELINA: A boy who was dead, coming back to life.

NATALIE: Like in a hospital when someone's heart stops. It happens all the time.

FELINA: Someone who...someone whose skull was shattered, who was paralyzed, is suddenly healed.

RON: How do you know so much about this?

FELINA: It's all over school.

RON: The details. Nobody knows those things. Not even Billy knew I was paralyzed.

MIKE: You were paralyzed? What is this, the late, late movie? "Godzilla Versus the Paralyzed Boy"?

FELINA: Ron, I know you don't know me. But I wouldn't do what you're planning –

RON: What do you mean?

FELINA: Jump.

CHERIE: You just got here, how do you know that?

NATALIE: "There are more things in heaven and earth, Horatio, than are dreamt of..."

MIKE: What!

CHERIE: It's a line from Shakespeare. We're studying it in senior English. Really, Natalie, I don't think now's the time –

NATALIE: Just trying to be funny. Trying to stop these three idiots –

FELINA: At least we agree they should be stopped. Think, Ron! Even if you do survive...

RON: They won't jump; they're too chicken. Mike's a bully. He thinks being bigger than anyone else makes him special. He's not so special.

MIKE: I'll jump; you'll see. Don't back out on me now.

FELINA: Please, Ron Pagliani! Do reconsider.

RON: Ron...Pagliani? Why – Have we met before?

FELINA: You...and my little sister have met.

RON: What? I don't –

FELINA: She lives on the other side of the highway, about halfway from here to your house.

RON: Who are you!

FELINA: I told you my name's Felina. I'm new here.

RON: But if your little sister –

FELINA: It's a little too complicated for a human mind –

MIKE: Human? What are you talking about?

FELINA: Please don't jump.

RON: You don't understand. I have to. I really have to. So will you excuse me? *(He steps around her and heads for the door.)*

FELINA: Remember, every life is precious.

RON: *(Turning back)* What did you say?

FELINA: Every life...is precious.

FRANK: What are you, some kind of religious nut?

FELINA: I'm...Felina.

MIKE: Things are getting weirder and weirder.

RON: Not for long, Mike, at least for you. Let's go. *(RON crosses right, leaving the school. The others trail behind.)*

MIKE: You're not really going to do this?

RON: What's the matter, man, you scared?

MIKE: Only a dopehead would –

BILLY: I think he's backing down, Ron. You got nothing to worry about.

FELINA: Don't! You'll only make it worse.

MIKE: Worse? Nah. I didn't intend to back out.

FELINA: Please, Ron Pagliani. Please listen to me. You saved my little sister's life! Please don't throw a life away.

CHERIE: What are you talking about, Felina?

FELINA: Ron knows, I think.

NATALIE: I thought you said you saved the life of a kitten.

CHERIE: Oh, wait a minute, I get it. This is some kind of joke, right? Ron saved a kitten. Your name is Felina. A feline is a cat.

FELINA: No! I'm telling the truth.

RON: *(Looking at her strangely)* Did someone send you here? Someone like Mer –

FELINA: No! You must never say that. No!

RON: I...I'm sorry. I didn't mean –

FELINA: *(Smiles reassuringly.)* It's OK.

FRANK: Do you have the feeling we're watching a movie with subtitles that don't make sense?

RON: Enough! I want this to be over and done with. *(He rushes to the tree and begins to climb. Part way up he turns.)* Mike, Frank, you coming? Or is the air too thick to breathe up here?

FRANK: You're the one who got us into this.

BILLY: Don't, Ron. How are you sure – I mean, I know what happened last night. But...

144

RON: *(To MIKE)* **Big talk, but you don't back it up. Right?**

MIKE: OK, I'm coming. You're not going to call my bluff.

FRANK: We'll just see who's chicken, right, Mike?

MIKE: Shut up, Frank.

FELINA: Please don't do it! Ron...will live. You will not live.

FRANK: What...are you talking about? You act like some...fortune teller. You a gypsy or what?

FELINA: There are some who say my race has gypsy blood. Originally, we came from Egypt, though. My own ancestors, I mean.

CHERIE: This has gone far enough. You've got to come down.

RON: All right. Here goes. *(RON climbs to the top of the tree, stands on one of the branches and assumes a diving position. The lights flash wildly on and off, on and off. The girls scream. The lights come up to reveal RON lying on the ground, unmoving, his arms at an awkward angle. A puddle of blood is spreading around him.)*

NATALIE: Oh, my God. Oh, my God.

CHERIE: I'll go call an ambulance. Damn you, Mike! Damn you! Get off that tree. You too, Frank. You see what you've done. *(FELINA hurries over to RON and kneels beside him as MIKE and FRANK climb down.)*

FELINA: I understand, Ron Pagliani. You felt you had no choice. But you did. Those of my race know not to give up. Not till the very end. That is why – people often say we have nine lives. *(As the lights slowly fade to black, we hear the sound of an ambulance siren coming closer and closer.)*

Scene iv

AT RISE: The action occurs in a room in a TV station where guests wait to be called out for the "Winston Jepson Show," and the television studio itself. They are in different areas of the stage and are defined through lighting. MOM and RON are sitting in easy chairs at right angles to each other.

MOM: Are you nervous?

RON: Yeah, how about you?

MOM: A little. *(Chuckles.)* A lot.

RON: I'm sorry, Mom. It was dumb. I shouldn't have done it.

MOM: No. By the time they called me, you were OK. So I didn't have to think –

RON: *(Being punny)* I certainly made a splash though!

MOM: Ron, it isn't funny.

RON: I know. I keep thinking what if – what if Mike and Frank had jumped.

MOM: Since you jumped first –

RON: Even so, Mike is one stubborn kid.

MOM: What do you mean?

RON: He's big – tall and heavy – never fitted in, you know? Like... like me, I guess.

MOM: You're imagining things.

RON: I'm not. Just once, let me say it.

MOM: What is it? What do you want to tell me?

RON: The drugs, Mom. They were a way of belonging.

MOM: Belonging!

RON: I know. Not the best group of kids to get in with...

MOM: You really always felt...different?

RON: It's nobody's fault. It's the way I am. Other kids too. We don't fit in. We try in different ways. Mike bluffs his way through things. Being a bully. Billy...tries to be a regular guy. Doesn't want anyone to know. And me too. We're all outsiders.

MOM: You never told me you felt this way.

RON: I've tried. But it's not something you talk to your mom about.

MOM: I suppose not. I never meant to block out the way you're feeling.

RON: It's just that I'm not...not really good at anything.

MOM: That's not true! You're –

RON: I don't play sports 'cause I'm...I don't know. I'm...

MOM: A klutz?

RON: *(Smiling)* I wouldn't put it exactly that way. But yeah, that's what I am.

MOM: I used to be a klutz.

RON: You!

MOM: I got over it.

RON: You really felt that way?

MOM: I did.

RON: How did you get over it?

MOM: It didn't seem important anymore. After high school and a year of college...

RON: How come you didn't finish? I'd want to finish!

MOM: I met your father. He wanted me to, but I was impatient. It didn't seem important. It would have made things easier for us both.

RON: I didn't know.

MOM: I guess there are lots of things we don't know about each other. At least, you get good grades.

RON: Sometimes I wish I didn't. Sometimes I try not to. But in the end...I can't help myself. That makes me an outsider too.

MOM: You said you try not to...Ron, that's not good, is it?

RON: I wouldn't want anyone else to find this out. The guys at school. But it's like I have to know everything. There are all these subjects, all these things I'm interested in. I want to know why things are, why and how they work, where words come from. *(Shrugs.)* Dumb, huh?

MOM: You may...have lifetimes to explore them.

RON: What?

MOM: It's true, isn't it? You were given these lives.

RON: I threw one away.

MOM: One, Ron. You still have more than anyone else.

RON: Can I ask you something?

MOM: Yes?

RON: Did you really...I mean, did you really think I'd go back on...

MOM: You made a mistake; you saw that and admitted it. You have a strength of character, Ron, that few people seem to have. I'm sorry I doubted you.

RON: *(Kidding)* If you don't watch out, Mom, you're going to embarrass me.

MOM: *(Laughs.)* That's the whole id –

YOUNG WOMAN: *(Sticking her head through the door)* It's time. Will

you follow me? *(MOM and RON rise. MOM gives RON a wink. He smiles. They follow the YOUNG WOMAN. In a few moments, the lights fade and come up on the television studio. Seated behind a small, rectangular table is WINSTON JEPSON. MOM and RON are seated in the two chairs, RON in the one closer to JEPSON's table.)*

JEPSON: **Ladies and gentlemen, welcome to the "Winston Jepson Show." I am Winston Jepson, and my guests today are Ron Pagliani and his mother Liz.** *(Applause. JEPSON faces RON.)* **So you're the young man whose name has been bandied about all over the city today?**

RON: **I didn't do anything...wonderful.**

JEPSON: **Maybe not. But diving off the top of a thirty foot tree and landing on your head on the macadam surface of a parking lot certainly is spectacular.**

RON: *(Smiling)* **I suppose you could say that.**

JEPSON: *(To MOM)* **So, Mrs. Pagliani. May I call you Liz?** *(MOM nods.)* **So what do you think of your son's feat, Liz?**

MOM: **I suppose it taught me...to listen to him, to believe in him.**

JEPSON: **In what way?**

MOM: **Friday night when he came home from the game...he'd gone to the game with Rockland High.**

JEPSON: **Yes?**

MOM: **He told me he'd saved the life —**

RON: **Mom!**

JEPSON: **What is it? Something wrong?**

RON: **It's — I told Mom something I promised not to tell anyone but her. I asked her to promise too.**

JEPSON: **Does it concern what happened yesterday at school?**

RON: **Yes. But I want to say something. It was a dumb thing to do.**

JEPSON: **Dumb or not, it's unbelievable. Can you tell me about it, Ron?**

RON: **I let a couple of other guys get to me.**

JEPSON: **School chums?**

RON: **Hardly...chums. A couple of guys I know. They heard something a friend of mine said.**

JEPSON: **A friend?**

RON: That's right.

JEPSON: What did this person say?

RON: He's said he'd seen me...this sounds stupid too...that he'd seen me rise from the dead.

JEPSON: Rise from the dead. Do you believe this, ladies and gentlemen? *(Boos and cheers mingled with applause)* **Can you explain?**

RON: Like I said, part of it I can't. It's the promise I made.

JEPSON: It involves your ability to...rise from the dead.

RON: Yes.

JEPSON: Surely, with something so wondrous, so...miraculous, you shouldn't keep it a secret.

RON: It's not like other people can do it.

JEPSON: You say your friend told other students –

RON: My best friend. We live close to each other. I hadn't seen him before the accident –

JEPSON: Accident? What sort of accident is this?

MOM: He was hit by a truck. A tractor-trailer rig. The driver ran over him and kept on going.

JEPSON: How do you know this?

MOM: I didn't believe him either. That's the thing of it.

JEPSON: You didn't believe it? Will you elaborate on what you mean?

MOM: I'd rather not if –

RON: It's all right, Mom. *(To JEPSON)* I used to – I mean I got hooked –

MOM: Ron, you don't have to do this.

RON: I do. I want people to know that anyone can do what I did.

JEPSON: I'm lost here. I thought you said no one else could do it.

RON: That's not what I meant. I was talking about something else.

JEPSON: Do you want to share it with our viewers and those here in the studio?

RON: I was hooked on drugs. I went through treatment. Now I'm clean, and I intend to stay that way. The program – I've been drug-free only a short time. But I'd never take them again. I wouldn't. But no one knows that...for sure. I mean, I'm the only one –

MOM: What he means is that when he told me what he did, I naturally assumed – No, I take that back. Knowing Ron as I do, I don't think it was at all natural to assume it.

RON: Mom, it's OK.

JEPSON: I'm...I didn't realize any of this. Nobody informed me –

RON: It's not something I'm proud of.

JEPSON: But if you're clean, maybe you have a right to be proud.

RON: *(Shrugs.)* Anyhow, I was hit by the semi, and this friend saw it happen. I felt incredible pain – my arms shattered, my skull crushed.

JEPSON: If your skull was crushed, how could you know –

RON: Only for an instant. Terrible pain. The worst you can imagine. And then I woke up in the middle of the road. It was night. There was little traffic.

JEPSON: *(Lightly)* If I may be so impertinent, what were you doing in the middle of the road at night? *(The studio audience twitters.)*

RON: I saw a kitten, frozen in fear. And this semi was coming.

JEPSON: *(Astounded)* You tried to save this kitten's life at the risk of your own life?

RON: Yes.

JEPSON: But isn't human life –

RON: I guess I've always been different. I've never figured it that way.

JEPSON: So did you save its life?

RON: I did. When...when I woke up, I heard its meows growing fainter and fainter.

JEPSON: And how is it...that you regained your life? I don't mean I'm doubting you because I'm not. There's too much evidence to the contrary. Police, medical people, photos. Of yesterday, I mean.

RON: I shouldn't have let them get to me.

JEPSON: Who do you mean?

RON: The other two boys.

JEPSON: Tell me about the jump. You knew you could survive it?

RON: Yes.

JEPSON: How did you know?

RON: Because...it had happened before.

JEPSON: If you hadn't died, could you have risked permanent injury? Paralysis? Brain damage?

RON: I guess I didn't think of that. But then...diving headfirst onto a parking lot –

JEPSON: I see your point. *(Pause)* There was intense pain this time?

RON: In my back. Because of the way I hit. But the pain ended quickly.

MOM: Thank heavens I didn't know about this till afterwards.

JEPSON: That he'd jumped?

MOM: Yes. Till he had...healed himself.

JEPSON: Healed himself?

MOM: Regenerated, whatever.

JEPSON: You knew this would happen, Ron?

RON: I knew. But that's the part I can't tell you. How I was sure of it.

JEPSON: You can do this any time you like then?

RON: To a point.

JEPSON: I don't follow.

RON: I can do it a certain number of times.

JEPSON: How many times?

RON: I can't...

JEPSON: You'd rather not say?

RON: It has to do with the promise.

JEPSON: If I asked you now, could you climb to the top of that light tower? *(He indicates an indefinite area somewhere in front of his desk.)* Could you demonstrate?

RON: I could.

JEPSON: I'm not asking, mind you.

RON: That's good because I wouldn't do it. *(Laughter from the studio audience)*

JEPSON: Why is that?

RON: I told you. There are only a limited number of times... *(Suddenly FELINA rushes onto the set and stands left of JEPSON'S desk.)*

JEPSON: Well, what is this? We have a surprise guest. At least it's a surprise to me.

151

FELINA: I'm sorry. I don't mean to interrupt your program –

RON: Felina, what are you doing here?

FELINA: Think what you're doing, Ron, that's all that I ask. You have a great gift. You have to learn to use it wisely. I heard Mr. Jepson mention the light tower.

JEPSON: Young lady!

FELINA: Yes?

JEPSON: What business is it of yours what Mr. Pagliani –

RON: She's my friend.

MOM: You've never mentioned –

FELINA: Our friendship...is rather recent. *(To RON)* It is a gift, do you understand? A person, of course, is free to throw away a gift...

JEPSON: So is this perhaps your girlfriend?

RON: A friend.

JEPSON: *(He nods to someone off the set. YOUNG WOMAN carries in another lightweight chair and places it in between RON and MOM, who scoot either way to make room.)* **Curiouser and curiouser. How did you manage to get past the guards** –

FELINA: I came just in case – It's not important.

JEPSON: Maybe not to you. But if one person can get in –

FELINA: I promise you, Mr. Jepson, your security is still effective. Because of my background, which I won't go into –

JEPSON: For now, I'll accept what you say since I seem to have no other choice. So...what is the urgency that brings you here?

FELINA: You saw the newspapers, the news programs, the photos.

JEPSON: As has virtually everyone else in the area.

FELINA: Would you want a son or a brother or even a friend of yours to go through –

JEPSON: You have a point. Even knowing recovery is assured.

FELINA: All I want to ask is that Ron consider what he does or he doesn't do.

JEPSON: May I ask you something?

FELINA: You may ask.

JEPSON: Your speech. It seems a little more formal than that of the usual person your age.

FELINA: I suppose that's true.

JEPSON: Maybe you could explain.

FELINA: I'm new to this life.

JEPSON: To this life?

RON: She means to this area of the world? Am I right?

FELINA: Of course.

JEPSON: You've recently moved here then?

FELINA: My...benefactor made it possible. The opportunities here...

JEPSON: *(To RON)* I suppose that means then, you would not again consider doing this sort of thing...

RON: Killing myself? Probably not.

JEPSON: Would you explain that?

RON: Unless there was a very good reason.

JEPSON: Like saving the life of a kitten.

RON: Well...right. *(Once more the audience twitters.)*

JEPSON: Ladies and gentlemen, will you show your appreciation to Ron and Liz Pagliani and...to the mysterious Felina for appearing on our show? *(There is thunderous applause. In a moment the stage lights fade and are replaced by work lights which indicate the interview is finished.)*

MOM: Thank you, Mr. Jepson, for...

JEPSON: Yes?

MOM: For not insisting Ron say things he didn't want to. For not insisting he jump –

JEPSON: I would never insist that he jump. I doubt I'd even have let him do it. But you're welcome. *(To RON)* Thank you for agreeing to be on the show. *(He holds out his hand. RON and JEPSON shake hands.)* My assistant will show you... *(Laughing)* Well, I don't suppose she needs to. The mysterious Felina *(Smiles to show he isn't serious)* will show you out. *(To FELINA) But* before you go –

FELINA: Yes?

JEPSON: How did you get past the guards?

FELINA: *(Laughing)* Well...you might say I come from a long line of escape artists.

JEPSON: I suppose it has to do with where you're from?

FELINA: You could say that.

JEPSON: But you're not going to tell me. *(FELINA shakes her head. JEPSON shrugs.)* **Well, at least I tried.** *(He exits Stage Right.)*

MOM: Ron, I have to be getting back to work. Can I drop you off at school?

RON: No need, Mom. It's just a few blocks.

MOM: You're sure? *(RON nods.)*

FELINA: Mrs. Pagliani?

MOM: Yes.

FELINA: You son is an exceptional person.

MOM: *(Surprised and amused)* **Thank you. I heartily concur.** *(The work lights go to black as MOM crosses left and exits. RON and FELINA cross slowly Down Center where the lights come up.)*

RON: I'm glad you came.

FELINA: Thank you.

RON: I mean it was nice to have you here. But the things you said were important.

FELINA: Yes.

RON: There's something Mer didn't tell me, isn't there?

FELINA: What do you mean?

RON: The way you talked about the gift. How did you know all this anyhow?

FELINA: You are a very perceptive young man – for a human being.

RON: A human being! What do you mean?

FELINA: *(Puzzled)* **Exactly what I say.**

RON: Aren't you...human too?

FELINA: I'm human, for the time being. At least, mostly I am.

RON: Mostly?

FELINA There's this part that isn't. *(She pulls her hair back to show she has the ears of a cat.)* **And...** *(Making sure no one is watching, she takes off the long coat she's worn throughout.)* **This!** *(She has a long tail.)*

RON: I don't believe it. *(FELINA smiles.)* **Are you really the kitten's sister?**

FELINA: To your way of thinking. We reckon things a little differently, however, since we come from different litters.

RON: Can I ask you something?

FELINA: Yes?

RON: How old are you?

FELINA: Cat years or human years?

RON: Cat years.

FELINA: About fifteen.

RON: What does that – I know. When we had old Fluff – the one who died a long time ago – we had a chart that showed a cat's age compared to a human's. In the first year, a cat develops much, much faster. I think...that the first year of a cat's life is equal to fifte –

FELINA: A little over a year in your way of looking at it.

RON: But then it slows down, right?

FELINA: Even so, I age much faster than you.

RON: But – I like you, Felina. I really...like you.

FELINA: Mer Heptaphanes was right. You are an unusual human being.

RON: If you stay human...will you continue to age –

FELINA: You asked about the gift. You said you thought there was more to it.

RON: Is there?

FELINA: There is more.

RON: Will you tell me?

FELINA: No, Ron Pagliani. That's something you'll have to figure out for yourself. *(The lights fade to black.)*

Scene v

AT RISE: Within a few seconds, a dim light shows on the table in the PAGLIANI'S kitchen. The phone rings insistently. MOM rushes on Stage Left and picks up the receiver.

(MOM is talking on the phone, but the words are indistinct. Within a few moments, RON enters rubbing his eyes. MOM hangs up.)

RON: Was that the phone, Mom?

MOM: Yes.

RON: Who'd be calling at this time of —

MOM: It was Billy's mother. He's in the hospital. In ICU.

RON: ICU?

MOM: Intensive care.

RON: What happened?

MOM: Last night he was in a fight. Two boys beat him up.

RON: That can't be! He's a hemophi —

MOM: He wants to see you. His mother thinks...I know this is hard, Ronnie. She thinks he may be dying.

RON: He wants to see me?

MOM: Come on, Ron, we've got to hurry. Get dressed and I'll take you to the hospital. Maybe there are some vending machines. Or you can eat in the hospital cafeteria.

RON: I'm not hungry, Mom. How can I think of food when —

MOM: I'll give you some money. I'll stay as long as I can, and then I'll have to go on to work. I can't miss any more time. *(As lights fade to black, we hear RON speak.)*

RON: They think he may...be dying?

Scene vi

AT RISE: The action occurs in a hospital, first in and around the intensive care unit and then a ward in the opposite wing of the building. In the second ward, there is a different sort of ICU unit.

(As the lights come up, BILLY is lying in a hospital bed, eyes half-closed. He is connected by tubes to two plastic bags hooked to portable metal stands.)

NURSE: I'm sorry, you can't stay long. But since he's been asking for you...

RON: Is he —

NURSE: He's doing as well as can be expected.

RON: But is he going to...

NURSE: *(With compassion)* I'm sorry, but that's all I can tell you.

RON: Thanks. *(He crosses to the bed and stands looking down at BILLY.)*

BILLY: *(Opening his eyes)* **Ron, you came.**

RON: Of course, dummy. You know I – I'm sorry. I shouldn't kid around when –

BILLY: Dummy. Who you calling a dummy?

RON: You, ya dummy!

BILLY: I suppose a guy who dives headfirst off a tree onto a parking lot is smart.

RON: You got me there, guy. *(Pause)* **So how are you doing?**

BILLY: I'm scared. This has happened before...but never –

RON: You're going to be OK.

BILLY: Hey, just 'cause some of us have a whole bunch of lives. That's what you said on TV.

RON: *(Seriously)* **I know; it's not fair.** *(Beat)* **Especially when I throw mine away.**

BILLY: Hey, it's okay. I didn't mean anything. I wanted to see you. I wanted to apologize –

RON: Apologize? For what?

BILLY: For telling everyone. If I hadn't, you wouldn't have jumped.

RON: It's over with.

BILLY: You sure?

RON: You really are a dummy. *(Seriously)* **So...what happened?**

BILLY: It's internal. Kind of serious.

RON: Who did it?

BILLY: Mike and Frank ganged up on me.

RON: What!

BILLY: I went to a movie. I was walking home. Guess they were waiting. *(Suddenly MIKE comes rushing inside followed by the NURSE.)*

NURSE: I told you you can't go in there.

MIKE: I've got to see him. Just for a moment, please. *(Not waiting for an answer, he hurries to the opposite side of the bed from RON.)*

RON: Hey, I don't think –

MIKE: I'm sorry. I mean, God, Billy, I didn't know – I never knew –

BILLY: OK!

MIKE: *(Crying)* **I mean it. I'd never want to do this to you. I'd never want to do this to anyone.**

BILLY: I didn't want people to know. I didn't want to be treated like I'm different.

NURSE: I'm sorry, you'll both have to leave. Doctor needs to examine –

MIKE: I'm going. *(Turns to BILLY.)* Can you forgive me?

BILLY: I...I don't know, Mike. I really don't know.

NURSE: Boys, please.

RON: See you, guy. *(He leaves the immediate area of the bed.)*

BILLY: So long. *(MIKE lingers for an instant staring at BILLY and then turns and hurries after RON. DOCTOR enters Stage Right.)*

DOCTOR: Are you the O'Brien boy's friends?

RON: Yes.

MIKE: I – I'm the one –

RON: We're his friends!

DOCTOR: You can wait out here if you like. Down the corridor is a lounge.

MOM: *(Enters Stage Left and crosses to RON.)* How is he?

RON: I don't know. He looks – I'm afraid, Mom. I'm thinking of when the crane fell and Dad bled –

MOM: What happened exactly? Mrs. Llewellyn didn't tell me who was responsible for –

RON: I think Mike better tell you. Mike, this is my mom.

MIKE: *(Very shaky)* I didn't know. I never knew that Billy...is a hemophiliac.

RON: Mike is one of the two guys who – the ones who climbed up the tree with me.

MOM: I see.

MIKE: He said those things about my sister.

RON: Being on drugs like me, you mean.

MIKE: Worse, a whole lot worse.

RON: What do you mean?

MIKE: The drugs fried her brain! She's dead.

RON: I'm sure Billy didn't know.

MIKE: I know he didn't. Nobody knew. My family kept it a secret. Billy knew she took drugs. His mom and my mom always talk. Mom must have said something about Betsy, maybe even that she'd dropped out of school. Billy overheard.

MOM: I'm sorry.

MIKE: *(Tears in his eyes)* **We fought all the time. But...I love her. I still love her.**

MOM: I thought you said she had died.

MIKE: Her brain's dead. The rest of her...might as well be.

MOM: You mean...she's on life support? *(MIKE nods.)*

RON: I used to know her. Know who she was. Remember the high school play, Mom? The one we went to when I was starting junior high. That was her, wasn't it, Mike?

MIKE: *(Miserably)* Yeah. That was Betsy.

RON: She played the lead.

MIKE: The part of Gwendolen.

MOM: She was wonderful. The perfect Gwendolen. Wilde must have had her in mind when he wrote the play.

RON: I thought she was in school.

MIKE: Julliard. It's all she talked about. And then – she started fooling around with drugs.

RON: I know what that's like.

MIKE: I guess so.

RON: Where is she?

MIKE: What?

RON: Where is she?

MIKE: Here.

MOM: In the hospital?

MIKE: Different part. Where they keep all the hopeless cases.

MOM: Hopeless?

MIKE: The other wing. Like here, it's supposed to be intensive care. Nobody really cares.

MOM: Mike, listen, somebody cares. Someone wants to keep her memory alive.

MIKE: Yeah, my sister, the doper. Just what O'Brien said.

RON: Can I see her?

MIKE: What for?

RON: Tell me where she is.

MIKE: *(Defiantly)* I said it's the other wing. I don't know why you want to see her.

MOM: I've got to go.

RON: See you after school, Mom. *(MOM exits Stage Left.)* **Show me where she is.**

MIKE: Haven't you caused enough trouble?

RON: What!

MIKE: If you hadn't been hit by that truck.

RON: Oh, yeah, like I tried to be hit by the truck.

MIKE: Sorry. I guess I'm upset. Don't know what I'm saying.

RON: I think I can help your sister.

MIKE: What?

RON: Let me try.

MIKE: If you think you can help my sister, you're even weirder than I thought.

RON: Thanks a lot.

MIKE: I'm worried about Billy. What if –

RON: Worried about him or worried about you?

MIKE: OK, I admit it. Both him and me.

RON: Yeah. I'm worried about him too. But let's worry about your sister right now.

MIKE: What's that supposed to mean? I told you her brain is dead.

RON: You saw what happened, didn't you? After I dived off the tree.

MIKE: How did it happen? How could something like that ever happen?

RON: I want you to give me a promise. One you can never break.

MIKE: Depends on what it is.

RON: Maybe I can help your sister; maybe I can't. I mean, if I can save my own life. If I can bring myself back from being dead –

MIKE: Oh, God! Do you – I mean do you really think –

RON: I don't know. Show me where she is.

MIKE: Sure.

RON: Will you promise not to tell anybody I tried. It's like I'm some kind of freak who can rise from the dead or give one of my lives to others.

MIKE: *(Unbelieving)* **One of your lives?**

RON: Whatever. Will you promise?

MIKE: Sure. But...what about Billy?

RON: Your sister's already dead. You said so yourself.

MIKE: More than a week now. She was supposed to graduate this year. Had a series all lined up. On TV. She always wanted to be... this great actress or something. *(Pause)* Come on, I'll show you.

(The lights dim on the area surrounding BILLY's bed and come up on another hospital bed. Just as they do, RON and MIKE enter the area.)

MIKE: She's in there. I don't want to see her.

RON: There's a nurse. Can you talk to her, hold her attention, so I can get in without being seen. *(MIKE shrugs.)* Will you try?

MIKE: *(With little hope that RON will succeed.)* I'll try. *(He exits Stage Right. RON looks around to see if anyone's watching. He stops at BETSY's bed. She lies curled in a fetal position. RON kneels by the bed and picks up one of BETSY'S hands.)*

RON: Betsy. Hi. Do you remember me? Ron Pagliani. I used to see you sometimes on the way to school. I don't know if you ever knew me or not? I saw you in a play once, Betsy. A couple of years after Dad died. Mom took me to it. *The Importance of Being Earnest.* You know what? That was the first time she and I did anything together after Dad died. The first time we went anywhere, except to get school clothes for me and stuff like that. I was twelve then. But I thought you were wonderful. So much better than anyone else.

I almost threw my own life away on drugs. I did throw my life away for nothing, a different way. I'll never do something like that again. Betsy. If you wake up, you'll be fine. But you have to promise me, OK? You have to promise...no more drugs. Please, Betsy, no more drugs.

BETSY: *(Opens her eyes.)* What – Where am I? I feel...strange. *(Suddenly alarms begin to sound.)*

RON: You're going to be fine, Betsy. Believe me, you're going to be fine. You have to be because I don't want to waste another life. Do you understand!

BETSY: Who? I –

RON: I gotta go. *(He races as fast as he can straight Downstage from the bed. The lights come up near the edge of the stage as they slowly fade on the hospital bed. The sound of the alarms becomes muffled.)*

FELINA: *(Enters Stage Right and crosses to RON.)* **Mer knows what you did. She thinks it's a very fine thing. She says she thinks you are no longer a kitte – a boy. She says that maybe now you're a man. A good man.**

RON: Billy! I've got to go back and see if Billy –

FELINA: William O'Brien is fine. His bleeding has stopped...miraculously.

RON: What!

FELINA: Five lives left, Ron. That's what you have now. Your first life. The one restored after the accident. Another when you dived from the tree. The fourth, Michael's sister. Mer says that maybe it is better that you give no more away. Mer says that perhaps it is better to use these lives you have left to better the lives of all others.

RON: I don't understand.

FELINA: You have many lives, many, many lives of a cat. Lives to study and find ways to improve all of life.

RON: What about Billy? I have to try.

FELINA: I told you William O'Brien is fine.

RON: How can that be?

FELINA: Mer used up nearly all her remaining power. Perhaps she will fade away. Perhaps she is no longer needed in a world such as this. When she had all her great power, the world was simpler, more trusting. She told me that. She told me to tell you.

RON: She stopped Billy's bleeding? But why?

FELINA: She puts her faith in you, Ron Pagliani.

RON: In me?

FELINA: She says sometimes myth has to give way to reality, and so she has passed the torch. I do not know what that means.

RON: Are you going to school?

FELINA: I? No, I don't think so.

RON: It's almost time.

FELINA: I think I'll be going back home now.

RON: Home? Where is that?

FELINA: Very far away...for most of the human race. But not so far for someone like you.

RON: You sound as if –

FELINA: As if...what?

RON: Will I see you tomorrow?

FELINA: Perhaps you will.

RON: Perhaps! Felina, that isn't good enough. I...I like you. A lot. Don't you know that?

FELINA: As I said, Mer has used up most of her power. Only a small bit is left. Once it is gone, there will be no more.

RON: Yes?

FELINA: *(Crying)* If she is able...

RON: What? If she is able to what?

FELINA: There will be a full moon tonight. If she has power left, it will be magnified then.

RON: I don't know what you're saying.

FELINA: Since I already have this form, it may be easier.

RON: Are you saying you may be able to remain a human being?

FELINA: We may never meet again, Ron Pagliani. Look for me though. If you look hard enough, you can find me.

RON: Felina, please. I don't want to look for you. I want you right here.

FELINA: On the other hand, maybe I'll see you in school tomorrow. *(She crosses toward the Stage Right exit.)*

RON: Felina!

FELINA: *(Turning toward RON)* **Good-bye, Ron Pagliani. Mer was right. For a human being, you are a very nice person.** *(FELINA runs Off Right. For a moment RON is left standing there in the light of morning. Then the lights fade to black.)*

(Curtain)

Production Notes and Considerations

"The Boy With Nine Lives" is a melodrama in that fate does intervene in many ways — Ron's rescuing the kitten (which, of course, can be a stuffed animal), Billy's having hemophilia, Mike's sister's condition, and Ron's mother being a single parent. There is little actual humor. Yet even though the piece deals with some serious subjects, it is not meant to be heavy.

There is an unfairness in the characters' lives, as seen in Billy, Mike, and Ron's problems, as well as in Mrs. Pagliani's having had to rear Ron by herself. The taking of drugs has been a problem for two characters. There is Billy's illness and Mike's sister's being in a coma.

"The Boy With Nine Lives" also has elements of a romance comedy or at least the possibility of romance between Ron and Felina.

Ron, of course, is the protagonist, and so the action concerns what he will do with the seven additional lives he receives. Although Mer Heptaphanes calls him a good person, we know he has had problems with drugs. So, as an audience member, we want to root for him. But does he have enough strength of character both to continue to stay away from drugs and ultimately to do what he knows is best or not?

A ladder can serve as the tree. Ron can either jump or not. If he does, he perhaps can land out of the audience's sight on mattresses or a trampoline. Then when the lights come back up, he can be lying in the audience's sight.

The scenes frequently change location, which of necessity demands that the set be fairly simple. Curtains can be used or flats painted in a neutral shade. The locations can be more easily defined and suggested through the use of area lighting.

The major characters in "The Boy With Nine Lives" are more realistic and fully developed than the characters in many of the other pieces in the book. Because of this, you might want to analyze them more in detail to see what they are like and why they are like this. What is important to them? What are their goals? What makes them tick? What are their relationships with each other?

If you are playing any of the minor characters, you may want to individualize them in some way not necessarily suggested in the script. Do remember, however, that these characters such as the Nurse, Jepson, Jepson's Assistant and even Mer Heptaphanes, Frank,

Cherie, and Natalie need not and should not be as fully developed as the central characters. To try to make them complete or three-dimensional would take away from the main thrust of the plot — Ron's responsibilities, his prior involvement with drugs, and his relationship with his mother and with Felina.

If need be, there can be an overlapping of roles. Cherie and Natalie also can play the nurse, Jepson's assistant, Mike's sister, and so on. Frank can play the role of Jepson. The director can decide on which roles it's most practical to double up on for any particular production.

Another Sort of Forest

Romantic comedy usually is gentle in showing the complications the hero and heroine face in their quest for living "happily every after." But it is involved with more than love. In its earliest and purest form, which developed during the nineteenth century, romanticism involved the spiritual and the ability of human beings to transcend the physical world and discover the ideal truth of existence. That definition certainly fits "Another Sort of Forest" and in ways applies to "Nine Lives."

"Another Sort of Forest" is somewhat similar to "Pails by Comparison" in that it relies on incongruity in bringing characters from the past into the present. However, its humor is more gentle. In fact, the piece is a little melancholic or sentimental. Because of this, it could be called romantic comedy in that a happy ending is implied. The piece is unusual in that only half of the romantic pair appears on-stage.

Although the two characters start out as somewhat two-dimensional, as the piece continues, we learn more about them and see that they have a depth that is lacking in the characters of Jack and Jill.

Although there is humor, there is a poignancy in their unwillingness to trust one another, though looking back, it is easy to see that from the beginning Marie recognizes John. Yet she is afraid — perhaps that he has changed too much, and by implication, so have all the others whom she hasn't seen in many decades. She also fears that the situation has changed too much, that the man she loves no longer loves her.

There is humor in the word play, and, similar to "A Tale of the Bog," in the mixing of old and new expressions and ways of speaking. Although there are clues throughout as to who the people really are, it is not confirmed completely until the end. Even then, the man Marie loves is never actually named.

CHARACTERS: MARIE, appears to be 15-18; JOHN, appears to be about 19.

SETTING: The corridor of a high school.

AT RISE: MARIE enters Stage Left and crosses toward Center Stage. A moment later JOHN rushes on Stage Left and calls to MARIE.

JOHN: Will you wait a minute? *(MARIE turns her head.)*

JOHN: Please.

MARIE: *(Facing him)* **Who are you? What do you want?**

JOHN: My name's John.

MARIE: Juan?

JOHN: John. I said my name is John.

MARIE: Juanito. My little John.

JOHN: Don't you have me mixed up with someone else?

MARIE: No, I don't think so. Why?

JOHN: OK, what's your name?

MARIE: Marie.

JOHN: What a nice name for a pretty maid.

MARIE: I am not a maid. I teach high school literature classes. Not that there's anything wrong with being a maid, you know!

JOHN: Hey, if you teach English, you must be aware that there's more than one definition of maid.

MARIE: Damsel, girl, nurse, virgin! Is that it? And which of these am I? What are you implying? I warn you to be careful.

JOHN: I am implying...it's been a very long time.

MARIE: A long time? What do you mean?

JOHN: Myths and legends, if they're good ones, they live forever.

MARIE: We haven't experienced forever, so how could you say that?

JOHN: You know what I mean.

MARIE: I'm not certain of that at all.

JOHN: Did you know that names often have a common base?

MARIE: Of course, I know that, why do you ask? Paddy, Patrick, Patricia, Tricia, Trish!

JOHN: Mary, Marie, Maria, Marian!

MARIE: How dare you?

JOHN: I don't understand. I've searched a long time.

MARIE: Searched?

JOHN: Do you not remember?

MARIE: What on earth do you mean?

JOHN: Earth, yes. Those such as we are doomed to wander the earth...

MARIE: Are you a lunatic too?

JOHN: What sort of literature do you teach?

MARIE: What sort of literature? Poetry, of course. Fiction. Drama.

JOHN: Myth and legend.

MARIE: That enters into it.

JOHN: May I ask you another question?

MARIE: Another question. It seems to me you've been asking many questions without my permission.

JOHN: Two questions then.

MARIE: I don't know why I should answer.

JOHN: Question one: English lit or American lit?

MARIE: English, not that it should concern you.

JOHN: Why are you so...hostile?

MARIE: Is that your second question then? If so, I shall be going.

JOHN: It was not my second question.

MARIE: I don't know why I stand here talking to you. I have better things to do.

JOHN: I'm sure you do know why.

MARIE: You're a very impertinent young man.

JOHN: Young? Am I young?

MARIE: You appear to be nineteen or twenty.

JOHN: Appearances can sometimes be deceiving. My second question concerns *your* age.

MARIE: My age?

JOHN: And your name?

MARIE: Isn't that really two questions in one?

JOHN: I'll ignore that for the moment. If I appear to be nineteen or twenty, you yourself appear to be sixteen. At the very oldest seventeen or eighteen.

MARIE: Is that a question?

JOHN: It wasn't phrased as such.

MARIE: Get on with it then.

JOHN: How is it that a...woman, who appears to be fifteen or sixteen...

MARIE: Now you've changed it.

JOHN: I've had longer to observe. May I proceed?

MARIE: Get on with it. I do have a class to teach.

JOHN: How is it that one who appears so young is already a teacher?

MARIE: How can I answer? Some of us age more slowly than others. Appear to, I mean. Time passes the same for everyone, of course.

JOHN: Except if one takes into consideration –

MARIE: What is it you are implying?

JOHN: I think you know.

MARIE: Perhaps.

JOHN: Why have you chosen English literature? With a name like Marie, one would think you were French, or since you called me Juanito, perhaps even Spanish. María.

MARIE: I was being facetious. I was speaking in code. My brain is muddled. All of the above.

JOHN: I don't think so.

MARIE: What do you mean?

JOHN: I think the remark was deliberate...yet deliberately disguised.

MARIE: Whatever do you mean?

JOHN: Juanito. That is what I mean.

MARIE: You are speaking in riddles.

JOHN: No more than you, m'lady.

MARIE: "M'lady." Now who's being facetious or muddled or speaking in code?

JOHN: *(Simply)* He misses you.

MARIE: *(Hopeful)* He does?

JOHN: Indeed. He's searched both far –

MARIE: Must we be trite?

JOHN: Trite sayings at one time were fresh, as new as the glint of morning sunlight on the tip of an arrow.

MARIE: That's true, of course.

JOHN: Will you come with me then?

MARIE: Juanito?

JOHN: Yes, Juanito.

MARIE: It really is you?

JOHN: You didn't know.

MARIE: How would I? It's been years.

JOHN: Years, but still you look as you did –

MARIE: A curse, if you ask me.

JOHN: Aye, it is a curse.

MARIE: Where is he then?

JOHN: We followed you, and then lost your trail.

MARIE: Where is he!

JOHN: He's teaching. Like you. The ancient arts. Do you teach *The Canterbury Tales*? You used to love them. I remember your telling those of us who had not yet learned to read –

MARIE: Yes, I did.

JOHN: And do you still?

MARIE: Sometimes, when I gaze out my window, I think I see them setting off, telling their tales.

JOHN: Aye. 'Tis sad to long for the old days.

MARIE: The new have much to offer.

JOHN: Tell me, if you could, would you trade away the new –

MARIE: Of course! Ah, my Juanito. Things are so much better now in so many ways. Still –

JOHN: The heart yearns?

MARIE: I suppose you could put it that way. *(Urgently)* Tell me where he is.

JOHN: *(Not unkindly)* I told you he was teaching.

MARIE: *(Vulnerable)* Where?

JOHN: Not far. Not far at all.

MARIE: How did you find me?

JOHN: It's taken...many years.

MARIE: I suppose it has.

JOHN: Why did you come here?

MARIE: It was breaking apart, dissipating. I couldn't stand it. I wanted to get as far away –

JOHN: He would have followed. He did try to follow.

MARIE: We were torn apart...in the mist of such dissipation, one

171

tends to lose one's vision.

JOHN: Yes.

MARIE: *(Pleadingly)* Tell me.

JOHN: Ironic. He's teaching physical education at the college.

MARIE: The college? What college?

JOHN: On the other side of town.

MARIE: It cannot be! How long –

JOHN: Three years, at the end of this term.

MARIE: Oh, my God!

JOHN: Another cliché pops to mind.

MARIE: Ah, yes. So near...

JOHN: ...and yet so far. Not anymore.

MARIE: What's he like?

JOHN: Much the same as he was when...the end came.

MARIE: I've missed him. I've missed him so much. Not a day goes by, hardly an hour –

JOHN: He's kept your memory alive as we all have.

MARIE: Take me to him.

JOHN: You said you have a class.

MARIE: Fie on my class!

JOHN: Fie? Does anyone still say "fie"?

MARIE: *(Grabbing his arm)* You're right. No one does. I haven't used it myself since –

JOHN: I know. *(They begin to stroll slowly to Stage Right.)*

MARIE: Physical education? What area? Is it –

JOHN: What else would you expect?

MARIE: And the others?

JOHN: A few here and there. More all the time. *(Both stop.)*

MARIE: Are there any plans – I mean –

JOHN: The time is past. We keep in touch. Spread across the vast continents of the earth.

MARIE: I thought I might see them.

JOHN: There're phones and snail mail, of course. E-mail. GIFs that can transmit pictures. Chat rooms.

MARIE: Yes, one does have to keep up. Is he teaching –

JOHN: What else? His team always wins. They enter the national championships? Compete in the Olympics. But it's only sport now, and a minor one at that.

MARIE: *(Crying)* Oh, John, I've missed you all so much.

JOHN: I know. Nobody realizes, I suppose, that even though the place, as you say, dissipated into mist...

MARIE: The legends – The people, I mean –

JOHN: Yes.

MARIE: He really wants to see me?

JOHN: *(Gently)* As you say, not a day goes by, hardly an hour –

MARIE: 'Tis good to hear you say't.

JOHN: I parked in the faculty lot.

MARIE: Ah, Juanito. Little John. No one can give a legend a parking ticket!

JOHN: *(Laughs.)* Would 'twere true.

MARIE: You said his team does well. And he himself?

JOHN: Still splitting those arrows in the middle of the target.

MARIE: I never would have doubted it.

JOHN: I'm sure that's true, Maid Marian. *(They exit.)*

(Curtain)

Production Notes and Considerations

In this play, because there is more depth to the characters, there is more emotion which should be played as honestly as possible. While "Pails by Comparison" is strictly burlesque, though it does deal with equal rights, this play touches on several deeper feelings. Running through it are several themes: fearing to trust or believe; yearning; a sense of lost time; a longing for something that never again can be, and yet the idea that we must make the best of things, no matter how they differ from our expectations or beliefs of what should be.

All that's needed for staging the piece is an empty space.

If you are playing Marie, you may want to determine what sort of person she is, particularly in relation to Robin Hood, and why she doesn't at first want to admit that she recognizes Little John. Actually, she has conflicting feelings, in that she does refer to him as Juanito, which in Spanish does mean Little John.

In playing John, you may want to figure out why he and not Robin has searched for Maid Marian and how he feels about her reactions to him after their not seeing each other for many decades.

What sort of relationship do you think the two of them have? How do they feel about each other?

A Day at the Beach

Although "A Day at the Beach" is a one-act play, it is different from the majority of plays. Similar to "Father Knows Better," it has a thematic structure. That is, there is no plot, nor does it deal with a particular social issue. It is centered around the idea of how six teenagers interpret the events of their afternoon at the beach.

The play has some underlying themes, but nothing that really ties the whole piece together. One of the themes is the surprise a person can have at a character or personality trait shown by someone we've known for years.

It also shows the differences among people who still remain friends. The situation is somewhat exaggerated, or at least unusual, in that the three girls and three boys have been friends since primary school and have maintained the group as their primary friendship and support circle all of this time.

The play is meant to be humorous, though it is a soft kind of humor, not boisterous, even though the characters do say some pretty outrageous things, both about themselves and about the others.

CAST: JON, TANYA, MICHELLE, JAMES, BEN, JERRI FAYE, all 16-17; MR. HERNANDEZ, early 40s.

SETTING: The action takes place in a city park near the beach.

AT RISE: The characters appear on an empty stage. JON stands Down Center. The others, spaced randomly, stand or sit on park benches. MR. HERNANDEZ sits on a park bench Stage Right. Beside the bench, hidden from the audience's view, are several partially filled trash bags and various trimming, digging, and hoeing tools. As each of the characters delivers his or her monolog, the others react appropriately.

JON: OK, here's my side of it. What really happened. See, it was last Thursday, and we went to the beach. The whole gang of us. Me, Tanya, Michelle, James, Ben and, of course, Jerri Faye. Friends since grade school. All since first grade, except Ben and Michelle. Ben moved here a year later and Michelle two years after that. In third grade, we were all in Mrs. Sargent's room. Friends a long time, you know what I mean?

Anyhow, we went to the beach. Like to swim, and the girls to sunbathe. I mean Jerri Faye has this big towel with a picture of Mr. Spock. Belongs to her Mom. We'd packed a picnic lunch, all of us chipping in. They have this big fire ring, where it's OK to burn wood or whatever. Who has wood on the beach, right? So we decided we were going to go up a block or two, where there were houses with big yards and see if we could get some dead branches. Nothing wrong with that, is there? Not like we were stealing or anything.

We should have had a better plan. Some of us should have stayed at the beach and only two or three of us gone to look for dead limbs. But no, Ben insists we're like Siamese sextuplets, or whatever. We all gotta stick together. The six musketeers. So there we are all marching along like some dumb parade. Pretty suspicious right off. Six kids in swimming suits sneaking along in back alleys in single file. This little old lady was sitting out under this big lawn umbrella at a glass-topped table staring at us. "We better forget all this," I tell the others.

"Nah," James says, "that woman's so old she probably can't see us without her glasses, and I don't see any glasses."

I shrugged. Seemed like I was the only one who thought we should head back. And I admit, sometimes I'm wrong. Not often. *(Chuckles to show he isn't serious.)* But no, they insisted. So anyhow, here we are – can you picture this? – all hunched over tippy-toeing down this alley when Tayna whispers real loud, "It's a cop car." "A what?" someone asked. "Policeman!" Tanya yells, all in a panic. "Run, run. Let's go."

So here we are, all six of us, and this police car going *reeeeal* slow. I say we should have just stayed there and talked to the man. What could he have said? We weren't breaking any laws. Yeah, I know, tippy-toeing down some alley in a silly line, in swimming suits and nothing else, what are we going to say? What's the policeman going to think – that we indulged a little too much? Sure, of course, I tried booze once. Well, beer, actually. Couldn't stand it. Hated it. Wondered how anyone could drink that stuff. I was thirteen, and my cousin sneaked me a sip. Wow, Mom was really mad. I was grounded for a week, you know. Not even allowed to see my cousin again till a whole year later. I don't mean like I'm a sissy or anything. I just don't like the taste of the stuff.

So anyhow, this guy in a police cruiser pulls up and asks us what we're doing. And, man, Ben has to tell him this dumb story about how we're playing follow the leader. Follow the leader! Who in his right mind's going to believe something like that? Man, I haven't played that dumb kind of game since I was five years old! Well, OK, maybe thirteen or fourteen. *(Laughs.)* Nah, I'm just kidding. Gotta find a little bit of humor here, right?

So what do you think? This policeman doesn't believe us. Asks us to go to the cop house. Jerri Faye says we don't have a car, so how can we do that? "It's only two blocks" he says. "But we don't have shoes!" Michelle pops out. "Hasn't stopped you so far, has it?" the policeman asks.

You want to know the worst thing about all this? Who the

cop was. Friend of my Dad's. Poker buddy. Bill Hernandez. I mean they play every week. And *sometimes* a whole group of 'em, Mom included, takes off for the real thing – Las Vegas. Can you imagine that? Sin City, and my mom gets her nose all out of joint 'cause I had one sip of beer. I'm bitter about that? You bet your life I'm bitter. Who was it who said, "The punishment should fit the crime"?

Anyhow, I guess Mr. Hernandez didn't recognize me at first, or at least pretended not to. So here we are, this cop car driving down the street real slow and us walking along, trying to act casual-like, beside him. Too casual, if you ask me. I mean, who really walks down the street whistling, or looking up at the sky, or holding her head up real high like she's better'n anyone else? Try it some time. You and a couple of friends walk down the sidewalk barefoot in swimming suits and try to look nonchalant. The more nonchalant you try to look, the more stares you're going to get. Believe me.

So what happens then, just as we get to the door to the police station? Jerri Faye goes all nuts and starts yelling about how she forgot Mr. Spock. Now if that doesn't convince a policeman that we're on something, I don't know what would. I mean, here she is, the pitch so high it stabbed through my brain, yelling how she forgot Mr. Spock.

Well, I guess I can see her point. She wasn't supposed to use the towel. It was some real big deal, given away at a convention or something. Science fiction convention. Guess her mom used to be a big Trekker or whatever they're called, and this old actor, Leonard what's-his-face was there at the convention and personally handed out the towels. I mean Jerri Faye knew all that stuff, so why did she take the towel anyhow?

At the same time Jerri Faye's shrieking and wailing about her towel, Ben is all worked up about leaving all the food right there on the beach. And he starts talking about how he's hypoglycemic and he just has to eat right away or he's going to pass out. And Michelle yells at him to shut up, or everyone's going to think we're nuts, everyone at the station. As if they don't already, the kind of circus we're putting on. I mean, she and Ben are going steady, but she starts yelling at him, just like she's his mom or something, about how he's supposed to carry this little plastic bag of nuts and grains with him all the time. Then all at once she turns to me and says, "Why didn't you think of putting the food in the car so someone doesn't steal it?" "Me?" I say. "Why me?"

And then it sinks in. The car! Dad's car. Dad's pride and joy. The one thing he's proudest of in his whole life, though who knows why! It's this restored VW beetle, or whatever he calls it. Hardly room for all six of us to squeeze in anyhow. Someone always has to crouch in the "way back." That's what my brother used to call it when he was a little kid. The space behind the back seat. "Can I ride in the way back?" he'd start screaming every time we went anywhere.

Well, that has nothing to do with anything. What does have something to do with anything is that I'd parked the car at a parking meter. The plan was to feed the meter a couple of quarters every time it got hungry. Cheaper than the parking lot, I thought! And we were all going to chip in. But what if it was towed. We had our clothes and everything in there. My wallet. My wallet! So very politely, I asked the policeman if I could go check on the car. And he says he just wants to ask us a few more questions. Then he takes a good look at me. "Say, aren't you Rick's son?" he asks.

Oh, no! Now I'd be in trouble for sure. My dad's old poker buddy would call and tell him what had happened. "Yeah," I say real soft, like I didn't want to admit it. 'Cause I didn't. "And could this be your dad's Volkswagen we're talking about?"

"That's right," I say, trying to be calm about the whole thing, but everyone else is yelling about I don't know what. Jerri Faye's towel, Ben's food. Then out of nowhere, like he's really challenging this policeman or something, James says: "Do you know who my father is?" Like his father's someone important who can get us out of this jam. No disrespect or anything, but James's father runs some kind of computer or something for the Navy. So how's that going to help?

"No, son...I don't. Why don't you just tell me?" "Oh, no, that's all right," James says. I'm still trying to explain that I've got to get back to the car, and I hear Michelle asking James what he thinks he's doing talking to a policeman like that, and he whispers something and runs for the door.

"Halt!" Mr. Hernandez shouts. And it's just like the movies or something. I mean, I almost expected him to go for his gun. James was right by the door, and Mr. Hernandez goes over to him and asks him what he thinks he's doing. "If my dad finds out about this, I'm dead," James says. Hernandez starts to laugh. "So you thought you'd just run away?" He takes James by the arm and leads him back to the desk, lets go of him, walks around to an empty seat behind the desk and sits down. He plops his elbows on the top, folds his hands, and rests his chin on them.

"OK, now why don't you kids tell me exactly what you were doing?" he asks. As calmly as I can, I try to tell him. We don't have charcoal. But we do have hamburger meat and hot dogs. And marshmallows. And nobody thought to bring any wood so we could use one of the fire rings on the beach.

"So you see," Tanya jumps in before I can go on. "We were really doing a public service." "What public service is that?" Mr. Hernandez says, as if he can't believe this whole thing's happening. "Well..." Michelle says then, "maybe not public, but sort of...of private?" Like she was sticking a little question mark at the end. "Would you care to explain?" Mr. Hernandez asks. By this time half the people in the police station are standing around, grins on their faces as if they're really enjoying this.

"Uh, well," Ben says, "You see..." "Hush up!" Jerri Faye screams, and I'm really surprised because she's always been such a quiet girl. She's my girlfriend, besides my friend. So I should know, right? Wrong! "Hush up! Hush up! Hush up!" she goes on. "Now just a minute, young lady," Mr. Hernandez says. "I'd like to hear what this *gentleman* has to say."

Then Ben comes out with: "It's just like...like Michelle says!" "Ben!" Michelle screams, "Do you have to tell him my name. Ben turns to her, mouth open, like his jaw's on a big loose hinge. "Not that you said *my* name or anything, right?" He turns back to Mr. Hernandez. "OK, what we were going to do," he says, "is look around and see if we could find dead limbs off trees. Like fallen off or...maybe even still on the trees. And we were going to clean 'em up. Carry 'em off."

"I see," Hernandez says, and now there's no hiding his sarcasm. "Just to be helpful and nice." "Not exactly," Michelle says. "We needed wood to start a fire to cook the food." Now I hear a couple of people chuckling and look around. I can tell all these police people are finding this really funny. And I'm getting steamed. Really mad 'cause I've got to see to Dad's car.

"I'll make a little deal with you," Mr. Hernandez says. "You like cleaning up dead wood so much. This Saturday we'll all meet at the park, say at eight a.m., and beautify the place a little. Now how does that sound?" "I can't!" Tanya screams. "I got to watch my little brother." "And I have my dance class," Michelle says. "And I've got football practice," Ben chimes in. And pretty soon everything's in an uproar again. Am I the only one with any sense? Am I the only one who sees the serious-ness of the situation?

I tried. I did my best, and finally they all stopped screaming. By this time, a police sergeant – a woman – comes walking up and hands Ben this package of sunflower seeds and raisins and stuff. And he gets tears in his eyes. Can you believe it? Tears in his eyes. "Thank you," he says. "I could've passed out, you know?" Right away he rips open the bag and starts chomping on this holy mess of cow's food. And by then everyone has quieted down. Maybe it was seeing that the police weren't just there to give us problems. Maybe it was seeing they cared.

JERRI FAYE: Oh, come on, Jon, that isn't the way it happened, and you darn well know it. The policewoman with the heart of gold? That's silly. I'm going to tell you what really happened.

First off, the Spock bit. The towel. Jon's right. We have all been friends, and I might add, despite many differences. Who knows why? If you do, tell me. Yeah, we went to the beach all right, not one of my very favorite activities. But sometimes you have to give a little. That's what friendship's about. And going steady. I'm going to be an artist, OK? Not that I'm the world's greatest painter. No, but I try hard.

So what is this thing about the girls sunbathing?! Jon knows I don't sunbathe. First, I'd rather be going to exhibits. Art museums or galleries. I don't think Jon enjoys it like I do, but he usually goes with me. Sometimes all six of us go. *(Laughs.)* Can you imagine six teenagers among all those ladies with light blue hair? *(Giggles.)* Maybe they're old punk rockers, right? *(Pause)* So here we are. The only teenagers in a group of old ladies and men. They give us the eye. I guess they think we're there to cause trouble. *(Seriously)* We're not. We're there – *I'm* there – to study brush strokes and technique and shape and form.

My point is, compromise. Since the others go to exhibits, I'm glad to do what they want...within reason. But sunbathing? Can you imagine anything so boring? Sure, if I wasn't going with Jon, I admit the beach is a good place to see guys. Not that I'd ever go up to them, talk to them. *(With mock coyness)* Of course, it depends on the guy. *(Laughs.)* I'm kidding.

What I started to say is I'm allergic to the sun. Weird, huh? But I am. It's like a ray of sunlight hits, and it's instant burn. Instant nausea. Maybe not that bad, but close. That's why I brought the towel. It's big. It covers me head to foot. I'm glad we always come late afternoon 'cause soon it's cooler; the sun's not so hot. We always have a picnic. I don't mean to make a big thing of this. It's not a big thing. I mean here it is the middle of August, and we've been here only three times all summer. That's why I'm willing to suffer. Funny, huh? Like...an artist is supposed to suffer for her art. *(Laughs.)*

Don't get me wrong. These guys are my best friends, my best friends in the whole world. There's almost nothing I wouldn't do for them. So that's why I had the towel. Other than being too hot for two or three hours, I'm willing to do it. I'm not a...what did they used to call them? A beach bunny.

And what's this bit about wood? You're going to find wood on a public beach? Even a...a *beach* bunny knows better than that. I suggested we go to the store and buy charcoal. Oh no, nobody had the money to spare. Then Ben says this thing about how much better food is cooked over wood. *(Doubtful)* Maybe. But like I said...wood on a public beach? Sometimes you can find wood at the supermarket. Like for fireplaces. But I don't think so. What kind of store is going to stock wood in the summer?

So what happens? Not what Jon said. It wasn't like: *"We* decided *we* were going to look for wood." No. Jon takes it upon himself to announce that we're going to go find dead branches. And it's like the rest of us don't have brains? Why did we go along with this? "That's nuts," I said, but nobody listened. At least Tanya was smart to suggest that some of us stay at the beach. Then Ben starts insisting that all of us have to stick together.

You know what? I think he had this premonition. He figured we'd get into trouble, and everyone should share in the blame.

So here we are, sneaking through town. Down side streets and alleys. And I forgot my towel. Dumb. Thank goodness, that section of town is kind of wealthy. Kind of? I'll bet three-fourths of the richest people in the county live right near that beach. So they planted all these trees. The streets and alleys are all lined with trees. Which was good. Picture this: the others are sneaking along, one behind the other, carrying twigs and pieces of wood. And here I am, slouched over, walking tippy-toe just like they are. Except I'm weaving back and forth from one side of the alley to the other just trying to stay in the shade. I start to burn in less than a minute. Laugh if you want, but it's true.

You know what? Maybe it was my fault; I don't mean the

whole thing. I mean that police officer stopping us. Probably thought the way I was reeling back and forth all of us were drunk or on drugs. None of that stuff for me. I want a clear head when I paint. *(With mock seriousness)* Yeah, well, OK, there is the linseed oil and turpentine! *(Forceful)* I'm kidding. I'm kidding.

Even after we started out, I tried to talk everyone into going back. Guess who insisted we go on? Jon! The one who claims he insisted we head right back to the beach. Just like I'm the one who insisted we grab dead tree limbs from people's backyards. Uh-huh. What I said was that if we wanted wood from people's yards, maybe we should ask them.

"Come on, Jerri Faye," James says, "they'd think we're casing the joint." "Casing the joint?" I tell him. "You been watching too many old movies." "You know what I mean," he says. "Anyhow," Ben butts in, "if we ask them for wood, they'll want us to do all kinds of work in their yards."

I'm serious. That's what they said just when I was all set to ask this nice old lady sitting out at her table under this big umbrella. But everyone's trying to shush me up. I should have gone back to the car.

Then, just as we get to the end of this alley where the old lady was sitting, Tanya goes completely berserk when she sees a police car. Were we breaking any laws? No. Had we broken any laws? Well, if stealing dead tree limbs is breaking the law, I guess we did. Sheesh!

So here's Tanya practically out of her mind, and here we are sneaking along like in a Saturday morning cartoon. What's the policeman supposed to think! You know, if we'd just been walking together – me having to keep in the shadows, of course, he wouldn't have noticed. A bunch of kids going to the beach or coming home. Happens all the time. It's summer, for gosh sakes! We live near the ocean. It's logical we'd be walking along near the beach.

The follow the leader thing was dumb. But who wants to go to the police station? So I said the first thing that came into my head. "We don't have a car." That was dumb, too, maybe even dumber than what Jon said. *(Kidding)* No, nothing could ever be that dumb. *(Again seriously)* But if you were a high school kid in this situation, the first thing you'd think of was what would happen when your folks found out. You'd try to get out of it however you could, am I right? *(Pause)* I didn't know the station was only two blocks away.

You want to know the worst part? Walking along the sidewalk with the police car right beside us. What if one of my friends had come by? Or my mom or my grandpa?

Just as we got to the door, I thought of the towel. I'd left it on the beach. Very quietly and very politely, I tried to explain to the officer. "Sir," I said. "I left this towel on the beach. One of my mother's most prized possessions." He looked at me kind of strangely. Who wouldn't? Saying a towel is someone's most prized possession. "You see," I said, "my mom was a Trekker. You know what that is?" He shook his head. I said, "It's like a fan of the old TV series 'Star Trek.' Not the one with Data and Whoopi Goldberg and that. The original. With Captain Kirk and Scotty and – Anyhow, my mom's favorite actor was Spock. *(Sarcastically)* And for your information, Jon, the *old* actor's name *(Pauses for effect)* is Leonard Nimoy."

Anyhow, when my mom was just a kid, a young kid, her dad took her to this sf [pronounced "ess eff"] convention. And Spock was there. Mr. Nimoy himself. And he gave Mom this towel with his picture, and in the background the Enterprise and stars and planets and space. Mom even slept with the towel. Then, when I was a little kid, she had it thumbtacked to the wall. Really. She did. Weird, huh? But it meant a lot to her, and I shouldn't have taken it.

Knowing Mom like I do, I was sure she wouldn't do anything...exactly. But she'd feel really sad. I mean really sad, and she'd let me know for days she was sad. Days and days and days. OK? So I asked as politely as I could if I could go get it. I don't know why Jon said I started to scream. I can show him what screaming is if he wants to know.

Maybe I did overdo it. But nothing like Ben when he realized he'd forgotten his trail mix. It was like it was the end of the world. I know he has hypoglycemia and has to eat sometimes. But all he had to do was look around and see the snack machine inside the door of the station. Plain as anything. Candy and crackers and trail mix. I mean, are the police going to beat him if he asks to use the snack machine? They going to get out the rubber hoses, the bright lights to shine in his eyes?

Then Michelle gets a little bizarre. Yelling at Ben about forgetting his Zip-Loc bag. Jon says he can't understand that. I can. I mean if it were Jon, I'd probably get a little weird too. I mean he's my boyfriend. I care about him. Michelle cares for Ben. Of course, it wouldn't help at that point. But she was upset.

Yet, like I said, all Ben had to do was use the snack machine. It's not like I could get Mom's towel from the snack machine.

Then Jon, Mr. Cool-Calm-Collected, starts yelling louder than anyone. His dad's old car. This so-called restored Volkswagen beetle. Nothing against Jon's dad. Everyone collects strange stuff. I should know, huh? I've seen better looking cars in the junkyard! OK, it's nice that he lets Jon drive it practically any time he wants. If he didn't, the six of us would be stuck with no way to get anywhere. *(Giggles.)* And speaking of stuck? Have you ever tried to get six grown people into a Volkswagen beetle?!

I shouldn't laugh. I'd be upset too. Especially when he realized he'd left his wallet back at the beach. And if the car was towed. You know what, though? It was Jon's idea to park at the meter. To park all afternoon in the lot is only five bucks. We said we'd all chip in. None of us has much money, I know, but divide five dollars by six people, and what do you have? Very little, but a lot of time saved in running back and forth to a meter.

I did feel really sorry this cop was a friend of Jon's family. So there was no way Jon could get out of this one. If I'd been him, I'd have been plenty scared too. I mean he had as much a right – more of a right really – to get upset than any of us. And he did! No matter what he says, he did. He was yelling as much as anyone.

And then...looking back this is really funny. James asking Mr. Hernandez if he knew who his dad was. Like James's dad was some big shot or something. And I thought, oh, no, don't do this. You're just going to get us in deeper. But then to try to make a run for it. Might have made it too, until Mr. Hernandez says, "Halt where you are." Just like on TV. "Halt where you are." Jon says he was scared the policeman would grab his gun. I didn't think of that. I was thinking of the cop shows I've seen on TV and how this was just like they are. Afterwards... then I was scared.

Anyhow, I see that everyone else within hearing range is looking at us and smiling. And I felt stupid.

Then Mr. Hernandez asked what we were doing walking along carrying these teeny pieces of wood. Jon tries to tell him about the picnic, and Tanya jumps in with the stupid thing about a public service. That's OK, but Michelle has to make it worse with the private service bit. What was she talking about? A funeral?

Then Ben jumps in all hyper, and I try to get him to stop. It could only make things worse. "Let it be, Ben," I said. "OK. You're just going to make things worse." He looks at me and turns back to Mr. Hernandez. And very calmly I say, "Hush up. Why don't you just hush up, Ben?" I can see it's a losing battle when Mr. Hernandez asks him what he was going to say. But I'm always the cool one in times of trouble. I'd accepted that the towel was gone, that I was sunburned, that Ben needed to eat, that James would get in big trouble, that the car might be towed, that we had a lot of stuff in the car, that we'd be lucky to see the light of day the rest of the summer. But that's the way it was. The calmer we were, the more quickly we could... *(Losing her temper)* go back to the dumb car!

I have this absolute horror of being laughed at. Like when I was a little girl, my uncle teased me all the time. Everyone laughed. I hated it. Nobody knows how much I hated it. In spite of that, I was the only calm one.

When Mr. Hernandez said we had to help at the park, I was glad. It meant the whole thing was over. Sure, I'd have to give up some painting time. I'm working on a seascape. Ship out in the distance. Sea gulls overhead. A pelican on the beach. Seaweed. Foam.

TANYA: Everybody's ignoring the most important thing here, the car with Jon's wallet and some of our things, and all the stuff we left on the beach. That's what's important, right? That's what I was worrying about. Not all this other stuff. Well, OK, I did worry a little, but not all the much. I mean it was an innocent thing. All anyone had to do was talk to Officer Hernandez to find that out. My mom's not unreasonable. She understands...most of the time.

One thing I do want to say though. And here's what it is, OK? I'm sorry, Jon, but Jerri Faye's right. About the car. You could have saved us a lot of worry if it had been parked in the lot, and it would have cost maybe a dollar more. It's a quarter every fifteen minutes for the meter; five dollars at the lot. Just plain silly. I know that's not really my business, since most of my things were on the beach. Which also was pretty dumb.

The whole thing is I don't know why we had to go for wood. Do you know what I'm saying? Why didn't someone bring wood from home or a bag of charcoal, OK? Then we wouldn't have to be running around and leaving our things behind. And I'm really sorry, Jerri Faye, but I do like the beach. If that makes me a...beach bunny, fine, I don't care. That's just the way it is. I like the sun; I like getting a nice deep tan. I know the health warnings, but I use a good lotion.

You know, when Jon was telling about all this stuff that happened, he said we packed things for a picnic. Really? Well, I beg to differ. I packed it. *(Turns to the others.)* You guys were only too willing to bring all your little grocery bags of hamburger and buns and pickles and chips. But who provided the picnic basket and the cooler? *(Faces the audience.)* You know where we got that basket? Mom brought it back from South America. Yeah, after she went there with the money she received in the divorce settlement. The cooler doesn't matter that much. But the basket is...the only word is elegant. But that's fine. I'm only too happy to bring it along.

Jerri Faye kept complaining about a tattered, beat-up old towel. Well, I suppose I can understand about her mom having it all those years. She was worried about getting into trouble, and I guess I'd be too if my mom felt that way over some stupid...towel. But if it was that old and tattered, I think I'd throw it out.

You know, I not only provided the basket, and with Mom's permission, I might add, but the wicker holders for paper plates. They're from South America too. And Mom's second best silverware, not some cheap plastic junk. I mean, in my family, we never use that white plastic silverware. Just because you're on a picnic doesn't mean you have to be a barbarian. I suppose the rest of you don't agree. But so far as I'm concerned, the things you use are indications of the person you are, the values you have, the way you look at life.

It's like – well, as Jon says we've been friends practically forever, the six of us. And I think that's pretty unusual, don't you? A lot of kids are best friends for years. But a whole group? Not so likely. We're lucky that no one moved away or got angry or something. And I'm *glad* we're all good friends. But some-times...and I even hate to say this...it takes an effort. It really does. Jon's car, for instance. And I agree with Jerri Faye here, it really isn't a classic any way you look at it. Fine, it takes us places, if that's all that's important. But should it be? I mean, six almost adults, squeezed into that little VW thing. Come on, who's kidding whom here? Do you really like that? I mean, I'd take Mom's car in a minute, if I could. But she needs it, OK? She never knows when she might have to go somewhere. Anyhow, she didn't really think it was important I get my license when I was sixteen. And you know what? I didn't...No, I really don't want to be misleading, all right, to lie. I wanted my license to give me a little bit of independence. But it's a small thing. It is. It's not like she doesn't trust me. She's worried. Out on the road could be dangerous. That's what she says. Why it's more dangerous for me than for her, I don't understand.

And you know what? Sometimes I get a little sick of traipsing around to all these cultural things. I hate to say this, but I think maybe Jerri Faye is a little too pretentious. I mean, we've all met people like that, right? Uppity. Culture vultures! That's what Mom calls that sort of person. Just like vultures swooping down on anything that looks like it has the least bit of taste. And you know the sorts of things vultures like.

I'm sorry. Really. That wasn't very nice. But I do get tired of this art stuff. Why do I go then? I don't very often. Poor Jon, though. Stuck with it just about every darn time Jerri Faye wants to go. I go because we're friends. That's what friends do. Support each other, you know what I'm saying? But OK, I admit it, sometimes I want to kick back and watch Oprah or sometimes the soaps. I admit it. I like the soaps. *(On the defensive)* Anything wrong with that? All right then!

Maybe I'm spoiled. I've been accused of it often enough. Not like Mom is rich. Or Dad either. One thing they've always agreed on – even though they're divorced – is that they didn't want me ever to work until I had to. At least through high school, and maybe even college...if I go. Though I doubt that I will. They both had it rough. Took Dad years to get through college, trying to support Mom and me and my brother. So I guess I'm lucky.

Anyhow, I don't want you to get me wrong about Jerri Faye's art exhibits. I appreciate her coming to the beach when the sun bothers her so much – well, not as much as she lets on, I'm sure – but she does burn really easily. I know that. All that ugly red skin. Too bad she can't tan like I do. Well, I guess we're all different. That's the way it's supposed to be.

Jerri Faye says we didn't have money for charcoal. I suppose she's talking about me not wanting to chip in. OK, I didn't have much money. And the thing Ben said about wood. I don't *think* so. Who really can tell the difference between hot dogs or hamburgers cooked over wood or cooked over charcoal? I mean, I'm sorry to argue that point. I really am. But when it comes right down to it, who cares? I mean that, Ben. What really is the difference?

It's not that I wouldn't have chipped in; everyone knows that. It's just that I feel that I shouldn't have to. Jon either, though all of us were feeding quarters into the parking meter all day. But you know, if I'd realized what kind of day it was going to be, I'd have bought the whole bag of charcoal.

And I know I mentioned this before too, but it really bothers me. Jerri Faye is one of my very best friends ever in the whole world. But did she have to make that remark about beach bunnies? I know who she was talking about, and you do too. We can't all be smart like Ben and James and Jon, or as talented as Jerri Faye. But that doesn't mean everyone who isn't has a head full of nothing but oxygen. Anyhow if I studied more, I could get good grades. My interests are too wide for that. Lots of other things I like besides school. Movies, the cheerleading squad. OK, that is a part of school, but you know what I mean.

But that's not the problem right now. That's not what we're talking about. What we are talking about is all the dumb things that happened at the beach. Or the town really. Jerri Faye is right about one thing. Going for wood was a stupid idea. Really stupid. I know some of you wouldn't consider this important, but it is to me. Look at my nails. *(Holds her hands out front to let the audience see.)* You see what they're like. I worked hard to get them like this, and I'm not going to risk breaking one to pick up dead tree limbs. OK, maybe that makes me selfish and like my head's full of nothing but air. You know what though? My nails are important to me. My one big extravagance. Keeping a regular appointment at the nail place.

On the other hand, I wasn't going to be left alone on the beach either. Not by myself. Not with all the boys wandering around. Boys and men. College guys, I mean. I'm attractive, you know what I'm saying? I can't help that. *(Giggles.)* Not that I'd really want to, OK? I mean, let's be honest here. Just the same, I don't want a bunch of guys I don't know hanging around when I'm all alone.

So what choice did I have?

Jerri Faye wanted to stay. OK, I understand that. Even if she'd stayed by herself? Who's going to take a second look at someone covered head to toe in a ratty old towel, only her nose sticking out and even the nose all in shadow. Not that she's unattractive. Don't get me wrong. She *is*; she's a very good-looking girl. Really. But I'd be the one having to deal with all those beach-bum Romeos. See what I'm saying?

Oh, I tried, like Jerri Faye said. I was the one who suggested we stay at the beach – four of us. Or five maybe. I mean how much wood are we going to need to find for one little bitty fire? I thought that's what we were going to do.

Then Ben says we should all go for wood. I have to admit it was kind of fun though. Like a big adventure. It made me think of when the six of us were kids and went hiking or riding our bikes. Or skateboards. Ever notice how it's only ever guys who seem to ride skateboards? Not with us! The six musketeers: all for one, and one for all. So Michelle and Jerri Faye and I got skateboards too. Bet all six of us made quite a sight racing down the sidewalk. We did it for only one summer. Our moms got together, I guess, and decided it wasn't very ladylike.

And talking about Mom, I was a little hesitant about leaving her stuff at the beach. But I figured we'd be gone maybe ten minutes tops. *Wrooong!*

But like I said, it was an adventure, and we did get to see how the rich folks live. Like I'm going to live someday. Laugh if you want, but it's true. I'm going to live here in this town someday, not just visit to go to the beach.

The dumb thing was stealing the wood from backyards. It's stealing, all right. And trespassing too. I figured maybe some of the places had burglar alarms – maybe even the kind where if you reach through the beam of a light, it goes off and alerts the cops. Like when we were reaching through fences and gates for dead limbs. Do those things work just for buildings? Or gates and fences too? I don't know. Or I figured maybe it was that old woman out in the yard sitting under the umbrella. Maybe she called the cops. So, of course, I got upset when I saw the policeman. OK, I admit, I went crazy. Like if we're hauled into jail for breaking the law, what's my mom going to think?

The cop asks what we're doing, and Jon says we're playing follow the leader. Dumb? Yeah. I have no idea why he'd say something like that. But I do understand Jerri Faye's saying we didn't have a car. So what if it was only two blocks? Who wants to walk two blocks beside a police car with everyone watching?

Worst of all was at the police station. Everyone yelling about everything. Ben about his food. Jon about the car. Michelle yelling at Ben. Jerri Faye screaming at just about everyone. I mean, I was the only calm one. Would you believe it? I mean, for heaven's sake, we aren't five-year-olds. Nobody wanted to be there, but screaming isn't going to help. I felt like screaming on the inside, but I didn't want all those people watching. I suppose I can understand Ben needing his food. And James's dad really is awfully strict. And like I said, I can even understand Jerri Faye being upset too. About the ratty old towel. And Michelle yelling at Ben. It's because she cares. That's fine. I mean we're all friends, but I don't really have a boyfriend, you know. Who's left? James. I like James OK. But nothing's ever going to happen between him and me.

It bothered me that everyone was looking at us. I mean I was upset. But then again, I suppose I'm used to it. Cheerleading. Plays. The beach. People look...I mean, they do. Always. And I can't do anything about it.

So no matter what the others say, I did not scream. I repeat. I did not scream. I may have mentioned having to take care of my little brother Saturday mornings. My mom works. The cosmetics counter. Rexall Drugs. Can I help that? I can't help that. So it was going to be a problem. I'd have to tell Mom. I knew I couldn't pretend I was going somewhere else. You know, I'm glad I didn't spend my money on charcoal. I could use it for a babysitter for my brother.

MICHELLE: OK, so what can I tell you about all this? Everyone's had their say, and they're all wrong in some pretty important ways. Have you ever noticed that any time people tell someone else about something that happened, the people doing the telling always make themselves look good? Yeah, well, just think about the differences in what everyone said. Who's right? All of them are about some things. But most of the time you noticed, they disagreed about all but a few of the details.

Not me. My uncle always said I should be a journalist. When I tell something, it's clear and correct. That's what I want to do. Get a job on a newspaper and work my way up. City editor or editor maybe. Not women's reporting or society or lifestyle or whatever. Nope. Like Uncle Bob says, a hard-nosed reporter. That's what he is.

So we'll stick to the facts. The important details concisely at first and then elaborate. Who? When? Where? What? Why? How?

OK. On Wednesday, August 21, at approximately 3:42 p.m., six teenagers from nearby Stockville arrived at the public beach in Ocean Point. According to one of those involved, sixteen-year-old Michelle Farnaby of 1324 Second Avenue, Stockville, the six teens, three boys and three girls, friends since primary school, planned to spend an hour or two sunbathing. This was to be followed by a picnic at a fire ring at the north end of the beach.

Jonathan R. Miller, the driver of the auto, a red 1959 Volkswagen belonging to Jonathan *M.* Miller, father of the aforementioned Jonathan, parked the car at a parking meter. The teens then piled out of the car, gathered their belongings – beach paraphernalia, a picnic basket and cooler – and headed for an area just south of the fire ring.

One of the girls, seventeen-year-old Jerri Faye Berlin of 758 Palm Ave., Stockville, immediately rolled herself into an antique towel, complaining of an allergy related to her exposure to sunlight. The others proceeded to spread out their towels.

The six teens spent slightly more than two hours talking, swimming, and generally passing the time in what might be described as a pleasant manner.

Wait a minute. Just wait one minute. I have to work on that. That last paragraph. Sounds like a women's page/society/lifestyle story, if I ever heard one. *(Speaking as though reporting a solemn event)* The guests of Mr. and Mrs. Dashiell Dash-hound spent a pleasant evening aboard the Pinta Santa Maria, the Dash-hound's 320-foot yacht, moored in a little cove off the coast of a Martian canal. The hit of the evening was Martian Marsha Marshmallow, demonstrating the Martian stomp. A good time was had by all. *(Normal voice) Yuuuck!* See what I mean? That's not for me.

This really isn't a news report though, is it? So I'll be a little less impersonal. Sort of like maybe a feature story, OK?

For some reason we had no charcoal. Various theories were given, but no reason was proved, other than that no one had brought any. So we had no way of cooking the picnic lunch we'd brought. That is, each of us agreed ahead of time to provide certain things. It was suggested we buy a bag of charcoal; the suggestion was voted down. One of us suggested we look for wood in the city of Ocean Point. We proceeded to do so.

Yuck, what is this?! Now I sound like a police report.

I don't mean to talk that way. I really don't. I'm just trying to tell you what happened in a solid, objective way. Take the word "pleasant." That's a subjective word. Its meaning isn't precise. What is pleasant? Watching a tennis match may be pleasant for me, but maybe you hate it. Maybe you'd rather watch a ballet, OK? I hate ballet, ever since Mom decided I'd make the cutest little ballerina and made me this icky pink outfit with bows and ruffles for my first recital.

195

Whoa, now that's *really* subjective.

Where was I?

The six of us went looking for dead limbs off trees in back alleys and backyards. Hold it! I guess you can't be a journalist constantly. What I mean is, why do we always end up in some stupid situation? Does it ever fail? Well, hardly. Like Tanya said, we used to go bike riding. Let's take that first. All right. The first time, James has a flat tire. No one has a kit to fix it, or a pump. And, of course, no spare. And we're miles from home. Twelve or thirteen years old, all of us. And we can't just leave James. So we decide we have to walk along with him. So we all push our bikes. Ten miles from home. I'm serious. And then, guess what? Big rainstorm. Out of nowhere. Not even predicted. And so we're slogging along, James's bike worthless, all of us soaked to the skin. And Tanya starts complaining about the blisters on her feet, and Ben's plastic bag of food got all soggy. Tell me, how does plastic get all soggy? I'm serious. Supposed to be watertight, right? And then this big semi comes along and hits this puddle of water. You guessed it. Now we're not only wet. We're covered in mud.

I could go on. Tanya mentioned we often went hiking. This one time we got lost. We'd been on the same trail two dozen times. Took a wrong turn. And we're all tired and hungry and Ben's plastic bag is getting empty, and finally hours and hours later – it's dark by now – we see this big light coming toward us. Should we be scared or not? We don't know. We're out here in the woods, off the regular trail, and is this someone trying to rescue us – or is this someone who wants to chop us up and stick us in some oven with Hansel and Gretel? Well, OK, it was a couple of high school kids. They showed us back to the trail. They said they'd been looking for hours and were really tired. They had to stop for a while and rest. We could wait if we wanted or go on ahead. We went on ahead. We got out to the main road, and there are all these people waiting. Like half the town of Stockville knew we were missing, and the other half didn't want to miss out on any excitement.

Anyhow, we're all safe and back with our families, and everyone's too happy and hyper to go home, when someone asks where these two guys are. The ones who found us. Everyone else who'd been searching had wandered back by now. They said they were going to stop and rest, we said.

They got lost. Next morning bright and early we're all out looking for *them*. It's true. Every time. So why should I have expected anything different when we went on the picnic? Well, to tell you the truth, I didn't. But these guys are my friends. They've always been my friends. And hey, Tanya said it. It was an adventure. Just like every time we get together it's an adventure.

Anyhow, I don't mean to blame anyone. But it was dumb. We should have bought the charcoal; we shouldn't have been wandering along the street like criminals. It's stupid, stealing dead wood! To get hauled in for something like that?

I don't even want to go into all the stuff at the police station. It was weird. Everyone thinking he or she was the calm one, when everyone was screaming. So there I was, just standing back and watching. Except I was getting a little bit miffed when the people at the station started smiling and laughing. Who likes being the butt of a joke? And here they were, ten or twelve police officers and clerks and a dispatcher and... *(Frowns and shakes her head.)* It doesn't matter how many there were, or what they were. Why does it matter?

Don't misunderstand. I really do want to be a reporter. Maybe someday a foreign correspondent. But I don't have to act like one every minute of my life.

You know what, though? I don't plan to get married. Not for a long time, at least. Maybe never. I haven't told Ben. I don't suppose it matters. How many high school romances do you know of that last? Ron Howard maybe. You know, the child actor who became a movie director? He and his wife met in high school. But that's unusual. It isn't going to happen in my life. Oh, I'm going to miss Ben. I am. Is it really less than a year till we go our separate ways? *(As if just realizing what she said)*

Oh, God.

I'll miss them all. A lot. A year...sort of seems like a long, long time. But it's not. Mom always says the older you get, the faster time flies. She's says it's because you've lost the markers, the transitions. From primary to middle school to high school. You don't have to think, "In one more year, I'll graduate. Then I'll have four years of college, and then three years of college, and then...." *(Pause)* The years just go on.

I was scared. Even though I'd been in a police station two or three times with Uncle Bob, when he was talking to a detective about some crime. But that's a whole different thing. I never expected –

You know what? It makes me angry at all the exaggeration about what I said to Ben. I may have become just a little flustered. But I didn't scream like Jon said. And all right, it was really silly to say we had no way to get to the police station. I knew it was two blocks. It was dumb. What else can I say?

But everyone else did dumb things too. I'm willing to admit what I did. Everyone else is trying to blame the other person. Not me. I don't do that. I'd never do that.

Friends. You learn something new about them every time you see them. And some things aren't so flattering. I mean I never would have believed Tanya's thing about how she attracts all these boys. Does she really believe that?

Anyhow, I knew Mom and Dad would be really upset when they found out what happened. I mean there's this dumb dance class. Yeah, I'm still taking lessons. Don't ask me why. Mom wants me to, that's all. I'll never be a dancer. I don't want to be a dancer. But I got upset 'cause I knew I'd still have to pay for the lesson whether I went or not.

JAMES: Did you hear her? Michelle, I mean. I can't believe it. You can't say you were uninvolved and then say you're willing to admit your involvement. I ask you, does that make any sense? And Tanya. I can't believe her either. Is she really that stuck up? Get serious. Are guys really going to bother her constantly at the beach? We've known each other for years. And I never saw that side of her. And Jerri Faye and Jon. It was wild.

There's no use in going over the whole thing again. Everybody's heard it so many times by now that they're sick of it. OK. So I'm just going to try to explain a few things.

First, everyone has a comment on my trying to run away. All right. Maybe I was wrong. But I felt it was worth a try. We aren't criminals. We didn't really do anything wrong. And for gosh sake, Tanya, don't talk about trespassing and stealing. I mean, do you really think sticking your hand through a fence to pick up a piece of dead wood is trespassing? And taking dead wood is stealing? If it's from somebody's woodpile, of course. But limbs that have fallen off trees? You can't believe that. Can you?

See, the thing is, we haven't done anything wrong – seriously wrong anyhow – all the years we've known each other. *(Glancing at the others)* Come on now, have we? What's the most serious thing we ever did. Stealing oranges from someone's tree? Stealing pieces of wood? *(He turns once more to the audience.)*

None of us have ever been in trouble, big trouble. Right? Wrong. To my dad any kind of trouble is big trouble. Stealing oranges. Do you guys know what happened when he found out about that? Confined to my room for a week. *(To the others)* Remember when I told you I wasn't feeling well after school every day for a week? I lied. Confined to quarters! Right. That's what he calls it. Over one stupid orange, and it wasn't even that good an orange. Green and dried up at the same time.

That's why I tried to run. I think maybe you would too. Let's forget all about who wanted wood and who forgot charcoal and who screamed at somebody else. That isn't important.

(To the audience) **Tanya** said my dad is strict. Doggone right he's strict. Like he was in the Navy for twenty years. Retired, but still works for the military. All that discipline and control and order.

So I'm on the track team, sprints and long distance both. Not many guys do that, huh? Well, I do. I figured if I could make it out the door, I'd use my sprinting ability for a couple of blocks and cut into a side street. Then I'd just keep on going. Going, going, going.

How far is it, anyhow? Ten or eleven miles. I'd make it home even before it was time. If I was lucky, nobody'd notice Jon didn't drop me off. If Dad noticed, I'd have to make up some excuse. But I had miles to think up that excuse. Ten miles? I've run that far. I've run further than that. A couple of half-marathons, and I'm only sixteen.

I want to go to college, see? And that's the only way I'll get there. Track scholarship. That's why I work out every day, every day of my life. Haven't missed a day since I started in seventh grade. I mean it. Not a day. OK...except for the week when we stole the orange. It's important to me. Maybe to get nationally ranked. Maybe...make the Olympics. At least the U.S. national team.

So I heard all this complaining about who did what. All this screaming and yelling. And all of you trying to say you were the one not making any noise. That you were the calm one.

Nobody heard me saying anything till I asked if that policeman knew who my father was. I don't say things. I act on them. Maybe it'll get me in trouble someday; maybe it won't. But at least I don't stand around just waiting and yelling. Anyhow, you think a cop's going to shoot an unarmed kid who's done nothing wrong? Nah, I don't think so.

I guess that means maybe I'm the only one of us got any nerve, any guts. That's all I got to say. *(Glancing at the others)* I don't mean to put you down, any of you. You're my friends. My best friends. My only friends, really. Yeah, maybe some guys on the track team, but nothing like you guys. But I mean, come on. OK?

BEN: Like James, I haven't got much to say. I mean what's left? You've heard this so many times now, I'm sure you're sick to death of it. We did a lot of dumb things, that's all. Like my insisting all of us go looking for wood. No matter what Tanya thinks or Jerri Faye or anyone else, I did it only 'cause I figured we'd need a lot. Have to take a lot back to the beach. It's not like having big logs that burn for hours, you know.

Nobody's fault. Nobody to blame. Anyone can forget charcoal, right? Yeah, right, except doesn't it seem a little weird that not even one of us thought of it till we were there on the beach? I mean we even planned which fire ring we wanted.

Yeah, I know. It's nicer to use wood there. But charcoal would work. Or we could find a grill. There are some of those around too. Back further, near the road. So why didn't we go buy some charcoal? Or see if one of the stores had wood? I've heard so much talking I can't remember who said what. But somebody said stores don't carry wood this time of year. Those bundles you put in a fireplace. Maybe they don't. But wouldn't it be better to look first?

And then, how could I forget my package of trail mix? Maybe the sun affected me, just like it affects Jerri Faye. I mean it. That plastic bag is such a part of me, it's almost like an arm or a leg. I'm never without some food. I know what can happen. And if any of the others had the problem I do, they'd get all panicked too. And OK, when I'm starting to get really panicky and feeling lightheaded and all that, I'm going to think about snack machines in police stations? Yeah, sure I am.

And I'm sorry Jerri Faye, but it was really nice of that woman to do what she did. Maybe she does have a heart of gold. I didn't see anyone else getting me anything. None of my *friends* putting money in the snack machine or even pointing it out to me. I had some money. OK, so I was wearing a pair of trunks and nothing else. But all the swim trucks I've ever seen have a little pocket in front. And I always keep some change there or a dollar bill. Like for when I run out of food.

Aw, well, it's over and done with. No use beating it to death anymore. Right? And like Michelle said, it's just another weird thing like the things that always seem to happen anytime we go anywhere together.

So I say, let's forget it. *(Turns to the others.)* **What do you say?** *(The OTHERS make motions showing they're about to give in. Suddenly MR. HERNANDEZ stands, and picks up the equipment by the side of his bench.)*

HERNANDEZ: Break's over. Time to get back to work. *(He hands the tools and garbage bags out to the others.)*

(JON, JERRI FAYE, TANYA, MICHELLE, JAMES, and BEN indicate in individual ways their reluctance to continue, though they finally comply with the implied request. They pantomime picking up trash and dead limbs, trimming trees and hedges, weeding a patch of flowers and so on. MR. HERNANDEZ walks Downstage and addresses the audience.)

HERNANDEZ: I tell you it was the funniest thing you ever saw in your life. At least in a police station. It was easy to tell right off the kids hadn't been doing anything all that bad. I mean, what can you do dressed in nothing but swimming suits? But I did get to wondering what on earth they were doing sneaking along like that. Little kids, sure. But kids that age. Sixteen, seventeen. Then one of them pops up with the follow the leader bit, and it was all I could do keep from cracking up right in front of them. I mean it. I nearly lost it. Then the girl, Jerri Faye, she says they can't go to the station 'cause they don't have a car? I had to turn away on that one.

Why did I take them in if I knew they weren't doing anything wrong? What do you think? I wanted cheap labor. What else? Of course, that's not it. I'm just kidding around. Why I did it was to make them think next time they go sneaking around stealing pieces of wood. *(Laughs.)* **Dead limbs off trees? Do you really think anyone's going to arrest them for that? Send them to juvenile hall? Put them in isolation? Give them a diet of bread and water?**

They're right. It's a small town. We hardly ever have big problems here. And they're all good kids. Right off, of course, I recognized Rick's son. I've seen him grow up from a little runt of a thing. Two, three years old. But I went along with pretending I didn't. I knew right away it was him and his best buddies. We play poker every couple of weeks at Rick's house. Actually, I've met every one of them. At Rick's house. So it isn't like I haven't seen them before.

So what you might ask then am I doing here at the park on my day off? *(Leans forward, confidentially.)* **OK. Let me tell you. I**

volunteered, oh, way back, months ago, to do the end of the summer cleanup and maintenance at the park. Sure, I got a lot of other citizens helping out. It's for a good cause, right? Everyone likes a nice clean park. Old folks to play chess or checkers. Young kids on the swings. Teenagers walking hand in hand.

So with the cleanup, you can always use a few pair of extra hands. Well, I guess instead of jawing at you any more, I better be getting back to work, too. *(He pulls a pair of pruning shears or a hand hoe or other small tool from his back pocket and starts to turn away. Then he turns back.)* **Oh, yeah, a couple of other things. I'm not such a bad guy, you know. Rick's car – it wasn't towed. When I parked the cruiser? One of the other guys was just coming outside. I gave him a quarter, asked him to check since I know Jon always drives to the beach and always parks at a meter. Who wouldn't recognize that old junk heap of Rick's? Classic. You gotta be kidding me.**

And about the kids getting in trouble at home? I wouldn't let that happen, especially with James. I know about his father, how important his running is, how it would kill him to miss a day. Rick and I have talked about that. I mean the father's a nice man. But he could teach the military a thing or two about discipline. I called the families, said I really needed the help at the park. Said I'd run into the kids near the beach, and that I recognized them, and that I asked for their help.

I told the families the kids gave me excuses. But I also told them how important this was. You know what? I even called that ballet teacher. She's not going to charge Michelle. And I asked my brother's girl – they live in Stockville – if she'd mind doing some babysitting. And I talked to the coach, too – an old high school classmate of mine.

Nah, I'm not such a bad guy. You might even say...I have a heart of gold. *(He turns and crosses Upstage where he begins to work as the lights dim to black.)*

(Curtain)

Production Notes and Considerations

Even though, as a couple of the characters tell the audience, the group has had a lot of misadventures, they never before have been taken to a police station, which is a stressful thing to happen to almost anyone, particularly a person who is law-abiding. But it is in situations of stress or upset that facets of a personality surface that even close friends have never seen before.

Actually, nothing much happens during the play. Everything up until the very end is a reflection of what happened when the six teenagers didn't have wood or charcoal to make a fire on the beach.

The characters are very much different from each other. When presenting this play, try to figure out all the differences you can among the characters and how this is shown on the printed page and how you can bring it across to the audience.

For instance, Tanya is very much different from Michelle, not only in what she says about herself, but in her basic attitudes. How do you know this? Why do you think it is so important to James to have a goal he's already stuck to for years? How can you show such intensity to an audience?

The play, of course, is a series of connected or thematic monologs delivered by the six teenagers and the policeman. They are not of equal length. Can you see a reason for the play's being written this way? What do you think it is? What is the purpose of bringing in the policeman at the end?

In ways this sort of play is easier to present in that you don't have to interact much with other characters, nor do you have to worry about cues. However, you do have to analyze your own character in relation to the others, and, despite the problems brought out in the different speeches, you still have to project a sense of friendship or comaraderie.

Once more the staging can be simple — a few park benches. For atmosphere, you can include two or three trees, some statuary, and maybe a hedge or two.

The Smyth's Tale

Comedy usually deals with a departure from what is considered sane or normal in society. Yet *Theatre of the Absurd* (or *Absurdist Drama*), most popular in the 1950s and 1960s, is just the opposite. It tries to show normal individuals in an insane, abnormal world. The term "absurd" does not mean the writing is preposterous. Instead, it refers to the absurdity or futility of human existence.

Generally, Absurdist Drama is nonsensical and repetitive. The "human condition" rather than the individual characters is important, since the characters often behave like robots and speak with illogical or disjointed dialog. Theatre of the Absurd maintains that nothing is good or bad in itself. Only what human beings attribute to something can make it either moral or immoral. Truth is to be found in disorder and chaos, because everything is equally illogical. In pure Theatre of the Absurd, the playwright tries to show the absurdity without making judgments about it.

In Eugène Ionesco's *The Bald Soprano*, the characters most often speak recognizable words and sentences, but overall they make no sense; they are non sequiturs. Although there is the appearance of struggle and conflict, there is no movement toward the solving of a dramatic problem, something that does occur in most plays. Samuel Beckett's *Waiting for Godot*, which was probably the most important play in calling attention to Theatre of the Absurd, begins and ends with two characters waiting for someone named Godot, though the audience never discovers who or what Godot is or why the characters are waiting. The play contains two acts, which easily could be switched without seriously affecting the outcome.

Theatre of the Absurd still continues to influence the writing of plays. Many written after the Absurdist movement began to decline have touches of Absurdism in the dialog or situation. However, these more recent plays often have further meaning than the futility of life.

Theatre of the Absurd can be humorous or serious in presenting its message. Ionesco's one-act play, *The Bald Soprano*, (1950) is much funnier, for instance, than is his full-length *Rhinoceros* (1960), which has a touch of the tragic in its tale of human beings randomly turning into rhinoceroses.

"The Smyth's Tale," which follows, is utterly lacking in any meaning, except in reinforcing the Absurdist viewpoint that life itself lacks meaning. The play's theme is that much of everyday life seems nonsensical or meaningless. To communicate this message, "The Smyth's Tale" uses a number of comic devices such as automatism, surprise, and exaggeration.

The bizarre coincidence of all the characters having a garden similar to the one Langford describes is an example of automatism. There is surprise, or the unexpected, at the many twists and turns the dialog takes, and in the fact that nothing at all has specific meaning. Even that which seems to head in a particular direction quickly veers off into nonsense.

Of course, the idea of using nonsense language, words, or situations is not unique to Theatre of the Absurd. Rather it has been around in many forms for centuries. An example is "The Valedictory Speech," which appears later in the book.

CAST: LANGFORD, 14 to 16; NARDA, 13 to 15; CALIDA, 15 to 17; SIDDELL, 16-18; and the NARRATOR, any age.

NOTE: All the directions are to be read aloud by the NARRATOR, who should sit or stand or lie or float Stage Right or Stage Left. This character, male or female, or perhaps another sex altogether, if such can be found, should watch the action, as if deeply engrossed, but should deliver all the directions to the audience. Thus, it would be of great help if the character had two sets of eyes, or even one set very widely spaced. That perhaps may pose a casting problem that is somewhat difficult to solve.[34]

NARRATOR: The action occurs somewhere in a universe, perhaps our universe, perhaps only yours. Whichever universe it is, it contains four chairs or stools or settees or rocks on each of which a body can seat itself. It is the season of the year, and school is perhaps in or out of session. All four characters are high school students, or not. As the curtain rises, the lights come up, the candles are lighted, the fireworks begin, the parade passes by, the circus comes to town, the state fair proves this year not to be so fair, the four of them sit, stand, sprawl, or squat around gossiping. Quite naturally, the talk turns to Jonathan. Perhaps the reader knows why this occurs, or perhaps the actors or the director. The writer does not. So shall it be, henceforth and forever in the governing of the affairs of humankind...or sometimes not so kind, alas. And a lackey. And a lad. And a dog. And a cat, who also may play these roles, if they wish.

Hence our journey begins.

LANGFORD: There were two things Jon hated, you know? One was his name, Jonathan Paddington Puddington Smyth. The second was his condition.

NARDA: That's because of the way people talk of the girl next door.

[34]Should the cast list and/or the "Note" be read aloud? Only the Narrator can answer that question. But is he, she, it going to answer? We can only wait in wild anticipation to discover the answer.

I don't understand it. What's so bad about her?

CALIDA: Who said she was special?

SIDDELL: Jon Puddelly, Paddelly – whatever – always said that there was something really weird about the garden.

LANGFORD: Do I perhaps detect a hint of foreshadowing? All right, I'll go along with it then. "What garden?" I shall say, as expected. Thus: "What garden?"

NARDA: Jon's my boyfriend. It was arranged, you know. We've been dating now since 1875.

CALIDA: That doesn't make any sense.

LANGFORD: Why should everything on earth make sense?! Now here's how it was when I was a child.

NARDA: A child? Aren't you a child even still? The same age now that you were two years ago...in July, I think.

SIDDELL: As I once said: "Tendrils of fog, echoes in still water."

NARDA: Jon said all that about the girl next door.

CALIDA: No! It's because he hates his name so much. Piddlety Puddlety. That's OK. But anyone with a name like...

NARRATOR: She speaks the name with utter loathing.

CALIDA: Jonathan!

NARDA: Of course, all of our names are perfectly normal.

LANGFORD: What are our names?

SIDDELL: I'm sorry. I forgot to introduce you. I should have done it when we met in fourteenth grade. Normal school. After college when we lived together in that big old house in New York City.

CALIDA: Under the subway?

LANGFORD: Get to the point!

NARDA: Yes. It is a pointed conversation. Particularly since I have all this homework to do.

SIDDELL: My world, my time – destroyed by pestilence.

NARRATOR: Speaking with a sense of wonder.

SIDDELL: But this world is a forest primarilyeval.

CALIDA: Don't you mean primeval?

SIDDELL: That too, of course.

LANGFORD: So where are you from?

NARDA: Philadelphia cream Cheesits. Potato chips. All crumbled up in a waste bin of fortuitous odoriferousness.

NARRATOR: Calida speaks with near adoration. Or actually it could be far adoration if her physical body is not close to the physical bodies of the others.

CALIDA: Pretty, oh, so pretty.

NARDA: Smell cannot be pretty! One sees with the ears cocked back to the side of the head. But a reeking aromatic scent cannot be...

NARRATOR: Narda's speech and manner become extremely derisive.

NARDA: ...pretty.

LANGFORD: I hate to disagree with you, Frank, but think of it as music class.

SIDDELL: Music class?

NARDA: Get with it, Susan. "A Pretty Girl Is Like a Melody." You know very well that's true.

SIDDELL: Which reminds me, Darwin, you're both pretty girls. You and Rudolph.

LANGFORD: I'm a boy!

SIDDELL: What a ridiculous statement. Of course, you're a boy! Everyone knows that.

NARDA: Let me come to his defense. I assume it's because we don't know everyone's name. Mine is Narda.

SIDDELL: Mine is Siddell.

CALIDA: Mine is Calida.

LANGFORD: Mine is Langford.

SIDDELL: Like someone once remarked. A name like Jon Smuddington Smiddington Partington –

LANGFORD: Are you sure that's right?

CALIDA: No, silly goose. We're the ones who are left. Narda, Siddell, Langford, and me.

NARDA: What sort of name is "me"?

LANGFORD: Your name is Narda. You know very well it's Narda.

NARDA: That's not exactly what I meant!

SIDDELL: Not exactly. I'd say, in fact, you're far from the truth. Narda. Wasn't she a gymnast once? Long, long ago. My great-grandfather's third wife's new husband said that she came

209

from Eastern...Kentucky.

NARDA: Eastern Europe. And my name's Narda. Hers is Nadia, Nadia, Nadia, Nadia!

LANGFORD: Very strange. Why would someone be called Nadia-Nadia-Nadia-Nadia?

NARDA: For emphasis, you silly duck.

LANGFORD: Emphasis. I don't think so. That name's nearly as bad as "Jon."

CALIDA: Jon's not a gymnast.

SIDDELL: This is the silliest continent I've ever been on.

LANGFORD: Nice, finally, to meet all of you. But I was saying –

NARDA: You were? But you led us to believe you've always been Langford.

NARRATOR: A little past annoyance but not quite to fury, he says...

LANGFORD: I am!

CALIDA: Why's he so angry?

SIDDELL: Beats me. I think he wants to tell us a story. Isn't that our purpose in convening here today?

LANGFORD: You know it is.

SIDDELL: Well, then, Petrucchio, why not begin?

LANGFORD: Langford! My name is Langford.

NARDA: Who is?

SIDDELL: Please, please, let Langford tell us his story.

CALIDA: Then I suggest we all sit down.

NARRATOR: The strange thing here is that they all have been sitting or standing or some of them have or haven't. The director simply has to advise them on this.

NARDA: I prefer to sit up.

LANGFORD: What difference does it make whether we sit up or down?

SIDDELL: It's a directional thing, Langford. I see that you haven't had geometry or geology or *National Geographic* delivered by little Venusian boys and girls to your doorstep.

CALIDA: Grammatically, shouldn't that be: "delivered to your doorstep by little Venusian boys and girls"?

NARDA: Oh, gracious, no. It's Paper Eaters Anonymous from

beyond the Milky Way.

SIDDELL: I prefer Snickers myself.

LANGFORD: Snickers, snickers. Every time I want to tell my story, there are always Snickers.

NARRATOR: Whether he means to refer to the candy bar or not, nobody knows but Langford. If you're curious, you must ask him. He may not tell you, but then again he may not.

CALIDA: Yes, but we still haven't settled whether we're sitting up or down.

SIDDELL: English is a funny language.

NARDA: I always thought it was Germanic.

CALIDA: Germanic. Oh, my God! I brush my teeth, and wash my hands, and pour Lysol over my head. And still these horrible Germanic...things keep coming out of my mouth.

NARDA: There, there, it's all right. Just listen to the story.

CALIDA: I can't believe hearing a story will rid my mouth of germanics.

LANGFORD: Neither can I, but I want to tell it. Now once and for all, let's sit down.

NARRATOR: They sit or walk or jump or skip or stand. Maybe they even saunter.

LANGFORD: All comfy?

SIDDELL: Rather philosophical question, eh what?

CALIDA: A watt? You mean like in wiring and switches and...

NARDA: Switches? Reminds me of my cousin Ruthie Bobby. Used to be with the old Atlantic City Braves. She was a switch hitter.

SIDDELL: She could bat right-handed or left-handed?

NARDA: Bat? Whatever do you mean?

NARRATOR: Langford, tapping his foot.

LANGFORD: Your cousin? You said your cousin was a switch hitter.

NARDA: No, no, no, you misunderstand. She made cakes. Vanilla cakes, chocolate cakes.

SIDDELL: For the Atlantic City Braves?

NARDA: Heavens, no. What gave you an idea like that? She was a pinch hitter. When the coach thought the players were getting sloppy at the plate, he called in Ruthie Bobby.

LANGFORD: To pinch hit.

NARDA: To pinch them. To switch them. To feed them cake. Fed it to them right there on home plate.

LANGFORD: On home plate!

CALIDA: Obviously, the poor girl tortured these people for pay, and then brought plates from home to feed them.

SIDDELL: Any fool can see that.

LANGFORD: Can you, Siddell?

SIDDELL: Of course not. I'm not a fool. I was just citing sources which, when examined, will prove –

CALIDA: Yes, isn't it wonderful that we can sight things. Right now, I sight the three of you and even parts of myself. My hands, my arms, my feet. Well, not really my feet since they're covered by shoes and socks.

LANGFORD: Ankles too!

NARDA: Of course, two ankles. Do you have to be so obvious?

LANGFORD: Oblivious. I have to remain oblivious, or I'll get so angry I can't tell my story.

NARRATOR: Calida, speaking with a genuinely regretful tone...

CALIDA: Oh, I am so sorry. You were going to tell us a story.

SIDDELL: I love stories. My mother used to read stories to me every night before she tucked me into my little crib with the decals of bunnies and chickies. I so looked forward to the day that I could tell stories myself.

NARRATOR: Langford speaks through clenched teeth, each word separate and distinct.

LANGFORD: But right now I am the one who is telling the story.

NARDA: Oh, fiddle faddle, I must not have been listening. I didn't hear any story.

NARRATOR: Langford rolls his eyes.

LANGFORD: It's because I haven't started it yet.

SIDDELL: But you said –

NARRATOR: Langford holds up a warning finger, then waits a couple of beats before beginning.

LANGFORD: Here it is. Are we ready?

NARRATOR: All, including Langford, nod once very slowly in

unison, and then once again.

LANGFORD: And no one will interrupt.

ALL: No! Yes!

NARRATOR: They all pause.

ALL: Yes! No!

NARRATOR: Langford really hams it up in the following speech.

LANGFORD: Outside my window is a garden where dead leaves live and hopping birds make sounds like elephants. It's a magical place where vines stretch across the roof of a tumble-down garage and limbs of a magnolia tree frame vines of bougainvillaea.

NARRATOR: Langford glances from one to the other, pausing for a beat to stare at each face. He is pleased to see that all are enraptured by his tale.

LANGFORD: Sometimes I go there when no one else is around, and the most wondrous things occur. Last Tuesday morning, the third of July, along the fence bordering the lawn, separating it from jungles of twisted limbs and dark, frightening shadows of night-bumping things grew rows of flags – American flags just beginning to bud.

CALIDA: How wonderful. How very, very wonderful. Do you want to know why? The same thing happens to me when I look out my window.

SIDDELL: And mine.

NARDA: Mine, too, you know. I'm so glad for the corroboration!

CALIDA: Corroboration?

NARRATOR: The others stare at her and frown. They hiss simultaneously.

THE OTHERS: Shhhh! Shhhh! Shhhhhhhhh!

CALIDA: Oh, never mind, you always have to spoil everything.

LANGFORD: Where was I? Oh, yes, the flags. Behind them – the flags, I mean – sprouted a row of tiny drums, stems like little green drumsticks stretching above them. Suddenly –

SIDDELL: What!

CALIDA: Do go on, please.

NARDA: Reminds me of a movie I saw once. A very old movie. I

213

believe it was called *Gone With the Wind.*

SIDDELL: No, it was only a breeze. Just wait and see.

NARDA: Perhaps you're right.

NARRATOR: Langford, furious.

LANGFORD: May I continue?

CALIDA: Of course, you poor dear.

NARRATOR: Langford laughs.

LANGFORD: I wasn't angry. I was only kidding. Wasn't I kidding, Siddell?

CALIDA: If only Jonathan Piddling Paddling Puddling – whatever – were here, he'd have seen that you continued with this.

LANGFORD: I'm trying.

NARDA: Aw, poor Langie.

LANGFORD: Langie? No one has called me Langie since old Mrs. Smyth.

CALIDA: Jon's grandmother.

NARDA: No, you nit. Langford is referring to his third cousin, seven times removed. Am I not right, Langie?

LANGFORD: At this point, I simply know that no one has called me Langie before this very day.

SIDDELL: But you said –

LANGFORD: I was wrong. I made a mistake, OK?

CALIDA: If it's a mistake, how can it be OK?

LANGFORD: It was a rhetorical question, nothing more. Now here's where the story picks up: In a gentle breeze...

NARRATOR: Siddell nudges Narda and mouths the words...

SIDDELL: I told you so.

NARRATOR: Langford gives them a dirty look before continuing.

LANGFORD: ...the wind came up and the stems beat against the drumheads with a mighty rat-a-tat-tat. I told my mom, but she wouldn't believe me.

NARDA: My mom wouldn't believe me either when I told her.

SIDDELL: Nor mine.

CALIDA: When I told my mom, she said she'd slap me silly if I didn't shut up. She didn't mean it. She's always saying things like that.

NARDA: Calida, please. I want to see how closely Langford's story matches my very own.

LANGFORD: "You're making it up, Tom," Mom said. I don't know why she called me Tom. She knows my name is Langford.

NARDA: My mom did the very same thing. Maybe it had something to do with the scent of the flags, the rat-a-tat-tat of the drums. A hidden message that only adults can recognize.

SIDDELL: I am nearly an adult, and I didn't recognize it.

CALIDA: Perhaps you have to be married to learn of these things.

SIDDELL: I suppose that's as good an explanation as any that's not as good.

LANGFORD: "Come and see," I told Mom. "Don't be silly," she said. Then she stuck her nose deep inside the book she was reading...or writing perhaps. "Herbs and Spices of the Continental Shelf as Discovered by Amerigo Vespucci."

NARRATOR: Narda, with a sense of awe.

NARDA: Now isn't that something? My mother was reading...or writing the very same book.

SIDDELL: Mine, too.

CALIDA: Not mine. She was reading...or writing "Spices and Herbs of the Continental Shelf as Discovered by Vasco de Gama."

SIDDELL: What an aberration. I truly am shocked.

NARDA: Shocked! I warned you the wiring was faulty in this room.

LANGFORD: Please!

NARRATOR: He goes back to the story.

LANGFORD: I was watching the flags unfurl and the drums beat when my best friend Bob showed up.

CALIDA: My friend Robert showed up.

NARDA: My friend Rob.

SIDDELL: My friend Ruthie Bobby.

LANGFORD: That's only to be expected. At any rate, I told Bob, "Of course, she's a witch. Every woman who lives in this town is a witch. And every man too, though some prefer to call themselves warlocks or hags or the three weird sisters. I'll be one, too," I told him, "and so will you."

NARDA: Why must everyone interfere that way?

SIDDELL: I think it's Jon's fault for hating his name so much.

CALIDA: You know, I never thought of that.

LANGFORD: I became very angry at Bob. I mean, just try to convince the rest of the world to believe in American moms and apple pie. So you know what he did? Of course, you don't, so that's why I'm going to tell you.

CALIDA: What a wonderful story.

SIDDELL: It nearly made me forget how hungry I am till you mentioned my mom's apple pie.

LANGFORD: I couldn't help it.

SIDDELL: Even so, what a fantastic way to spend our summer vacation.

CALIDA: Good-bye, Jon.

LANGFORD: How did you know?!

SIDDELL: We all knew.

NARRATOR: The others nod in confirmation.

SIDDELL: The mask is not enough.

NARRATOR: Langford...or Jon, if you prefer...is not wearing a mask. Narda crosses to him and gently touches his cheek.

NARDA: Be sure to get a good night's rest now, dear.

LANGFORD: That is *exactly* what I shall do. Then we'll see what happens.

NARRATOR: He frowns, shakes his head and continues to mutter to himself as he exits Stage Right or Left. He has a difficult time making up his mind.

NARDA: Now who would ever have imagined that?

SIDDELL: I really must be going. Shall I see you again?

CALIDA: I think it best that you don't.

SIDDELL: I guess that's it then.

NARRATOR: He shrugs and hurries off-stage.

NARDA: Ah, alone at last.

CALIDA: No, you're not. You're with me.

NARDA: So I can better guard against your revealing the secrets you learned today.

CALIDA: Good-bye then.

NARRATOR: She turns from Narda and hurries off-stage. Narda, to the audience.

NARDA: And so there you have it. On to the next exhibition.

NARRATOR: She bows to each chair or stool or settee or rock in turn and skips laughingly off-stage. Narrator pauses and then says, "There is a brilliant fireworks display on-stage. Unfortunately, the audience cannot see it because by now the curtain has fallen, also muffling the sound. Yet if they listen carefully, the audience may hear, way off in the distance, the mighty rat-a-tat-tat of tiny organic drums." The curtain closes as I say, "The curtain closes." The end.

(The curtain closes — or not.)

•

Production Notes and Considerations

As you work with "The Smyth's Tale," figure out where and how all the elements of comedy are used and how you might point these up or make them apparent to an audience.

The style of acting should be realistic, and the characters should not react with surprise or disbelief at anything that is said, except where indicated in the directions given by the Narrator. And even this "disbelief" is surprising in that the entire situation already is completely unbelievable or bizarre.

The Narrator can read the note aloud or not.

As most of the other plays in the book, "The Smyth's Tale" requires a simple set consisting only of some sort of seats for the actors. For the Narrator this can be a stool or chair, and for the other characters, it can be chairs, stools, papier-mâché rocks strong enough to support their weights, etc.

We Are, You Are, They Are

"We Are, You Are, They Are" uses many elements from Absurdist drama, but it is not pure Theatre of the Absurd. Rather, it is a satire of the educational system and many of its parts. The play satirizes pseudo-intellectualism, both on the parts of the teacher and the students. The latter is seen first in Dotty's attitudes and actions and later in Sally's change from being the "homecoming-queen" type to the supposed intellectual.

In showing the change the two girls undergo, the play pokes fun at the idea that students and teachers often fall into the pattern or stereotype that is predicted for them. This is further emphasized in the character of Bob, who is white, a good athlete, of a "certain religion," and who someday will be twenty-one. Here, of course, the situation is reversed from the usual in that what some bigots find desirable, such as being white, is now looked down upon.

"We Are, You Are, They Are" also pokes fun at the sort of education we receive in high school. Often it's vague and inexact. This is shown not only in June's talking about the Civil War as if it has just broken out, but is further emphasized when she inserts the non sequitur about Henry Ford. This is poking fun at learning isolated facts by rote, facts that have little meaning or application to our lives. Even June's reference to her "dripping nose" pokes fun at the gullibility of those who always believe what they are told.

Throughout the piece are Shakespearean lines which most often dribble away into nonsense, and occasionally, there is mention of a philosophy or historical fact. All are isolated, which is meant to reinforce the idea that much of education is memorizing facts, which means little to a student.

The teacher's speech about his background and philosophy of education also is presumptuous (as is his title of Professor Doctor Teacher) in that it means nothing since he wavers between student and teacher rights, trying to see which the students will accept as more important.

Another target for satire is emphasizing the unimportant, which, unfortunately, does occur at all levels of education. This is shown in the Authoritative Voice which comes over the loud speaker and seems to command utter fear.

In recent years, schools have come under attack for teaching distorted history. This includes such things as ignoring minority contributions to society, in perpetrating certain myths such as the George Washington cherry tree story, and in slanting the writing toward a particular viewpoint. This sort of thing is satirized in June's announcement and the reaction to it.

The play contains a lot of nonsensical dialog. Yet it has different purposes than does the nonsense dialog in "The Smyth's Tale." In each instance in "We Are, You Are, They Are," the nonsense language is meant to poke fun at something to do with education or with society in general. Following the same theme, there are lines that seem to make sense but don't. An example is the position to which Dotty has been appointed and which seems to inspire awe in all the other students and in the teacher.

The satire is gentle and not meant to hurt, though it is meant to point out a lot of deficiencies with the idea of their being changed.

CAST: JIM, 15-17; DOTTY, 14; BILL, 17-18; SALLY, 16-18; PROFESSOR TEACHER DOCTOR, 50s; JUNE, 15-17; authoritative OFF-STAGE VOICE, any age.

SETTING: The action occurs in a classroom of one of the largest secondary education institutions in the Western Hemisphere. There is a teacher's desk Stage Right, in front of which are two rows of six student desks, three desks to a row. There is a doorway Up Right Center.

AT RISE: As the play opens, JIM is standing Center Stage, facing the audience. He is a typical high school student in typical high school dress. DOTTY is seated at one of the front row desks nearest the audience. Her appearance suggests that she is an intellectual, and that she cares little or nothing about her looks.

JIM: *(To the audience)* **I go to this secondary education institution, one of the largest and most renowned secondary education institutions in the Western Hemisphere.**

DOTTY: *(To no one in particular)* **I have found that according to Sir Walter Raleigh's *History of the World*, sodium chloride and a Greek periakto[35,] when mixed together with a diminished seventh chord, result in a stream-of-consciousness technique similar to that employed by the late William Faulkner in his sonnets of Admiral Byrd at the Equator. Therefore, the tendency is to I sing, you sing, he, she, it sings. We sing, you sing, they shall have done been singed.**

JIM: *(Still addressing the audience)* **Dotty is studious. She's only four-teen. Yet next month she will assume the position of intellectual overseer at Harvard Girls' School where she will teach kindergarten children how to compose atonal operas and how to say thank you and please in Cantonese, Mandarin and orange juice.**

DOTTY: *(To the audience)* **The professor teacher doctor will be here shortly. That is to say, very soon he will arrive in this room in a building on the campus of one of the largest secondary**

[35]pronounced perry-ack´-toi

education complexes in the Western Hemisphere of the globe we call a planet and which according to most theories is referred to as Earth, at least in the English language. So far as anyone has ever been able to determine, in some other language, it might be called Wrigley's Spearmint Chewing Gum.

JIM: *(Turning toward DOTTY)* **How astute.**

DOTTY: *(To JIM)* **What else would you expect?**

JIM: **Yes, I would.**

DOTTY: **I've prepared my assignment so it will exist in a state of ideal perfection. Maybe New Hampshire or Spain. Whichever, I shall receive my A-plus for the day.**

JIM: *(Again to the audience)* **This class is small. There are just two other members of this class, which is small. This is because the professor teacher doctor tells far too much for many students to absorb. If the class were larger, there simply would be too much knowledge dispersed, too many notebooks to fill. And since this secondary education institution is ecologically aware, specifically in relation to trees and raspberry bushes, it's important that we limit class size.** *(He sits beside DOTTY at a desk on which are lying his textbook and notebook. BILL enters. He is the clean-cut, all-American-boy type. He carries a loose-leaf folder and several books.)*

BILL: *(Taking a few steps into the classroom)* **Good afternoon, fellow students. I'm a clean-cut, all-American-boy. I've come to class because, as you know, I'm from one of the most visible minority groups in the United States. I am of a certain religion, white, and someday will be twenty-one. I run the hundred-yard dash in 7.9 seconds. Or is it in 9.7? I suppose it doesn't matter. What *does* matter, however, is that I impress you, my fellow classmates, and the good professor teacher doctor that my ethnic, religious and national backgrounds are just as good as yours. That is the major reason I work so hard at being punctual, i.e., on time for each, all, and every single one of my classes at least twice every grading period.** *(He sits at one of the desks behind and downstage of JIM and DOTTY.)*

JIM: *(To BILL)* **Even though you belong to a minority, I'm willing to**

tolerate you. I'm even going to go so far as to wish you a good afternoon. Thus, I say, "Good afternoon, Bill."

BILL: Thank you, Massa James. I sure do appreciate it. You don't know how much that means to me. Why practically nothing is what it means to me, don't you see?

DOTTY: I shall have sung; you will have sung; he, she, it will have sung. We shall have sung; you will have sung; they shall have had been singed.

JIM: If only I had your intellectual capacity and your way with words.

DOTTY: Surely, you jest. No one – not even that vos Savant woman who writes smart-alecky answers in *Parade* magazine in the Sunday newspaper – can approach my intellectual capacity. But I am curious. What would you do if you had as many brains as I? After all, I already have been hired as the intellectual overseer as well as the overseer of intellect at Harvard Girls' School, the only position of any worth still open anywhere over the entire length and breadth of the world.

JIM: I haven't given it all that much thought.

DOTTY: Of course, you haven't. No one could. *(SALLY enters carrying two or three books and a notebook. Her appearance should convey the idea that she is dumb but beautiful.)*

SALLY: Good afternoon, Jim, Bill, and Dotty.

BILL, JIM, DOTTY: *(Simultaneously)* Good afternoon, Sally.

SALLY: I hope the professor teacher doctor isn't late. I don't want him to waste my precious time and hold the class over. You see, Mummy and Daddy bought me lots of nice clothes and lots of makeup and perfume and let me have my hair done every two days so that I will look nice when I attend this secondary education institution, one of the largest in the Western Hemisphere. Because they spend lots of money enhancing my beauty, though they certainly can afford it, I wish to make the best of my time spent here. I have few brains and am talented in few areas, but I do have my beauty and so am sure to be elected prom queen every year from now on, even after I receive my diploma.

BILL: I think you are the most beauti –

DOTTY: *(Interrupting)* **Brains count, nothing else.**

SALLY: Well, pardon me. *(She sits beside BILL.)*

DOTTY: "Thou bleeding piece of earth that I am meek and gentle with these butchers" who always charge outrageous prices even for the simplest cuts. *(The PROFESSOR TEACHER enters and pauses just inside the doorway. He wears an academic gown and mortarboard and carries a briefcase.)*

PROFESSOR TEACHER: *(Effusively)* **Children, children, children.** *(There is a pause while he crosses to the front of his desk and sets down his briefcase.)* **Please, this instant, take your seats.** *(The students exchange puzzled looks because they already are seated. They ad-lib such reactions as "He's kidding, right?" "We are sitting down, dummy!" and "Are you gaga?")* **I am as much in favor of intellectual discussion as anyone on the campus of this, one of the largest secondary education complexes in the Western Hemisphere. However, I also favor the niceties. That is to say we must teach ourselves – or if we are too dumb ourselves, then to have others teach us – to respect the opinions of everyone else and allow each to voice an opinion regardless of his intellectual thinking.**

SALLY: His intellectual thinking! Do I look like a male to you?

JIM: *(Snickering)* With that bod? No way, not a chance, unh-unh.

SALLY: How dare you speak to me –

PROFESSOR TEACHER: Students, please. *(Pause)* Please. And yes, you do look rather like a male. Does not a male have legs? Does not a male have arms? Does not a male have a head and eyes and a nose and a mouth? Jab us with a pin. Do we not bleed? Give us a head cold, do we not sneeze? Need I go on?

SALLY: Yes, please do.

PROFESSOR TEACHER: Children! Do mind your manners.

DOTTY: I apologize. *(Acknowledging the others)* He, she and he apologize. We are apologizing. We have done been apologized.

PROFESSOR TEACHER: Then I assume we are ready to begin today's lesson. *(DOTTY raises her hand, and the PROFESSOR TEACHER acknowledges her.)*

224

DOTTY: I have worked quite diligently on this assignment. And so I insist upon being heard and receiving my A-plus for the day.

PROFESSOR TEACHER: My dear young lady, do you presume to tell me, your honored professor teacher doctor –

DOTTY: Of course, sir, I do not presume to tell you how to conduct classes! Yet I, with my superior intellect, demand to be heard.

PROFESSOR TEACHER: *(Standing in front of his desk)* Fine, but first I think I should like to tell you a little about myself so you know where I'm coming from.

JIM: *(Puzzled)* Tempe, Arizona, isn't it?

PROFESSOR TEACHER: That is not precisely nor even exactly nor even remotely close to what I meant.

BILL: *(Explaining to JIM)* It's an obsolete use of a colloquialism, i.e., a slang term, street talk, cool jive, man, like dating back to the 1970s or 1100s, much in the manner as "Cool, Dude" or "Twenty-nine Skidoo."

JIM: Twenty-three.

BILL: No! White and someday twenty-one.

JIM: Pardon me.

DOTTY: "Thou bleeding piece of earth."

PROFESSOR TEACHER: *(Completely losing his temper)* Enough, enough, enough.

SALLY: Well, I never –

BILL: Absolutely never? You've got to be kidding. I do it all the time.

PROFESSOR TEACHER: *(Giving BILL a scorching look)* Young man!

BILL: Don't get huffy.

DOTTY: Huffy and puffy and blow the house down.

JIM: But what if someone lives there, an uncle or a cow?

BILL: I think violence is abhorrent. Despicable. Hateful. Know what I mean?

SALLY: No...what?

PROFESSOR TEACHER: As *I* was saying...I've always worked hard. My father was a fortuneteller with the Galactic Council of Elder Youngers, and my mother Secretary of State. I don't remember what state this was since we resided with the Galactic Council off the coast of Oahu or sometimes in

Washington, D.C., behind the Lincoln Monument in a little shelter we built there. So I struggled for every achievement. And due to my hard work and a little bribery and a lot of cheating here and there – mostly there – I was graduated *magna cum laude* from George Washington Junior High School. I spent the following year as a Fulbright Lecturer in Greece, studying the hieroglyphics of the nineteenth-century Indo-Chinese. And thusly, in my master's thesis in tenth grade at Elton John High School, I proposed the use of corrugated cardboard in the construction of interstellar rockets, which brought me renown and widespread acclaim. Subsequently, for my doctoral dissertation, I chose to write on a hitherto unheard of concept. The title...

DOTTY: *(So excited she can hardly wait to hear it.)* Tell me, tell me.

PROFESSOR TEACHER: The title? *(Pausing for effect)* *The Translation into Nineteenth-Century Indo-Chinese Hieroglyphics, as Practiced in the Country of Greece, the Immortal Nursery Rhyme, "Little Bo Peep."* Thus, I received my high school diploma.

JIM: *(Rising and applauding)* Bravo, bravo, Professor Teacher Doctor.

PROFESSOR TEACHER: As to my philosophy of education, I firmly believe the professor teacher doctor is always right, and his actions should never be questioned. He is to be acknowledged as the most superior of beings. By his very presence he demands respect. Yet, there should be complete freedom for the students. Because after all, they have just as many rights as he has. Thus they should be respected too, don't you think? Of course, you think, and therefore you are. What you are is...not up to me to say – but I do respect it. Just so you don't use spit wads and throw paper airplanes in this classroom at one of the largest secondary education institutions in the Western Hemisphere. *(He bows.)*

SALLY: Never have I heard a more stirring testimony of one's beliefs. It inspires me to greater heights of learning.

DOTTY: I shall emulate you always.

PROFESSOR TEACHER: I now open the floor to questions.

BILL: Well...uh, as you know –

PROFESSOR TEACHER: Yes, young man? Don't be afraid. You're safe in this haven of learning.

BILL: Maybe so. But as you know, I'm of a certain religion, white and someday will be twenty-one, and my batting average is 801.3333345.

PROFESSOR TEACHER: *(Extremely impatient)* Get to the point.

BILL: Something bothers me, puzzles me, drives me... *(Matter of fact)* pretty much nearly out of my head with deranged, mad and crazy insanity. *(A beat)* Psychosomatically speaking, of course. And nowhere in these ivied halls of learning have I heard it discussed. I even took nonorganic biology to try to discover the answer.

PROFESSOR TEACHER: I find that difficult to accept. Intellectual freedom is the very trademark of this institution where everything in all of existence, my existence at least, has been discussed.

BILL: No, sir, Monsieur Professor Teacher Doctor. It's something hidden. Something that's never, I'm sure, been brought forth for examination in this secondary education institution, one of the largest in the Western Hemisphere.

SALLY: My goodness, what could it be?

DOTTY: Will you tell us?

JIM: *(Eagerly)* Yes, please.

PROFESSOR TEACHER: Any subject can be discussed and debated and discoursed upon here. *(A beat)* Well, naturally, as you certainly must know, I mean any subject that is within the realms of good taste.

BILL: All right then. Babies.

DOTTY: Oh!

SALLY: Oh!

JIM: Oh!

BILL: I want to know where they come from.

PROFESSOR TEACHER: A worthwhile topic, one to tax your intellectual boundaries. Something I would expect to hear discussed only by students with the highest of intelligence.

DOTTY: *(Unsure of herself)* **Professor Teacher Doctor, if I may –**

PROFESSOR TEACHER: **Yes, Dotty. Don't be afraid.**

DOTTY: **Are you sure?**

SALLY: *(Encouragingly)* **Oh, we are, aren't we, classmates, and Professor Teacher Doctor?**

JIM: *(Simultaneously with PROFESSOR)* **Yes.**

PROFESSOR TEACHER: *(Simultaneously with JIM)* **Certainly.**

DOTTY: *(Chanting)* **Birds and bees, chickens and eggs, flowers, heart-shaped boxes of candy! Shortly thereafter, a baby starts to grow.**

PROFESSOR TEACHER: *(Applauding)* **Well done, child, well done. I couldn't have explained it better myself. Now if there's nothing else.**

DOTTY: **But there is.**

PROFESSOR TEACHER: **Yes?**

DOTTY: **It's something that has occupied my musings, my thoughts, my contemplations for many and many a day. Therefore on the basis of broad experimentation, I have formulated a theory.**

JIM: **Experimentation? What sort of experimentation?**

DOTTY: **All I can tell you is that it's astounding. It truly is astounding.**

PROFESSOR TEACHER: **Yes, child, get on with it.**

DOTTY: *(Clearing her throat importantly)* **Well.** *(She takes a deep breath and plunges right in.)* **I have found through a subtle combination of colors that the mixture of blue and yellow by no means results in red.**

PROFESSOR TEACHER: **Amazing! Imagine, for one so young.**

BILL: **Of course, you know, Herr Professor Teacher Doctor, that Dotty next month is assuming the position of intellectual overseer at Harvard Girls' School.**

PROFESSOR TEACHER: **The thought did escape my memory. However, that accounts for the fact that her observation and experimentation are so far advanced for one of her chronological age.**

DOTTY: *(Demurely)* **Thank you, Professor Teacher Doctor.**

SALLY: *(Eagerly)* **I know something, too.**

PROFESSOR TEACHER: What is it, my dear?

SALLY: Blue and yellow mixed together make green.

JIM: Oh, Sally, act your age.

PROFESSOR TEACHER: *(Chuckling)* Given the circumstances, it is a rather humorous remark, is it not?

BILL: *(To SALLY)* Why don't you use your brain! You never do, you know.

SALLY: *(Hurt)* Well, it does, doesn't it?

PROFESSOR TEACHER: *(Condescendingly)* Of course, but any child beyond the age of six months in any day-care school throughout the Canadian Provinces and the United States knows that much. Now if you had the same sort of inquisitive intellect as does the other female member of this class – Humph! But you with your preschool education should not presume to tell the rest of us, who have such obviously superior thinking mechanisms, a simple truth such as that. You completely waste your time and ours.

SALLY: *(Almost crying)* Red and yellow make orange.

PROFESSOR TEACHER: Tut, tut, my child.

BILL: Oh, brother.

JIM: *(Angrily)* I'm not your brother. Toleration goes only so far and not a smidgen further.

DOTTY: There, there, Sally. It's all right.

SALLY: Red and white make pink. *(The others show an actual physical aversion to SALLY by leaning as far away from her as they can.)* Blue and red make magenta. *(She begins to cry.)* Black and white make grey. Blue and black make blue-black, red and yellow and gold and brown make red-yellow-gold-brown. And everything mixed with everything else makes a big black blob.

PROFESSOR TEACHER: Young lady, I suggest you go to the powder room and powder your nose. You may use my puff if you wish. *(He takes out a large-sized body puff from somewhere inside his academic gown and holds it out to her. SALLY grabs the powder puff and rushes from the room. The repetition at the end of the speech should not vary either in tone or delivery from one instance to the next.)* Well, class, you have witnessed one of the saddest spectacles possible – the deterioration of a human intellect, human intellect, human intellect, human intellect, human –

DOTTY: Shut up! This minute!

PROFESSOR TEACHER: ...intellect, er, uh, yes. Sorry.

JIM: It's spreading like a disease. Earlier today, my neighbor told me he'd observed the dripping of rain down his window.

PROFESSOR TEACHER: Yes?

JIM: It reminded him, he said, of the elements comprising water – two hydrogen atoms ganging up on just one oxygen atom. Can you imagine? Overwhelm the poor little thing, they do.

PROFESSOR TEACHER: Well, yes, it certainly is appalling, but there appears to be no way of changing the situation, no matter how hard we try. *(He sits on the front of his desk.)* If you'll forgive an old man a nostalgic reminiscence. *(Pause)*

STUDENTS: *(Simultaneously)* Yes, Professor Teacher Doctor.

PROFESSOR TEACHER: At my first secondary education institution, the Benjamin Franklin Institute of Stoves, Kite Flying, and International Diplomacy, a group of students became so interested in their course work in a particular area of study that they all brought sack lunches to have an extra hour to meet with their instructor.

DOTTY: Merciful heavens! What did the board of education do?

PROFESSOR TEACHER: Do? You're joking, of course. What could they do? Expel the students outright? Give them detention? Fire the troublemaker? Certainly not. There would have been rioting. The students would have protested. The faculty, such as it was, would have joined with the students.

BILL: If it's not being too presumptuous of me to ask, who did what to change this terrible situation, and how did he, she, it, or they accomplish it?

PROFESSOR TEACHER: Well, a solution finally was agreed upon. And it all came about because of an insignificant little secretary in the office of the principle principal, rather than in the office of one of the more minor principals. It was her idea that when the grade reports were mailed, all the offending students were to receive straight "A"s, as it were – uh, was – uh, were.

DOTTY: Incredible. I must keep that in mind when I assume my new position.

JIM: And who would have thought...An insignificant secretary, you say?

PROFESSOR TEACHER: Yes, yes. And the outcome?

BILL: Please, Professor Teacher Doctor, don't keep us in suspense.

PROFESSOR TEACHER: They immediately made her the personal assistant to the superintendent of schools and let her have charge of press and public relations for the entire secondary education institution. Of course, that accounted for seventy-two students, counting fifty-three part-timers who had to take care of aged brothers and sisters and could attend only a certain portion of the day, usually only two hours and twenty-three minutes or thereabouts. It was an unusually large school, you see, much as this one wherein we sit, talk, dance, sing, run, play hide and seek, ride our tricycles –

BILL: And there was no more trouble?

PROFESSOR TEACHER: Quite so.

DOTTY: I sew, you sew; he, she and it, being very good dress designers whose work is always in demand, do a very great amount of sewing.

PROFESSOR TEACHER: Enough! Back to the lesson at hand.

JIM: Which is...

DOTTY: Which is...

PROFESSOR TEACHER: Which is, why the sky is blue.

DOTTY: Señor Professor Teacher Doctor, if I may be permitted to answer that question?

PROFESSOR TEACHER: Yes, Dotty. *(SALLY sticks her head through the entrance and listens unobserved. In her hand is the powder puff.)*

DOTTY: After long and careful consideration of why the sky is blue, I asked my father: "Daddy, what makes the sky blue?" A commercial pilot, used to the celestial heights and their near environs, he said: "Well, little tootsie." He always called me his little tootsie, you see. "Well, little tootsie," he said, "the sky is blue, and the trees are green because it would look weird as

231

perdition to have them the other way around."

PROFESSOR TEACHER: Brilliant, brilliant! *(SALLY now enters the classroom. There has been a transformation in her appearance. Her hair is pulled back severely, and she wears a drab sweater and thick glasses.)*

SALLY: Pseudo-intellectualism! That's what it is. And it's absolutely disgusting. *(The PROFESSOR TEACHER cowers at the onslaught of her words.)* **And neither do you frighten me with your red and green and blue and gold.** *(The PROFESSOR TEACHER slinks to one of the student desks and sits while SALLY crosses to front of teacher's desk. She is in absolute command of the situation.)*

I'll tell you what's right. You don't even know if you're using the additive or reflective theory in your discussion of color. Of course, you know the difference. Any child beyond the age of six months in any day-care center throughout the Canadian Provinces or the United States could write a discourse on the matter. And what makes the sky blue? Well, I'll tell you. The air gets so cold up so high in the atmosphere, stratosphere, ionosphere that just like a human being who is exposed to the elements of frigid sleet, snow, ice and shoveling out driveways in winter, it turns blue from a lack of warmth. Thus, all your assumptions, your hypothesizing, your theorizing, your conjecturing, your babbling nonsense about pilots of airplanes flying overhead? Really now, such silliness means not a whit! Absolutely nothing.

PROFESSOR TEACHER: *(Sinking to his knees in front of the desk in which he's been sitting)* **The intellectual guru has arrived. Let us all proclaim the news and bow to her vast and superior grasp of the knowledge of the ages.**

SALLY: Yes, my knowledge. As you know, we cannot all possess mere physical beauty. It is the beauty of the soul, the beauty of the psyche that count. The pure intellect bared unafraid before the Universal Studio Tour and Twenty-First Century Fox. So, students, show me what you have learned.

(The following three speeches are delivered in a frenzied manner.)

BILL: William Tell knew Tonto well, but William Penn ran around in the woods with Sylvia.

JIM: Biologically speaking, it takes a bone, a brain, and a hank of hair to create a human offspring.

DOTTY: I think, you think, he, she, it thinks. We think, you think, they think. At least I think they do.

PROFESSOR TEACHER: The square root of 196 is exactly two times eight, minus two.

SALLY: Yes, fellow classmates, you are dealing with absolutes and so are entirely correct, at least as much as one can be in such an overtly abstract manner.

PROFESSOR TEACHER: Fill me, fill me, with your knowledge.

SALLY: Very well.

PROFESSOR TEACHER: A.

JIM: B.

DOTTY: C.

BILL: D.

PROFESSOR TEACHER: *(Desperately hoping for praise)* **And sometimes even E.**

SALLY: Excellent, children, excellent. Keep going.

DOTTY: One.

JIM: Two.

BILL: Three.

PROFESSOR TEACHER: Four.

DOTTY: Five.

JIM: Six.

BILL: Seven.

DOTTY: Ate. You ate, he, she, it ated. We eaten; you aten; they eated.

SALLY: You're coming along. Be sure to keep up the good work. *(To the PROFESSOR TEACHER, in a haughty manner)* **I shall now resume my seat. I suggest you go on with the class.**

PROFESSOR TEACHER: Of course, oh, learned one. Of course.

BILL: I came to this secondary education institution to get an education. But primarily I wanted to prove to the world that despite my oppression, I could succeed. Now I find I haven't enough time to get to my next class.

233

JIM: Ah, you with your sheltered background. What do you know?

DOTTY: I know, you know, he, she, it knows. We knows; you knows; they sometimes doesn't know, though they always wish to.

SALLY: Remember to use your brain, Dotty, your brain.

JIM: I think, therefore, that we should take under advisement the reason for the chicken's crossing the road.

BILL: It's because someone at this secondary education complex has decreed that before students can receive diplomas, they all have to take two years of a foreign language, three years of English, three years of history, two years of math, four years of horseshoe pitching, six years of mud cakes, and on and on and on.

DOTTY: *(Simply)* The well-rounded student is the leader of the future.

PROFESSOR TEACHER: Right. Now, students, how many of you have read today's assignment? *(DOTTY hesitantly raises her hand.)*

SALLY: I wrote the book. I didn't powder my nose. While I stood out in the hall, I wrote the book, revised it and brought out a second edition. So here, pal, take back your professorial-teacher powder puff. *(She throws it at him. It hits him in the chest, covering him in powder.)* I have no need to puff myself up. I am much more than adequate just as I am, though my eyes do get puffy from all this reading. *(Melodramatic)* Yet I don't mind. It's worth it to have an IQ of seventy hundred and one points.

PROFESSOR TEACHER: For shame, for shame, silly Sally with your shallow ways. Yet, in the overall course of the universal rotations of the earth and the planets from here to infinity, I have only praise for James and William. Their minds are fresh. They have not been indoctrinated by the slanted writing of this text. *(JUNE enters. She is a typical high school student. She glances shyly around the room and beckons for silence.)*

JUNE: *(Apologetically)* I came as quickly as I could. However, the tidings I bring are not at all happy ones.

PROFESSOR TEACHER: *(Concerned)* What is it, my child?

JUNE: War has been declared.

DOTTY, JIM, SALLY, BILL, PROFESSOR TEACHER: *(Simultaneously)* War?

JUNE: I told you it wasn't pretty. Yes, war. Civil war. War between the North and the South.

PROFESSOR TEACHER: When?

BILL: How?

JUNE: As to how, I don't know. As to when, it was exactly at *(Pause in which she looks puzzled and shrugs)* some period or other during the eighteen hundreds.

JIM: *(Bravely)* Damn the torpedoes! I've just begun to fight.

SALLY: Will you go, Jim?

DOTTY: Will you go, Bill?

JIM: When duty calls, we must go.

BILL: *(Spinning around as if holding an assault rifle)* Ac-ac-ac-ac-ac-ac-ac. Bang. Bang. *Booooom!*

JUNE: There's no need for that.

PROFESSOR TEACHER: *(The inspired patriot)* No need. Why, girl, I've been thinking of joining up myself. My mother always thought I looked best in grey to match my blue eyes. Or...blue to match my grey eyes? *(Shaking his head in puzzlement)* One or the other, even though my eyes are green.

JUNE: The war is over; the battle's won. Appomattox and all that. General Grant is victorious.

BILL: Hallelujah!

PROFESSOR TEACHER: Praises be! I didn't really fancy myself fighting on some distant battleground.

JIM: And what for?

DOTTY: Maybe a Gettysburg address?

SALLY: Or one in Pittsburgh or Harrisburg or Bergen County, New Jersey. But lots of people live there already.

PROFESSOR TEACHER: It's a hard decision to make, and why?

JIM: Yes, why – to protect society as we know it from the spread of...gunpowder and elephants stampeding through the gates of the farmyards somewhere on the other side of the walls of this secondary education complex and even perhaps in some other state like Oregon. We shall not go.

DOTTY: Psst, Jim!

JIM: Yes?

DOTTY: We are in Oregon.

JIM: Really?

DOTTY: Yes, at least there or at some other location.

JIM: I didn't know that.

JUNE: But the war is over now. Brother against brother. Man against man. Women against beef cattle. I mean who wants to be stuck in the kitchen all day making roast beef and potatoes. Long live the fruitarians.

PROFESSOR TEACHER: And now the end has come. *(In near panic)* Why wasn't I informed? Why wasn't I informed?

JUNE: I did my best.

PROFESSOR TEACHER: You're not to be blamed. To err is human, to forgive is to forget all about the whole summation of the subjects covered in this class.

SALLY: *(A sincere compliment)* Nobly said. Most nobly said.

JUNE: And now if you don't mind, Professor Teacher Doctor, I must spread my tidings elsewhere.

PROFESSOR TEACHER: I understand. *(The frustrated actor)* Let not the light burn out. Through sleet and hail and storm of night, always keep it burning bright.

JUNE: *(Melodramatic)* You bring a sob to my throat, a tear to my eye, a dripping to my nose.

DOTTY: Such sentimental garbage.

JUNE: For you, maybe. But not for me. Because I always keep this thought before me. *(She sweeps to the door.)* Henry Ford mass-produced cars. *(She exits.)*

PROFESSOR TEACHER: Indeed, students, that was sobering news. But life does go on. And so, as you must see, that is precisely why I demand fresh minds and irreproachable moral character. However, with all of you arriving late and my having to sit here and wait for you, I attempted to shorten what I taught you – though I don't see why I bothered. But anyhow it didn't work out. I find I've unwittingly kept you overtime.

(The following three speeches are to be delivered in a rapid-fire, angry manner.)

SALLY: *(Jumping to her feet)* You had no right.

236

DOTTY: How dare you so insult the future intellectual overseer of the Harvard Girls' School?

JIM: *(Rising and facing DOTTY)* I demand the right to protest.

BILL: Who cares? I don't care. They don't care. Does anyone care?

PROFESSOR TEACHER: Students, students, students. *(The PROFESSOR TEACHER runs to his desk, opens the upper right-hand drawer and pulls out a Halloween noisemaker. Then he jumps up on his desk. Twirling the noisemaker, he speaks in an extremely condescending manner.)* Students, beloved children, I must insist you take your seats. *(The STUDENTS all stare at the PROFESSOR TEACHER.)* Gently now, gently. *(He jumps off the desk and reaches into the bottom drawer.)* You see, I have something for you. *(He lays down the noisemaker, and one by one pulls out five sack lunches.)*

SALLY: No! *(The STUDENTS all resume their seats.)*

JIM: You couldn't.

BILL: You wouldn't.

DOTTY: It's inhumane.

PROFESSOR TEACHER: *(During the dialog, he passes out the lunches.)* Oh, but I would. I certainly would. Remember that insignificant little secretary I told you about in the principle principal's office.

SALLY: The one with the scrupulous principles?

PROFESSOR TEACHER: Exactly. *(Pause)* Well, she's my wife now.... And that troublemaking teacher? You see him before you. So I suggest you follow me, students. Do as I do, and do as I say. *(He sits behind his desk.)* First, we take out the sandwich. *(He pantomimes his words and the STUDENTS follow suit.)* Then we carefully unwrap the waxed paper. And very carefully we bring the sandwich to our mouths. And so we realize now that very soon we all shall be receiving no grade lower than an "A." *(The PROFESSOR TEACHER and the STUDENTS begin to eat their sandwiches.)*

OFF-STAGE VOICE: *(Booming out of the loudspeakers)* Before you leave the room, *(Sarcastically)* Herr Professor Teacher Doctor, Sir! And all you insignificant little worms who call yourselves

students.

SALLY, JIM, DOTTY: *(Simultaneously)* **Oh, no! This is even worse than the lunch.**

BILL: *(Puzzled)* **What is?**

SALLY, JIM, DOTTY: *(Simultaneously)* **The maintenance engineer!**

BILL: The what?

SALLY, JIM, DOTTY: *(Simultaneously)* **Janitor!** *(The STUDENTS and the PROFESSOR TEACHER all cower in the worst sort of terror, one or two even attempting to hide underneath or behind their desks.)*

OFF-STAGE VOICE: Be sure the blinds on all the windows are even. Be sure the seats are lined up exactly. Or the consequences will be dire. Be sure there is no paper on the floor, no muddy footprints, no smudges on your desktops. Be absolutely certain to line up two by two when you leave. Turn out the lights.... *(The OFF-STAGE VOICE and the lights simultaneously fade to nothing.)*

(Curtain)

Production Notes and Considerations

This play, as "The Smyth's Tale," probably will come across best to an audience if you use a realistic acting approach, allowing, however, for exaggeration of character traits, such as the professor's superiority.

An exception to the realistic style is June's scene. She should use an overly dramatic style because the idea of going from classroom to classroom is overly melodramatic and silly.

There need be no specific set. The only requirements are four student desks and a teacher's desk and chair.

Somewhere in the Appellations

"Somewhere in the Appellations" exists simply for fun. Although it has no slapstick elements, it is closer to low than to high comedy since it contains many puns, considered to be a "low" sort of humor.

This piece relies largely on the device of surprise since the reader or viewer knows from just after the play opens to the end that there will be a lot of word play related to the character's names. This is close to automatism or the running gag in that the same sort of humor is repeated throughout, although it differs slightly each time. Another device is exaggeration since it would be next to impossible in everyday life to find an entire group of people who have such punny names.

CAST: TOM, MACK, KAY, HOMER, GILDA, SYBIL. All the characters are
  14 to 16.

SETTING: The action occurs outside a school building on the first day
  of class.

AT RISE: MACK is leaning against the railing of the front steps when
  TOM approaches. Here and there are other groups of students.

MACK: How you doing?

TOM: Hi.

MACK: Do I know you?

TOM: Maybe. I don't think so.

MACK: I thought I knew everyone here. Small place like this.

TOM: I don't know you.

MACK: What's your name?

TOM: Tom.

MACK: Tom what?

TOM: Tom Katt.

MACK: Tomcat? Oh, I get it. *(Thinks he's kidding.)* **I suppose you have
  a brother named Bob?**

TOM: Do you know him?

MACK: Look, kid, are you trying to be a smart aleck or what?

TOM: No, that's my brother.

MACK: What? Who's your brother?

**TOM: Alec. My brother Alec. The smart one in the family. He's a
  rocket scientist. Physicist really.**

MACK: Oh, sure, and I'll bet you have a sister whose name is –

TOM: You know my sister?

MACK: What do you mean, do I know your sister?

**TOM: She works at the mall. Thought you might have met her. And
  you said –**

MACK: *(Not taking any gaff from anyone)* **Oh, yeah, what did I say?**

**TOM: You were talking about my sister. I just thought you might
  know her.**

MACK: Bet she works at the pet store.

TOM: As a matter of fact, she does.

MACK: Look, I don't know your sister. I don't know your smart-

aleck brother...

TOM: But...you said you knew my sister's name.

MACK: It was a joke, kid. OK? All I started to say –

TOM: *(Angry)* A joke?

MACK: *(As if explaining to a three-year-old)* Yeah, like something that's funny. Something that makes you laugh.

TOM: Are you saying my sister's funny?

MACK: *(Holding up his hands, palms out)* No offense. You're new here, right?

TOM: No, it's my cousin Brandon who's Nue.

MACK: What?!

TOM: That's his name. Brandon Nue. We call him Brand for short.

MACK: *(Hitting his forehead gently with the heel of his hand)* I don't believe this. *(Shakes his head.)* Let's start over. *(TOM shrugs.)* What I mean is that you're a new kid in town, OK?

TOM: And I just told you I'm not Nue. But my cousin is. He's Brand Nue. Do you know him?

MACK: Let's just pretend I haven't said anything. We never saw each other. We never talked.

TOM: *(As if MACK hadn't spoken)* I don't see how you could get us mixed up. He's short and kind of chubby –

MACK: I can't believe this. I mean, I see this new...er...this kid who doesn't look familiar, and I decide to strike up this conversation.

TOM: Kidd? No! You really are mixed up, Mack. My name isn't Kidd. That's my mom's maiden name. But how would you know that?

MACK: Yeah, well how'd you know my name's Mack?

TOM: *(Big sigh)* Look, Buddy, I didn't know your name was Mack. OK?

MACK: You expect me to believe that? Then how come you know my first name, as well.

TOM: Your first name?

MACK: Buddy. Buddy Mack. *(Exasperated)* Man, I hate being saddled with a name like that.

TOM: Tom Katt's not such a great name either.

MACK: Couldn't you use your middle name. I mean this is your first day. At a new school, right?

TOM: Well, yeah.

MACK: So why not really start fresh. Use your middle name or something. No one else knows your first name, right?

TOM: I suppose not.

MACK: Then why not be T. ...Samuel, or whatever. Your middle name.

TOM: Wouldn't work. My family has this tradition.

MACK: Tradition? What's wrong with tradition? Turkey and dressing for Thanksgiving, picnics on the Fourth of –

TOM: This tradition's a little different. In my family, one baby born in each generation is named for the first ancestor who came here from the old country. Mom's maternal great-great-grandfather. Something like that.

MACK: *(Encouraging)* Yeah?

TOM: It's just ...

Max: What?

TOM: Nothing...It's just that – well, if the name had stayed like it was, it would be OK. But dear old great-great-great-grandpa decided his name was too long. He was in a new country, so he'd take a new name.

MACK: He shortened his name, you mean?

TOM: Yep.

MACK: What was it to begin with?

TOM: Polenski.

MACK: Polenski? What's wrong with – Oh, I see. I... *(He begins to laugh.)* Man, oh, man.

TOM: Thanks a bunch, Buddy.

MACK: Sorry, I didn't mean to laugh.

TOM: *(Giving up)* It's OK. Who wouldn't laugh? Tom Katt. Pole Katt. Tom Pole Katt. Anyhow, what was this joke about my sister?

MACK: Something really dumb.

TOM: I need a good laugh.

MACK: I was going to say that her name's probably Kitty.

TOM: It is!

MACK: What! I don't believe this.

TOM: Well, it's really Katrina. But everyone always...

MACK and TOM: *(Simultaneously)* **Calls her Kitty Katt.**

TOM: You know what? Let's just get it over with. My dad's name is Leo. I have a younger sister named Tabitha.

MACK: Tabby, for short.

TOM: And my mom's name is Allison.

MACK: Allison? What's wrong with that?

TOM: Nothing, I guess. Except everyone...

MACK and TOM: *(Simultaneously)* **Calls her Allie Katt.**

TOM: Uh-huh.

MACK: So, would you like me to show you around? *(Starts to cross Stage Right.)*

TOM: Surely.

MACK: *(Stops dead in his tracks.)* What did you say?!

TOM: "Surely."

MACK: Oh, I thought you called me by my middle name.

TOM: What's your middle name?

MACK: Shirley.

TOM: Surely what?

MACK: No! Buddy Shirley Mack.

TOM: Shirley! *(Begins to snicker and the snickers turn to guffaws. Gains control of himself.)* Sorry.

MACK: I know. What can I tell you? It's my mom's favorite name. Now that that's all over with, maybe I can introduce you around. Where you from anyhow?

TOM: Oh, I'm from...uh, we came to...I mean...we moved here from...

MACK: Is something wrong?

TOM: *(Angry)* What makes you think something's wrong?

MACK: Hey, idle curiosity.

TOM: All right. I'm from *(Gritting his teeth)* Wells, Indiana!

MACK: Wells, Indiana? Is there supposed to be something wrong with that?

TOM: Think about it!

MACK: Wells? Wells?

TOM: Ding, dong? *(KAY enters Stage Left and walks slowly toward them.)*

MACK: *(Smacking his head lightly with the heal of his hand)* **Dell. Ding, dong, dell, Tom Katt's in the *weeeeell*...** *(Puts his arm around TOM's shoulder.)* **Yeah, OK, I see what you mean.**

KAY: **Were you calling me, Buddy?**

MACK: **Huh?**

KAY: **You said, oh, Kay!**

MACK: **Oh, Kay. Yeah, OK. I'd like you to meet Tom. Tom Katt.**

KAY: **What?!**

TOM: *(Shrugs.)* **You live with it.**

MACK: **Tom, this is Kay Corralle.**

TOM: **Oh? Kay Corralle. Glad to meet –**

KAY: **Oooh! I hate that.**

TOM: **What? What did I do?**

KAY: **Oh, Kay Corralle. Get it! O.K. Corralle. Remember your history. The gunfight at O.K. Corral.**

TOM: **I didn't mean –**

MACK: **Kay's a little sensitive.**

TOM: **Aren't we all?**

MACK: **Hey, Homer?** *(HOMER enters and crosses to MACK, TOM, and KAY.)*

HOMER: **Yeah?**

MACK: **Like you to meet the new kid in town. Tom, this is Homer.**

TOM: **Homer?** *(HOMER mumbles something indistinct.)* **What did you say?**

HOMER: **I said my dad's a professor of Classical studies at the university.**

TOM: **Homer's not such a bad name.**

HOMER: **You don't think so? How about Homer LaGrange?**

TOM: **I don't get it.**

HOMER: *(Sings.)* **Home, Homer LaGrange, where the deer and the antelope...**

TOM: **I see.** *(GILDA and SYBIL enter left and cross to the others.)*

HOMER: **Oh, here come Gilda and Sybil.** *(Suddenly HOMER laughs uproariously.)*

TOM: **What's so funny?**

HOMER: *(Calling the two girls)* **Hey, come over here a minute, will**

you? *(GILDA and SYBIL cross to the others. HOMER tries to keep from smiling.)* **Gilda, Sybil?**

GILDA and SYBIL: *(Simultaneously)* **Yes?**

MACK: **There's someone I'd like you to meet. Just moved here. His name is Tom. Tom Katt.**

GILDA: **Tom?** *(Giggles.)*

SYBIL: **Katt?** *(Giggles.)*

HOMER: **Tom. This is...Gilda Lillie?**

TOM: **Huh?**

GILDA: **Something bothering you?**

TOM: **Sorry, I –**

HOMER: **And her best friend, Sybil Warfield.**

TOM: **Sybil – what?!**

GILDA: **Bet you can't guess where she's from!**

SYBIL: **Stop it, Gilda. Right this minute.**

TOM: **Where?**

SYBIL: **All right. I was born in Pennsylvania.**

GILDA: *(Teasing)* **Where in Pennsylvania, Sybil?**

SYBIL: **If you insist. Sybil Warfield from Gettysburg, Pennsylva –**

TOM: **Yeah, but wasn't that the Revolutionary Wa – Oops.**

SYBIL: **Darn you, Gilda.**

KAY: *(Changing the subject)* **Tom?**

TOM: *(Turns to look at her.)* **Yes?**

KAY: **Is your homeroom by any chance 201?**

TOM: *(Pulls a piece of paper from his pocket, peers at it, and glances up at KAY.)* **Yes, it is. How'd you know?**

HOMER: **We're all in room 201, Tom.**

GILDA: *(Striking a melodramatic pose)* **It was fated to be.** *(The bell rings.)*

MACK: **C'mon, I'll introduce you to our homeroom teacher, Mrs. Teacher.** *(All slowly cross to Stage Right exit.)*

TOM: **Mrs. Teacher!**

KAY: *(Giggling)* **Bet you can't guess her first name.**

SYBIL: **Come on, Kay, tell him.**

KAY: **Her first name is Ima.**

(Curtain)

Production Notes and Considerations

It probably would be best to use a realistic style of acting, rather than an exaggerated style, when presenting "Somewhere in the Appellations." Of course, you might want to think about ways to point up the names when you deliver the lines. One way is through pausing. Experiment to see what works best for you. The exceptions to this are the lines preceded by stage directions that tell more about how they might be delivered effectively.

The piece can be performed on an empty stage.

The Monolog[36]

From ancient Greek theatre to the present, there has been a mingling of the comic and the tragic in the same play. Yet the term *tragicomedy* is a contradiction in that a protagonist (a central character) who is truly noble, as the hero of a tragedy should be, cannot then come across as funny. Neither can a comic character possess the depth of a tragic hero. Yet many plays do mix elements. Although they often present an unhappy outlook on life, most are written in such a way as to be amusing.

Tragicomedy is perhaps the most difficult type of play to write since the playwright must advance the plot or portray the characters and situation without confusing the audience. The idea behind many plays in this genre is that life itself is a mixture of the serious or tragic and the comic.

Sometimes a situation appears to be comic, but later the theatergoer realizes that it is serious. Often the audience is jolted from comedy to horror, as happens in Edward Albee's *Who's Afraid of Virginia Woolf?* Sometimes it is difficult to separate the tragic and the comic at all.

Tragicomedy, according to some definitions, begins as a tragedy but ends happily. Yet there is so much overlapping of genres that it is impossible to find a definition that fits all plays that combine comic and tragic elements.[37]

The next three plays, which do combine tragic and comic elements, are much different from the others in the book because they do have a more serious tone. The first is "The Monolog," a one-person play in which a young woman, recently graduated from high school, is seeking her first real job in professional theatre.

Even though Sarah kids around a lot at the audition, she can't keep the director of the show from knowing things in her background that she has not shared with many others. It seems that she has both a need to talk with someone about this part of her life, while at the same time she wants to keep it hidden. The former impulse

[36]Thanks to Marla Bentz for allowing me to include this monolog.

[37]Some definitions include a separate category called *dark comedy* (not to be confused with black comedy which deals with what is sometimes called "sick humor"). According to this definition, even though there is a mingling of the comic and the serious, dark comedy begins with humor but ends on a somber or serious note, whereas tragicomedy is just the opposite.

wins out, maybe because of the pressure she's feeling in auditioning for a theatre that takes a different approach than most in the way it casts and produces its shows, and in fact, in its very purpose for existence.

Although fairly short, this is a play rather than a sketch or routine in that Sarah's goal, the inciting incident that begins the play's dramatic action, is to try to prove that she has worth as a person by being cast. Throughout the audition she struggles with this, as you will see, and in the end, she discovers a great deal about herself.

The play is true tragicomedy, with a total mixing of the elements of both tragedy and comedy. More than many characters in a tragicomedy, Sarah is a noble person, which is required for true tragedy. She is someone deserving of respect. She was a victim of sorts; her life took a turn she certainly wouldn't have chosen if she'd had the power to stop its happening. Yet she has to accept that what happened cannot be undone. Her only choice is to try to go on from there and succeed, both as an actress and as a person.

The situation is exaggerated in that in real life there probably are few times when anyone would have an audition such as this one...though it is possible.

CAST: Sarah, 17.

SETTING: The action takes place on an empty stage.

AT RISE: SARAH stands Down Center, neatly dressed to audition.

SARAH: **Hi, I'm Sarah Walker. Why did I say that? You know that already. This is the first time I've ever auditioned. Professionally, I mean. For an actual role. School plays, church, things like that, I auditioned, but never – I'm sorry, I already said that.**

You want me to tell you about myself. God, I don't know what to tell you. I'm seventeen. I graduated from the School of Performing Arts last month – Oh, yeah, I guess I did audition professionally. I mean I was in the chorus of a musical. But that hardly counts, does it? Nearly everyone in my class was in the chorus of that musical. And it closed after one night. It closed after half a night. Everyone walked out. Right in the middle of a number. Like a trail of ants. They trickled right out. And there we were, singing and dancing and...

I was born...I mean, this might be interesting. I was born in Liechtenstein. There aren't many foreigners born in Liechtenstein. Not many *people* born in Liechtenstein.

See, my parents were on this trip, and I was born early, and I was born in...

I came home when I was a week old. To British Columbia. Maybe I should explain that. My dad was working in British Columbia. I mean I'm not Canadian. Not that there's anything wrong with being Canadian. I'm not a Liechtenstinian eith – is that the word? Liechtenstinian?

Sorry, I'm babbling.

Mom said she thought I started performing the day I was born. She was just kidding, of course, but I can't remember when I didn't want to be an actress. Oh, God, I thought. It would be so wonderful. To be someone else, to be anyone else, to be a lot of other – I didn't want to be me. Never wanted...

So, anyhow, I was always singing and dancing and reciting nursery rhymes. My mom says I knew the whole "Night Before

251

Christmas" when I was a year and a half. A year and a half old, can you imagine? I'd say it at the drop of a pin. That's not right. Drop of a hat. That's right; that's what it is. Isn't it?

So, anyhow, I started singing and reciting poems and things in school and church and family reunions – I was never nervous. You might think I'm nervous. But I was never nervous. High-strung like a thoroughbred. That's what Dad said. He didn't know anything about horses. Never even saw a race. That's what he told me.

You're letting me babble on here. *(Laughs nervously.)* So maybe I could recite something. How about it? What do you say? Can I recite something?

Nah, I better not. You want to hear about my life. Well, there's nothing important. I grew up in – Oh, yeah, I used to play the accordion. Squeeze box is what Grandma called it. *(Broadly pantomimes playing an accordion.)* Bagpipes. That's what I thought the accordion sounded like. Don't ask me why. Same principle, I guess. Air squeezed in and out to make the sound. Bagpipes are always so, I don't know so...so mournful. Like the cry of a lonely siren *(Caught up in the mood)* luring sailors to deep, vast graves in the sea.

(Snapping out of it) But you don't want to hear about bagpipes; you know about bagpipes. The whole world knows about bagpipes. Maybe not the whole world.

(Takes a deep breath and expels it.) Where was I? Oh, yeah, so I grew up in Jersey. Newark. Can you imagine growing up in Newark? I didn't really grow up in Newark. I moved here when I was thirteen. I mean when I found out about the School of Performing Arts, and that the kids there got to audition for shows. Professional shows. Wow, you know. Anyhow, I came to stay with my grandma. And I went home weekends, except when I was in a *(Exaggerated French accent)* **tragédie ou comédie ou a lettle chanson ou danse nombair.** *(Seriously)* I didn't really want to go home. It was so strange going home. Back into all that – back into everything – I mean like Mom never even said any –

I'm making a fool of myself up here. Isn't that what I'm doing? Making a fool of myself. Well, so what? You wanted to hear me talk; you wanted to hear me sing and act. Did you want to hear me sing?

I don't have any brothers and sisters. Mom says who could put up with another one like me? She was just kidding...I think. *(Laughs and points straight ahead.)* Of course, she was kidding. *(Seriously again)* Except I know she and Dad would have been much happier if – I didn't ask them to be born, did I? And then the way he – I mean, nobody deserves to be tr –

(Brightly) Say, don't I get to read or something? Oh, yeah, the paper you handed me. *(She pantomimes looking at a sheet of typing paper.)* When I'm done telling you about myself, I'm supposed to read it, act it. But am I done telling you about myself? I mean, I'm done telling you about myself if you want me to be done telling you about myself. But, I can...Oh, well.

Yes, now. I see. It's on the paper here. You told me my audition piece was on the paper here. Nothing prepared, you said. A cold reading. Right here on the paper. OK, here we go. Here it is. *(Reading from the imaginary paper, almost to herself)* "To be or not to be..." Oh, sure, I know that. Everyone knows that. Doesn't everyone know that? *(Reciting in broad Shakespearean tones)* "To be or not to be, that is the question. Whether 'tis nobler in the mind to suffer the slings and arrows of outrageous for –" Hey! Wait a minute here. This is Hamlet. This is a boy. I mean, not a boy, but a man. A young man. Maybe not a boy; he is in college, I think. Isn't he? A college boy. Man. Isn't Hamlet in college somewhere? Sweden, Denmark, something like – Oh, yeah, of course, he's *from* Denmark. He's Danish. Danish? How do you get Danish out of Den – Lochtenstunian! Maybe that's what I'd be if we hadn't come home. To British Columbia. To Newark. To...Actually, I don't know why they brought me home. They never wanted – And so – anyhow, I was glad to live with Grandma. I had to get away. Oh, God.

Hey, wait! Whoa! Hold everything. The fine print. I see the fine print here. *(Quoting from the imaginary paper from which she'd been reading)* **This company was founded for the purpose of expanding gender and ethnic roles.**

(Puzzled) **A Dane is ethnic? So what am I? Aren't I ethnic already? I mean besides the way I look. See the way I look. And you have me playing a Danish white boy? I mean, hey, like they used to say, get with it! Ooh, sorry, I didn't mean anything. Wow, if I say stuff like that – I mean, if I keep on saying stuff like that, I'm really going to blow it, aren't I?**

So shall we try it again? "To be or not –" Expanding our views and our roles, is that it? You know I kind of admire that. No, really, I mean I do. I really admire that.

So, hey, should I try a little dance step? Why don't I try a little dance step? *(Doing a chorus line step)* **One and a two and a one and a two and a – Remember Lawrence Welk? Oh, God, when I was a little kid, I used to sit in front of the TV set when reruns of the "Lawrence Welk Show" came on. I wanted so bad to be one of those sisters, what were there names? You know, the sisters who sang and all that stuff on the "Lawrence Welk Show"? I envied them so much. And Patty Duke. Remember her as a little girl with her own TV show? And those old movies? Shirley Temple and Margaret O'Brien. I'd give anything if I could have had a life that was just a little bit like – That was normal, damn it!**

Sorry. I'm really sorry. You don't want to hear that kind – I mean. Oh, wow, you've just got to know how important this is to me. It's really important. More important than food and sleeping and...well, you know, don't you? Sure, you know, it's like the most important thing in the whole wor – Not really the most important. Grandma – well both Grandmas. And Grandpa...

(Mock serious) **I never knew my one grandpa. Now don't get the wrong idea. He didn't die or anything. He was one of those astronauts who went to the moon. The one you never heard about, the one they all kept quiet about. It was my grandpa. Went to the moon. A young man. And he liked the moon. And so he decided to live on the moon.** *(Trying to keep from laughing)* **No, really, my grandpa's alive. Both grandmas and**

grandpas. It's really my uncle who lives on the moon. *(Laughs.)*

My grandma was a singer. Mom's mom, and Grandpa played guitar. That's how they met. Isn't that romantic? Now isn't it? And it's the truth.

My other grandma plays the piano. Grandpa isn't musical though. He collects stamps.

So where was I? Oh, sure. A one and a – Nah! You don't want to see me dance. You want me to recite something? What? What can I recite? I know. *(Very hammy)*

"It was many and many a year ago
In a kingdom by the sea.
There lived a maid whom you may know
By the name of...Sara Lee?"

Funny. *(Almost pleading)* Isn't that funny? You see, that's my name. Sarah Lee, with an "H." Sarah Lee Walker. *(Parody of a western movie)* So, what do you think about that, pardner?

(Her normal voice) Are you just going to let me die up here? I don't mean really die. I mean die like in doing a terrible job, not knowing what to say or do. Or –

I got an idea. I'll tell you about my hobbies. *(Long pause)* I don't have any hobbies. The only thing I'm interested in is being an actress. That's my whole life's ambition. Everything else revolves around that. I'm being serious. I mean it. I know I've been kidding a lot, because, believe it or not, I didn't know what else to do. What else to say. But not now.

Why do people want to be actors or actresses? Why do I want to be an actress? I don't really know. It's just the most wonderful feeling in the world. Everybody watching and listening and the house so still you can hear a hat drop. *(Laughs and points.)* Got you again, didn't I?

(Seriously) No, but I mean it. It's not like I want to control people, or even that I feel I'm so important or special. *(Pause)* Even though I am. Important and special, I mean. Kidding. Just kidding.

(Seriously again) It's like I'm this instrument playing a duet with...God maybe? Or the consciousness of the universe. And

everything's aligned somehow. And I'm the chemical catalyst or the reed of a tenor sax or the sounding board of a piano. And if I've rehearsed and studied and am confident, well, it's like I'm playing and being played so the audience hears one pure, sweet note. Or a resounding chord.

(Changing abruptly) So you heard any good jokes lately?

You'd think with my wanting to perform and loving to be up here on-stage that I'd be pretty good at telling jokes. Well, I'm not. I always mess up the punch line. I forget it or something. I wonder why. I can say lines in a play just fine. Right intonation and emphasis. But I can't tell a joke. Maybe life itself's a joke. And we're stuck with one role. I was stuck in one role. A role I hated, till I moved in with Grandma and Grandpa. Can a person be an actress just because her life is – because she wants to get away, to escape – God, I'm seventeen years old. Why did I want to escape? Why do I still want...to...escape. *(Tears in her eyes)* It was like Mom didn't care. She knew what was going on. What Dad was doing to me. But she just didn't –

(An abrupt change) So, hey, do I have the role or don't I? I mean, I feel like I've been up here forever, and I haven't said a blessed thing. Haven't done a blessed thing. I mean I was always good at ad-libbing. When I was in junior high, before I went to the school of performing arts, I joined the speech club. You know, readings and contests and stuff. Well, I always did well with the impromptu event. Give me a subject, and whether I know anything or not about it, I can talk. I'll show you.

Give me anything to talk about, any subject. Say it's... quantum physics. All right? Ahem. Ahem. Good evening, ladies and gentlemen.

Quantum physics, huh? What made me think of quantum physics? I don't know what made me think of quantum physics. Black holes. That's it. Quantum physics and black holes.

(Orotund tones) Ladies and gentlemen, a discourse on black holes. What is a black hole, ladies and gentlemen? It's a hole in the sky. A hole in the sky that's black. Not brown, not green, not red. But black. Yes, people, it's black. And why is it black?

Well, because...it isn't really there. It's somewhere else. It's in some other universe. Ha! Didn't think I knew that, did you? A tunnel to the future or the past. Anti-matter.

But you can't go through a black hole. If you tried to go through a black hole, it's hard to tell what would happen besides being crunched down so you'd cover only one billionth of a billionth of a pinhole...

So thank you, ladies and gentlemen. My mother thanks you; my father thanks you; my grandmother thanks you; my grandfather thanks you. *(Her voice trails off.)* All of them... *(Sadly)* That's dumb. Mom and Dad wouldn't thank...they wouldn't give a damn. But the big thing is that I'll be on my own, and Dad can't – *(Realizing what she's saying)* What am I saying?! But if I can play at being someone else, at least for a while, I really can be that person, become that person, do you see? Everything's better. Everything's different. I'm different. And Dad can't do those horrible things anymore, and Mom can't pretend she doesn't know what – *(Panicky)* Oh, my God, I'm sorry. I shouldn't say things like – I'm...sorry.

(Brightly) So...what else would you like to know? *(Pauses as if listening to a response.)*

I can quit! I really can quit now. And I have the job. Oh, wow, I'll have to tell Grandma and Grandpa. And I'll tell Mo – *(Suddenly, she becomes dignified and composed, a young woman in command of her life.)* Thank you. Thank you very much. *(She nods and hurries Off-stage.)*

(Curtain)

Production Notes and Considerations

The plot is a subtle one, so if you are going to play this role, you and the director may have to do a lot of digging and analyzing of lines and character traits to determine the high points.

Try to be as genuine as possible. There are two styles of acting you should use. One is the genuine Sarah, talking to the director, concerned about making a fool of herself at the audition, and worried about how she's coming across in this sort of situation. The other is the "stage persona," only slightly different, but not the real Sarah. This is Sarah the actress combined with Sarah the role-player in life. She probably does not realize this about herself, but she must try to separate the role-playing she does in life from the acting she does on-stage, though in the company for which she's auditioning, this is not so important as it might be in other situations.

Sarah's stage persona is much more "on" than Sarah the real-life person. It should be fairly easy to figure out where she switches from one role or persona to the other. It's obvious, for instance, in her reciting of the poetry and lines that she's now the actress. Yet often during these times, a hint of her vulnerability still comes through. Always, this vulnerability is more pronounced when she is simply herself talking with the director.

An empty stage and general illumination is the only requirement for the setting.

Ghoul

"Ghoul" also is a tragicomedy (or a dark comedy) in that it is a mixture of the serious and the comic, but it ends happily. Actually, it changes from a completely serious tone in the first two scenes to the hint of the comic in the third. The final scene is close to farcical comedy, which is evident in the bizarre actions and exaggerations.

This is the first play in which the characters are in college rather than high school, though they are freshmen. Timothy U., the central character, is different in many ways. In fact, in order to point up his feelings of being an outsider, he accentuates his weirdness, going so far as trying to shock his roommate by praying to his literary hero Thomas Wolfe. Whether or not he is atheistic is not important in the confines of the play.

CAST: TIMOTHY U., 18; BOB, 18; DENNY SOBINSKI, 19; RON, 18; VIC, 18; four or five THEATRE STUDENTS, male or female, 18-19.

SETTING: The action occurs at multiple locations. First is a room in a dormitory for college freshmen. This contains a chest of drawers, two single beds, and two desks. Second is the college dining hall, which contains a round table large enough to seat four to six students. Finally, there is a cemetery that has tombstones, a street light, and two or three trees.

AT RISE: TIMOTHY is kneeling by one of the two single beds in a college dorm, his hands clasped, resting on the mattress. He doesn't glance up as BOB enters, carrying two suitcases.

TIMOTHY: *(Praying)* **Our Thomas Wolfe, who art in heaven, hallowed be thy name. Thy novels be read; thy writing be loved in the rest of earth as it is in Carolina.** *(Astounded, BOB stops for a moment and then crosses to the other bed. He turns, keeping an eye on TIMOTHY.)* **Give us this day our daily prose, and forgive us our writing blocks as we forgive your critics.** *(BOB sets down his suitcases, shaking his head. TIMOTHY rises and faces BOB. He grins.)* **There's no god. No heaven, except what we create in our minds. Thomas Wolfe is my god.** *(He holds out his hand.)* **I'm Timothy U. Landis.**

BOB: *(Taking his hand)* **Hi, Bob Thompson.**

TIMOTHY: **Since I arrived first, I took this side of the room, this bed, this half of the dresser.** *(He points to a large, squat chest of drawers.)*

BOB: **Fine, I have no preference.**

TIMOTHY: **Each one of us has preferences. We simply have to find what they are and not deny them. We have to be true to ourselves.**

BOB: *(Placing one of the suitcases atop a student desk by the bed)* **Maybe that's why I'm here. To find out my preferences, what I want out of life.** *(He opens the suitcase and pulls out socks and underwear, shoving them into drawers.)*

TIMOTHY: **Need any help?**

BOB: *(Surprised)* **You can hang these up, if you like.** *(He hands shirts* *and jeans to TIMOTHY.)*

TIMOTHY: *(Taking the clothes to the closet)* **I'm aware of my preferences. All of them. I know what I want.** *(He drapes a shirt around a hanger, shaping it just right so there are no wrinkles.)*

BOB: That's wonderful. But if that's the case, why are you even here?

TIMOTHY: Scoff, if you want to. *(He hangs up the pants.)* **But I'm going to be a writer.** *(He sighs deeply.)* **I may not last here, I don't know. I'll see what they have to show me. If it's nothing I like, I'll go south to the country where Wolfe was reared.**

BOB: *(Sounding puzzled)* **Thomas Wolfe? I've heard the name –**

TIMOTHY: *(Self-mocking)* **That's right. My lord and god.**

BOB: You're serious about that, aren't you?

TIMOTHY: *(He takes a few other shirts from BOB and returns to the closet.)* **Of course.** *(BOB shuts the first suitcase, slides it under the bed and opens the other. TIMOTHY hangs the shirts up.)* **I've been told that for freshman English, each person is required to do a final project. It can be a piece of fiction. I've written mine, a novella, I admit, influenced by my god. I showed it to the head of the department. He said it was more appropriate as a creative thesis for an MFA degree than a mere freshman project...** *(As the lights dim, BOB crosses Downstage and crawls into his bed, as TIMOTHY exits Stage Right. In a moment the lights come up in the bedroom. BOB is lying in bed, wide awake as TIMOTHY enters.)*

BOB: Tim?

TIMOTHY: Timothy U. *(Laughs.)* **What are you doing awake, Robert? Don't you have an eight o'clock class?**

BOB: It's Bob! *(Shrugging)* **Oh, all right...Robert.**

TIMOTHY: *(Surprised)* **Robert?**

BOB: *(Smiles.)* **I'm losing the war. School's been in session – what is it – a month? I haven't convinced you. I never will; I give up. My name is Robert and yours is Timothy U.**

TIMOTHY: Sorry.

BOB: To answer your question, yes, I do have an eight o'clock. An econ class.

TIMOTHY: Did I wake you?

BOB: *(Throwing back the covers, he swings his feet to the floor and reaches for a glass of water on the seat of the desk chair.)* **No, you didn't wake me. At least the noise didn't wake me. It's the anticipation, I guess. Because I know that –**

TIMOTHY: Sooner or later, usually later... *(He laughs.)* **I'll be back.**

BOB: It's none of my business.

TIMOTHY: Of course, it's your business. We're roommates... friends, too?

BOB: Sure, friends.

TIMOTHY: And if I'm keeping you awake –

BOB: Damn it, Timothy.

TIMOTHY: Timothy U.

BOB: *(Laughing almost hysterically)* **All right, for God's sake, Timothy U.**

TIMOTHY: You're tired. Too tired. After this I'll try to make less noise.

BOB: You don't make any noise now. It's just that –

TIMOTHY: What?

BOB: Where do you go every night? They roll up the sidewalks at ten. The town is dry, for God's sake. There aren't even bars. Even if there were –

TIMOTHY: I'm not old enough? *(He stands and crosses to his side of the room.)* **You're right. Anyhow, I have no interest in bars.** *(Sitting on his own bed, facing BOB)* **I go to a cemetery.**

BOB: What?!

TIMOTHY: That's right. Just outside town. It's quiet and peaceful. There are these graves. Young men, sixteen, eighteen, twenty, twenty-one. It gives me inspiration. I wouldn't tell that to anyone else, but I know I can trust you.

BOB: *(Chuckling)* **Yes, you can trust me.**

TIMOTHY: I've been writing this poem. An epic. The life of Thomas Wolfe.

BOB: *(Smiling, not unkindly)* **Timothy U., you're crazy.**

> *(The lights fade to black, and immediately come up on the dining table, around which are seated DENNY SOBINSKI, RON, and VIC. BOB and TIMOTHY join them and slip into the last two*

empty chairs. All may either pantomime eating a meal or actually eat a dinner throughout the scene. TIMOTHY has a notebook he scribbles in between bites.)

DENNY: *(Addressing BOB)* **I hear your friend here's a ghoul.**

TIMOTHY: *(Startled, looking at DENNY)* **What?**

DENNY: Perverted, undead.

BOB: What's this about, Sobinski?

RON: I hear tell he likes to sit in the cemetery at night.

DENNY: And you have to admit that *isn't* **a natural thing to do.**

TIMOTHY: What I do is my own business. Anyhow, what do you care?

DENNY: Looking out for the welfare of my buddies here.

BOB: *(Glancing at TIMOTHY)* **You want to leave?**

DENNY: Leave? You ain't finished eating. Come on, man. *(Indicating TIMOTHY)* **Him, I can understand.**

RON: *(Laughing)* **Yeah, ghouls and vampires and things like that don't eat food. They suck blood or eat decayed flesh.**

TIMOTHY: All I want is to eat my meal in peace.

DENNY: What are you writing there, ghoul? Seems you're always scribbling away at something.

RON: Maybe he thinks he's going to be a male Anne Rice – interview ghosts or vampires.

DENNY: That what you're going to do, ghoul?

BOB: Come on, Timothy. I have a couple of dollars. We can stop for fries at a fast-food place.

DENNY: *(To RON)* **You know what though? I hear tell this boy's a sissy, big time. Maybe he wants to be just like that woman.**

VIC: Anne Rice?

DENNY: Yeah. *(To TIMOTHY)* **Is that right, sissy boy ghoul?**

BOB: Tim!

TIMOTHY: *(To BOB)* **Timothy! It's Timo – Look, Robert, I came here to enjoy my meal. That's what I intend to do.**

DENNY: Whoa, will you listen to that. *(Imitates TIMOTHY, but speaks in a mocking, effeminate manner.)* **I came here to enjoy my meal, and that's what I intend to do.** *(To BOB)* **Why do you put up with that?**

BOB: We're roommates. Friends. That's why.

DENNY: Seems to me you're an all-right guy. I think you could find some better class friends.

BOB: Like you?

DENNY: What are you getting at?

RON: You could do worse. Denny Sobinski's got what it takes. Plays guard for the Cardinals, as I'm sure you know.

VIC: Probably be a starter next year or the year after. *(TIMOTHY tries his best to ignore the conversation.)*

DENNY: Anyhow, man, don't you know it ain't cool to eat with no ghoul? *(Digs his elbows into RON'S side, and both begin to laugh. He turns to TIMOTHY.)* **Ain't you the poet, ghoul? How's you like my rhyme?**

BOB: Timothy! Let's get out of here.

DENNY: Not when we're having such an interesting talk. Naw, you want to stay.

BOB: Timothy.

TIMOTHY: *(Slamming his notebook shut)* **OK, all right, I give up.** *(BOB and TIMOTHY start to rise.)*

DENNY: Look, Clements, isn't that your name?

BOB: *(Nods.)* **That's my name.**

DENNY: We ain't got no quarrel with you.

BOB: I'm not hungry. Anyhow, I have a one o'clock class.

RON: Come on, man. Denny's offering something important. His friendship.

VIC: Lotta guys on campus would envy you.

BOB: Envy me?

TIMOTHY: Football mentality, Robert. Sorry. A lot of jocks aren't like that. Some of them are.

DENNY: Hey, ghoul, watch your mouth.

TIMOTHY: Why don't you leave me alone? I'd like to finish eating.

RON: Thought you were leaving.

TIMOTHY: I changed my mind. I don't like being told what I can and can't do. Least of all by someone who has no authority.

RON: You little –

DENNY: Ron, Ron, it's OK. Let him say what he wants. I'm interested.

RON: What?! In a ghoul who spends his nights in graveyards, sitting on tombstones?

TIMOTHY: What do you care?

DENNY: Maybe he thinks you don't belong here. That's what I think.

BOB: Can I ask you something, Sobinski?

DENNY: Like I said, I ain't got no quarrel with you.

BOB: Who told you that Timothy –

DENNY: The ghoul?

BOB: That Timothy goes to the graveyard at night.

DENNY: Supposed to be a big secret or something? Hell, man, he sits right there in the open. Saw him a couple of times when I was driving past. Started checking around. A lot of other guys seen him out there, too. Know what I mean?

BOB: Why does that matter?

VIC: Hey, I got it. It's like in that movie. "Song of the South." This old black guy says everyone needs a laughing place. Somewhere special to go that's theirs alone. A place where they'll always be happy.

DENNY: Is that it, ghoul? The cemetery your laughing place?

RON: Sick, man! I tell you the boy's not well.

DENNY: Thought we decided it ain't no boy. Don't know exactly what it is. Can ghouls be sissy-boys, too?!

TIMOTHY: At least I have enough intelligence to speak the English language properly.

DENNY: Man, am I impressed. *(In TIMOTHY's face)* So what are you trying to tell me, that I don't know how to talk right?

TIMOTHY: Should be pretty obvious. *(Standing)* I'm going back to the room, Robert. Can't concentrate here, and I have an essay due.

RON: From what I hear, Denny, he's a sissy-boy, all right. Sits only on tombstones of young men, guys who died a long time back.

DENNY: *(Exaggerated)* Naw, that can't be true. You mean we got us a little –

VIC: The love that dare not speak its name.

DENNY: What's that, Vic?

VIC: That's what they used to call it. The love that dare not speak its name.

DENNY: You trying to tell me this here ghoul likes little boys?

RON: That's what I've heard.

BOB: Come on, guys, lay off, will you?

DENNY: How's come you're so concerned?

BOB: What do you mean?

RON: Just what he asked. What do you think he means?

TIMOTHY: Look, Robert, it's one thing to imply things about me. It's another –

DENNY: I don't imply things, ghoul. If I mean something, I'm going to come right out and say it. *(Glances at BOB.)* Like I said, I ain't got nothin' against your roommate. And I'm saying you're the one who likes boys.

TIMOTHY: I sit on the tombstones of young men, damn it! They're not boys. Anyhow, what if they were? I go there to think. For inspiration. It's peaceful and quiet.

DENNY: You mean you're admitting it then. That you like boys – er, uh, pardon me – young men?

TIMOTHY: *(Jumping up)* I've had enough.

BOB: *(He pushes back his chair and begins to leave.)* I don't believe you, Sobinski.

TIMOTHY: Stop it, Robert! Don't get yourself involved. *(TIMOTHY slams his tray hard against the top of the table and hurries Off - stage Left. BOB starts to follow, but DENNY grabs his arm. Bob struggles to get free.)*

DENNY: Let him go. You don't want to be with guys like him. *(When BOB sees he can't get away, he stops struggling.)* Good. Now sit down and finish your lunch.

(The lights fade to black, and in a few moments come up on BOB and TIMOTHY's room. TIMOTHY is throwing things haphazardly into a suitcase. BOB enters and stops.)

BOB: Tim!

TIMOTHY: Timothy U. *(Shakes his head.)* Sorry. I know it's silly. I never did explain the reason for insisting on that. Maybe now's my last chance.

BOB: What are you talking about? Where are you going?

TIMOTHY: To Carolina. Thomas Wolfe's home. I want to be just like him, you know.

BOB: A writer, I know. But what is this? You're just giving up?

TIMOTHY: *(Pauses in his packing and stares for a beat at BOB.)* Wouldn't you?

BOB: I don't know. Maybe I'd feel the way you do. I guess I probably would.

TIMOTHY: *(Checking to see that his belongings are all packed)* Anyhow, the reason for using "Timothy U." I've always wanted to be a writer, Rober – Bob. *(Smiles sadly.)* It's stupid enough to insist on my being called Timothy U. without insisting you be called Robert.

BOB: I don't mind. I really don't.

TIMOTHY: Anyhow, I've always wanted to be a writer. From the first time I was ever aware of books. Other kids...dream of being astronauts or firemen. Not me. Even when I was a little kid, I saw the power on the pages of books. Even before I could read, I did. And I wanted to be like those writers. People who put words on paper and had others read them. To me, that's the most important thing a person can do...at least, a person like I am could do. And I decided when I was six. In the first grade. I wasn't going to be just Tim Landis. Anyone could be Tim Landis. I would be... *(He stops for a moment.)*

BOB: I'm listening.

TIMOTHY: Timothy U. Landis. A name with power! Power enough to control words. A name people would see and remember. On the front of a book. Maybe dozens of books. Timothy U. Landis.

BOB: I guess I can understand that.

TIMOTHY: Silly.

BOB: It's not silly, Timothy U.

TIMOTHY: Tim. It's OK to call me Tim. I'm done with the pretensions. The silliness. *(Pause)* I'm still going to be a writer. The best doggone writer I can be. And on the cover of every book and on every title page of the novels I write, there it will be: Timothy U. Landis. But not in real life. In real life, I'll just be Tim.

BOB: Tell me something?

TIMOTHY: *(Shrugs.)* Yeah, what?

BOB: All these weeks, I've wondered.

TIMOTHY: Why I sit in the cemetery?

BOB: *(Laughs.)* Uh-uh. I'm used to that.

TIMOTHY: What then?

BOB: The "U" as in Timothy U. What does it stand for?

TIMOTHY: Nothing.

BOB: You mean it's just a middle initial?

TIMOTHY: I mean it's nothing at all. *(Self-mocking)* I told you it was silly. I wanted something to set me apart. A distinction. Something to make my name unique. Timothy Landis; that's common as weeds in a garden. But if I added a middle name. Something unusual. Or even a letter.

BOB: *(Smiling)* You made it up?

TIMOTHY: Yep. How many guys do you know who have a name that begins with U? Not many, huh?

BOB: *(Laughing)* Can't think of a one. Except maybe General Grant.

TIMOTHY: You see? *(Shrugs.)* I carried it much too far. Everyone thinks I'm weird. Stupid. Am I a sissy, Bob? In your eyes, I mean? Effeminate? Maybe even what they said. Do I come across that way?

BOB: No, you don't! Absolutely not. At the very same time, you *are* eccentric as hell!

TIMOTHY: *(Laughing so hard he has trouble stopping)* You're a gem, Robert. Bob. Truly a gem.

BOB: So...what's all this with the packing?

TIMOTHY: I told you. I see no reason to put up with the way things were at lunch. It wasn't the first time.

BOB: I know.

TIMOTHY: If I leave, start over...

BOB: Run away from your problems, you mean?

TIMOTHY: Sticking it out is sometimes highly overrated.

BOB: Maybe you're right. But I have a plan. Will you hear me out?

TIMOTHY: A plan?

BOB: I have a French class with a few guys from the theatre department. We've gone to the student union together a few times after class. I'm going to ask if they'll help. I'll bet they can even borrow some equipment and help set it up.

TIMOTHY: What equipment?

BOB: What I'd like to do...

(The lights fade to black. In a few moments, they come up on the dining room. BOB, DENNY, RON, and VIC are sitting around the same table eating dinner. It is two days later.)

DENNY: *(To BOB)* Good to see you, man. You haven't been around for a couple of days.

BOB: Been busy. You know how it is.

DENNY: See you decided to ditch the ghoul.

BOB: You could say that. *(Chuckles.)* When I got back to my room, I found him packing his stuff.

VIC: For what?

BOB: Said he was leaving school; didn't need it to become a writer.

DENNY: Good thing. This school has enough creeps.

BOB: Then he changed his mind.

RON: What?

BOB: Said something about his folks paying all that money for his tuition...

DENNY: Thought a big brain like him would be on a scholarship.

BOB: He told me he was offered one but turned it down.

DENNY: That doesn't make sense.

BOB: Said his folks thought the money should go to someone who needed it more than he did.

RON: Might have known he's one of the ee-fete!

DENNY: *E* Feet. What are *E* feet?

BOB: I think he means effete.

DENNY: Ain't never heard such a word. What does it mean?

VIC: Rich.

DENNY: Man, you're beginning to sound like the ghoul himself.

VIC: Hey, man, I really don't think –

DENNY: Relax, Vic. I was kiddin'.

BOB: I think the word really means self-indulgent or decadent. Even effeminate.

VIC: *(Challenging)* Rich! Just like I said.

BOB: Maybe.

VIC: What do you mean "maybe"? People have to be rich –

BOB: No offense, Vic. And I agree. To be totally self-indulgent, a person probably has to be rich.

DENNY: *(Laughing)* That's the ghoul, all right. Particularly that last thing.

RON: What last thing?

DENNY: Effeminate. Sissy-boy. *(To BOB)* Turned down a scholarship, huh? His family must be nuts, as well as rich.

BOB: I don't know about the nutty part. But from what Tim says, they aren't rich.

DENNY: Oh, yeah?

BOB: His dad's an electrician.

DENNY: You kidding me?

BOB: No. And his mom's a receptionist at a doctor's office.

DENNY: I don't believe this. Then why –

BOB: They have ideals, I suppose. Maybe misplaced...

DENNY: What do you mean, "ideals"?

BOB: Standards. Tim said his family felt they should always pay their own way when they can. If they can't, they do without.

RON: Not me, man. I want what I can get.

DENNY: The American way! Get what you can while the getting's good. Take my old man. Owns his own company. Makes computer software. Something to do with blueprints or building houses or somethin'. Never interested me. But when I got a football scholarship, you didn't see him yelling about no ideals. *(Laughs.)* That's for the...E feet, I guess.

BOB: Anyhow he decided to stay.

RON: And *(Mocking)* meditate with the ghosts out there in the cemetery.

DENNY: Now that he knows we seen him there, I wonder if he's got the nerve. I doubt it. Sissy-boy like him. *(Pause)* I think I'm gonna teach that boy a lesson. We'll just drive on by and see if he's there tonight or tomorrow...

BOB: He'll be there. He told me.

DENNY: *(Interested)* Oh, yeah. Why'd he tell you that?

BOB: *(Shrugs.)* I don't know. Said he wasn't going to allow anyone to scare him off. It was a matter of principle now.

DENNY: He's taking his life in his hands, man, I'm telling you. *(To RON)* What say we pay him a little visit?

RON: Why not?

DENNY: Damn ghouls. Gonna teach 'em a lesson or two. Ain't that right?

RON: Darn right.

DENNY: *(To BOB)* You in on this, man?

BOB: Tell me what time, and I'll meet you.

DENNY: Hey, man, I got a car. I'll drive you there.

BOB: I got a better idea. I'll wait till he leaves and call your room. Then I'll go on out there and make sure he stays.

DENNY: How you going to do that?

BOB: If he wants to go back to the dorm, I'll talk to him. Make sure he doesn't.

DENNY: You ain't such a bad guy after all, Bobby. I like that.

(*The lights fade to black. In a few minutes they come up dimly on the cemetery, which consists of a row of tombstones, perhaps plywood or cardboard cutouts, and maybe two or three trees. In the dim arc of light from a lamppost, TIMOTHY U. sits beside one of the graves. His notebook is open, and he is writing. DENNY, RON, and VIC enter Stage Right and cross to the edge of the cemetery. Outside the arc of the streetlight, they are barely visible. Throughout the scene, there are various noises and voices that sound otherworldly or as if coming from a great distance. DENNY, RON and his friends hear them, but TIMOTHY seems unaware.*)

DENNY: *(Stage whisper)* Where's Bob? He said he was going to meet us.

RON: What's the difference?

VIC: Maybe he chickened out.

DENNY: Naw, I don't think so.

RON: Hey, Denny, do you hear anything?

DENNY: *(Cocking his head and listening)* Yeah, maybe. What about you?

RON: Music. Some kind of music.

VIC: I say we get out of here.

DENNY: 'Smatter, you scared?

VIC: It's not that I'm scared. It's just –

DENNY: Yeah?

VOICE ONE: *(Ghostly, keening, eerie, the words barely distinct)* **Who is it who dares to come to our place?**

RON: **You hear!**

DENNY: **Someone playing tricks.** *(To TIMOTHY)* **Hey, ghoul.** *(TIMOTHY is engrossed in his notebook and doesn't react.)* **I'm speaking to you, sissy-boy. You going to answer me.**

TIMOTHY: *(Looking up, as if suddenly aware)* **Who is it?**

DENNY: **Sobinski. Like I said, we're going to teach you a lesson.** *(Suddenly, a silken web falls either from a tree branch or from the fly space and lands on RON's face. RON claws at it and screams.)*

VOICE 2: *(A raspy, gasping manner of speaking, drawing out each word, and seeming to come from all directions)* **Leave now before it's too late. Heed the warning; do not disobeyyyyyy.**

RON: **I'm going, man, I'm going.**

DENNY: **What the hell's happening?**

RON: **This thing, this thing on my face. Like a giant web.**

DENNY: *(Irritated)* **What's the matter with you? You probably walked into a spider web!**

RON: *(Managing to grab it from his face)* **If you don't believe me, just look.** *(As DENNY turns, the web is whisked away — back up into the tree branch or fly space.)*

DENNY: **I don't see nothin'.**

RON: **It was here, and then it was gone.**

DENNY: **Your imagination, man. Place has got you spooked.** *(Realizes what he's said and laughs.)* **Spooked, you get it?**

RON: **I wasn't imagining things, Denny.**

DENNY: **If you're so much of a chicken —**

VOICE 1: **Leeeeave, I teeeeeellllllll you. Leeeeeave now, and your life willlllll be spaaaaared.**

RON: **Hey, man, I'm going.** *(Suddenly, a hand reaches out from nowhere, grabs VIC's ankle and yanks. He nearly loses his balance.[38])*

---

[38]NOTE: If possible, black light can be used here. The theatre students can be dressed in black clothes with only portions of their bodies showing. The hand wears white gloves. A face is painted white while the rest of the body is dressed in black and so on. Otherwise, the theatre students can be dressed in black with white makeup on the parts of the bodies that are to be seen.

VIC: Eeeeeooow!

DENNY: *(So startled, he jumps and turns around.)* **What's wrong with you, Vic?**

VIC: **Something grabbed my foot!**

DENNY: **You probably tripped on a branch.** *(Calling to TIMOTHY)* **I might be a little more concerned if I was you, sissy-boy. If I was you, I think I might be leaving about now.**

VOICE 2: **Yessssss! Leave! Alllll of youuuu leeeeave. Youuuu Ronallllllllllllld Stiverrrrrrrrrs. Victorrrrrr Brownowskiiiiii.**

RON: **You can't tell me you didn't hear that, Sobinski.**

DENNY: **I heard, and I'm going to get to the bottom of this.** *(Suddenly a face without a body floats in front of DENNY. Invisible hands shove him hard; he stumbles back.)*

VOICE 2: **You are in graaaaave danger. Haaaa, haaaa, haaaaa, haaaaa. Graaaaave, graaave dangerrrr.**

DENNY: *(Recovering his balance)* **All right, that's it. I've had it. It's some kind of trick.**

RON: **Come on, Denny, let's get out of here.**

DENNY: **Some cheap trick. I don't know what's at the bottom of this, but I'm going to find out.** *(Suddenly, Halloween ghosts and skeletons drop from the trees or the fly space, perhaps four or five, perhaps eight or ten. They bob up and down amidst and in front of DENNY, RON, and VIC. We hear a CHORUS OF VOICES, chanting in unison.)*

CHORUS: **Do not doubt usssss. You are in dangerrrrr.**

DENNY: *(Starts to rush toward TIMOTHY.)* **We'll see who's in danger.** *(He grabs at one of the ghosts which quickly flies upward. He grabs at a skeleton.)* **Hey, ghoul, if you're at the bottom of all of this, I'm going to kill you. You hear me?**

CHORUS: **Killlll, killlll, killlll.** *(Bodiless hands grab RON and VIC and hold them fast. The two boys yell and scream and try to break free. The hands tie ropes around their ankles.)*

CHORUS: **Youuuuu had yourrrr chaaaaance. Noooow it'ssssss toooooo laaaate.** *(A group of bodiless hands grabs DENNY, twisting him one way, pulling him another.)*

DENNY: **What the hell's going on?**

273

TIMOTHY: Are you talking to me?

DENNY: What is this crap?!

TIMOTHY: I don't know what you're talking about.

BOB: *(Rushes in from Stage Left and crosses to DENNY and the others.)* Sorry, guys, I'm late.

DENNY: What's going on here?

BOB: What do you mean?

DENNY: *(Hitting at the hands but missing)* **Can't you see?**

BOB: See what? I don't see anything except you three guys.

DENNY: You haven't heard anything strange?

BOB: Strange? What do you mean?

DENNY: *(Trying to bat away the hands but never connecting)* **Come on, man.** *(Suddenly, a large net or web falls from above, enveloping DENNY. He fights to escape.)* **Stop it! I mean it.**

BOB: Who are you talking to?

DENNY: Whoever's playing tricks.

BOB: Tricks?

DENNY: Come on, man. All these hands grabbing at me. And this spider web or net or whatever it is.

BOB: This is a joke, right?

DENNY: You can't see it?

BOB: I don't see anything. *(Lights come up on a floating face, painted in a rictus of death. The floating face is VOICE 1.)*

VOICE 1: Youuuuu weeeeere waaarned. Nooooow yooooouuu muuuuust diiiiiie. *(Knives dripping blood appear in bodiless hands waving in front of RON and VIC and DENNY's faces. RON turns and runs quickly toward Stage Right. He is hampered by the rope on his feet and falls flat on his face just before he exits. He picks himself up and keeps on going. VIC hops after him, yelling and screaming the entire way Off-stage.)*

DENNY: I'll bet you think this is funny.

BOB: What are you talking about?

DENNY: Look, man, I thought I could trust you. I thought you hated the ghoul as much as I do.

BOB: I don't know what you mean.

DENNY: Well, I'm not scared, whatever you're trying to pull. *(With* *no warning, four or five pair of hands grab DENNY, twist him around, lift him up, throw him backward and catch him face up. It appears as if both he and the hands are floating in midair.)*

VOICE 2: Ghouls and ghosts arise from this mud
      and cover you in buckets of blood.

(A bucket of blood appears and is thrown into DENNY's face. He gasps and sputters and struggles to be free.[39] Unceremoniously, the hands release DENNY, who lands on the stage floor on his rear end. All the while, TIMOTHY is seemingly unaware of what is happening.)

DENNY: *(Rising and addressing TIMOTHY)* **Think you're pulling something funny! Just wait.**

CHORUS: Leave or suffer the further fate
      of all mischief makers who enter this gate
      with malicious thoughts awhirl in their minds
      for they will find
      that supernatural or not,
      we will seek you in any spot
      where you bully others. We make this vow
      you will be punished far worse than now.
      So go, and leave those who would never harm you.
      For if you don't, it shall be true. We'll get you.
      We will get you.

(Suddenly, the hands are gone.)

DENNY: You don't fool me. I don't know who you are, but you're as much flesh and blood as I am.

VOICE 1: Maybe that's true, but you don't know.

VOICE 2: Who we are. So we bid you go.

CHORUS: Everywhere we watch and wait
      and maybe soon determine your fate.
      Go now in peace, and in peace remain
      or we will surely meet again.

VOICE 2: And maybeeee neeexxxt tiiiiime the cooooonsequuu-uences will be moooore diiiiire.

---

[39]NOTE: The "blood" can be finely cut pieces of red cellophane or red tissue paper.

DENNY: Hey, man, if I find out you had anything to do with this –

BOB: You think I set this up?

DENNY: We'll see.

BOB: Maybe you should listen to what the voices say.

DENNY: Forget it! I'm not scared.

BOB: Seems to me your friends were.

DENNY: So who cares about them?

BOB: *(Shrugs.)* Whatever.

DENNY: I'm getting out of here. *(He pulls a handkerchief from his pocket and rubs the "blood" from his face.)* It's some kind of paint.

BOB: Maybe so. But I think I'd worry a little if I were you.

DENNY: Yeah, right. *(He stomps Off-stage Left. Once he's gone, the THEATRE STUDENTS and TIMOTHY begin to laugh as they gather under the streetlight.)*

VOICE 1: *(Speaking normally)* So what do you think?

VOICE 2: He acts tough, but I'm willing to bet he doesn't bother Tim anymore. Right, Tim?

TIMOTHY: Let's hope so. Anyhow, thanks a lot, guys. It was all I could do to keep from laughing.

BOB: So, ready to go back home?

TIMOTHY: Yeah, and you know what? No more trips to the cemetery. I think I have more friends among the living than the dead.

VOICE 1: Hey, looks like the guy's getting smart.

TIMOTHY: Maybe I am. *(To BOB)* I don't know how you pulled it all off. But thanks, OK?

BOB: It was fun, Tim. And I think we taught the guys a lesson. *(Chuckling)* I'm pretty sure we convinced Ron and Vic.

TIMOTHY: Sobinski, too. But I think I'm the one who learned something.

BOB: Oh, yeah? What's that?

TIMOTHY: The importance of friends. Not trying to act as if it doesn't matter. Not pretending to be weird just because you feel different.

BOB: Guess you're right. Everybody's different.

VOICE 2: Especially after tonight.

276

BOB: You can say that again.

VOICE 2: OK. Especially after tonight. *(All laugh as the lights fade to black.)*

(Curtain)

Production Notes and Considerations

In ways Timothy U. is similar to Sarah in that he is a vulnerable person. Similarly, he and Sarah both "act" to try to prove something. It is a kind of defense for both of them, putting a wall between themselves and the rest of the world. Sarah certainly isn't as deliberate about this as Timothy, who seems to believe the old cliché: The best defense is a good offense. This is the reason for his behaving so unconventionally. Yet it is easy to see that this wall of unconventionality he has built around himself is pretty thin. This comes across in his allowing his roommate Bob to break through the defense and get a glimpse of the real and lonely person inside. It also is apparent in the way he reacts in the dining hall.

Unlike Sarah, Timothy U. apparently had nothing specific in his life that causes him to behave as he does. Why then do you suppose he does so many weird things? Besides those already mentioned, what other things does he do to show that he isn't really all that he pretends to be? Can you point out instances of this?

Despite his pretenses, Timothy U. is the most genuine character in the play. He is the most fully developed, and Bob is next, though not nearly so well developed as Timothy. Why do you suppose this is so? Denny Sobinski, Ron, and Vic are caricatures, one-dimensional characters who seem to have no redeeming qualities whatsoever. Why do you think they are not more fully developed? The same, of course, is true of the theatre students. They are simply devices, who don't even have names.

If you were playing the roles of either Sobinski or Ron, it probably would be a good idea to try to develop them so they come across as real people. For Vic and the theatre students, this is not so important since they are there only to help Timothy U. realize that he needn't be so defensive nor need he feel so different from others.

This play is similar in staging requirements to "The Boy With Nine Lives." Different areas of the stage represent different locations. It probably would work best to switch from one location to another through the use of lighting.

Passions

(In memory of Rodney Shaffer)

"Passions" is a tragicomedy. Yet unlike the previous two plays, it ends on a somber note. Also, it is not as funny as any of the other plays. Instead, it is amusing in places because one of the three characters uses jokes and comedy as a defense.

This play is different from the other two in a couple of other respects. Dolly is college age, while the other two characters, Bruce and Tyler, are in high school. All three have somewhat old-fashioned names. This suggests a timeless quality and symbolizes that the characters are somewhat separated from others their age.

Another way in which the play is different is that it covers a great span of years, though most of it takes place within a few months. As the Narrator says, "Passions" is a memory play, based on events from years past.

All three of the tragicomedies are about people who feel different — Sarah, Timothy, and all three of the characters in "Passions." The one who feels the least different is Dolly. Yet she, too, feels a little bit out of touch with classmates because of her family's background. She was poor, and no one in her family has previously attended college.

CAST: BRUCE, nearly 16; DOLLY, 19; TYLER (NARRATOR), nearly 16; NARRATOR (TYLER, somewhere between the age of 28 and 50).

SETTING: The action takes place on a city bus, in the living room of Bruce's house, and in a park.

At RISE: The NARRATOR stands Center Stage looking out over the audience.

PROLOGUE

NARRATOR: "Passions" is a memory play – involving my friend, my very best friend until recent years. Because it is a memory play, it is bound to be colored by perceptions, individual recollections, and by changes in my own views of life over the past years.

It is important for you to know that I never met the play's second most important character. I saw Dolly, have only ever seen her, through Bruce's eyes. And his perceptions, of course, were colored by the situation itself.

This means that Dolly is twice removed from reality, and even reality itself is indefinable since each person perceives it through the lenses of our backgrounds and personalities. Thus the character of Dolly is destined to be slightly blurred and indistinct. She is built on what I perceive to be Bruce's view of her, removed even further in the tellings and retellings – both his and mine – of what actually happened. *(He nods to the audience and exits Stage Left.)*

Scene i

(The action in Scene i occurs in a crowded bus, which actually can be a simple stage with two chairs. The vehicle itself can be imaginary, the action of finding a seat pantomimed. DOLLY is already seated in one of the chairs. She is dressed in designer jeans and a T-shirt. She could be attractive, yet she wears no makeup, and her hair looks tousled, not by design but by accident or neglect. BRUCE enters Stage Right and walks toward the bus. He wears a suit and a felt hat, an outfit of a conservative dresser much older than he. He climbs

the bus's imaginary steps, deposits imaginary fare, and slowly walks toward the back. It is obvious from his actions that the bus is nearly filled. The bus starts with a jerk throwing him off balance, and he stumbles to the seat next to DOLLY, who holds a notebook and two or three textbooks in her lap. She has been watching his progress with a secret smile of enjoyment or perhaps anticipation.)

BRUCE: Seems like fate decreed I find this empty seat. *(Indicating the chair)* **May I?**

DOLLY: *(Smiling)* **Sure. Seeing how it's the only empty seat on the bus.** *(BRUCE sits, takes off his hat and places it in his lap. He's thin, with a smattering of freckles and fairly thick glasses, which also make him appear older than he is.)*

BRUCE: *(Glancing at her books)* **Student?**

DOLLY: Community college.

BRUCE: Oh, I didn't realize –

DOLLY: U. of Pittsburgh Regional Campus, actually.

BRUCE: *(Nodding)* **Junior Pitt.**

DOLLY: You, too? A student, I mean.

BRUCE: That's right. *(He doesn't mean to be misleading, but then again he finds the young woman very attractive.)* **Coming from my piano lesson.**

DOLLY: Music major?

BRUCE: I hope to be.

DOLLY: Undeclared major?

BRUCE: *(Obviously uncomfortable)* **Well...I suppose you could –**

DOLLY: I don't mean to pry.

BRUCE: *(His voice goes up a tone or two.)* **Oh, no.** *(He forces himself to speak more naturally.)* **That's fine. I mean, it's strange. I guess it sounds...silly or melodramatic or something, but it's like music is...** *(He shrugs.)*

DOLLY: It's OK. Go ahead and say it, if you like.

BRUCE: It's like music has become my whole life. *(Suddenly he's babbling.)* **I mean, we've always had this piano in the living room. My folks, I mean. And I never touched it. Never went near it. My mom plays a little; Dad, too, though not very often. But it was like suddenly it caught my attention. Ridiculous,**

isn't it? Fifteen years it sat there, and I hardly noticed it –

DOLLY: *(Assuming perhaps that he's her age)* **So what you're telling me is that you've been studying for only two or three years?**

BRUCE: Oh, no, no. Less than that. Much less than that. Though I... *(Suddenly realizing that he could be revealing his age if he goes on much longer)* **What I mean is –**

DOLLY: That your parents didn't have the piano the first few years of your life.

BRUCE: Well...what about you? I mean, what you're studying? Your major. You have a major?

DOLLY: *(Laughing)* **If I didn't know better, I'd think I'm having some sort of effect on you. You aren't always so nervous, are you?**

BRUCE: *(Taking a deep breath and letting it out)* **Nervous. No. Well...maybe. My first recital's tomorrow.**

DOLLY: That's exciting. It really is. At the school? Junior Pitt?

BRUCE: *Noooo.* **Actually, it's a private thing.**

DOLLY: Ah, too bad. I might have enjoyed it. What sort of music –

BRUCE: Classical. Strictly classical.

DOLLY: I assumed so. What I mean is –

BRUCE: Oh, I see. Composers.

DOLLY: Right.

BRUCE: Mozart. Chopin. But listen, you never told me –

DOLLY: My major? Can't you tell from my demeanor, the way I respond.

BRUCE: *(Puzzled)* **I'm not sure...**

DOLLY: I was certain it showed. The profs warned us. Take a few introductory classes and right away you want to analyze –

BRUCE: I think I understand.

DOLLY: Right. Psychology. I hope to become a clinical psychologist.

BRUCE: *(Puzzled, yet not wanting to show his ignorance)* **Clinical?**

DOLLY: *(Droll)* **Never did get on well with rats...or statistics.**

BRUCE: Rats or – I'm a little slow. You want to work with people instead of experiments in a musty old lab.

DOLLY: Right. You might not think it, seeing me. But I'm a people person.

BRUCE: I don't see why you feel –

DOLLY: Look at me. Mousey, right?

BRUCE: Certainly not!

DOLLY: A true gentleman, as well as a scholar...of classical music.

BRUCE: *(Getting in beyond his depth; hoping to change the subject)* You live here in town? Obviously, you do, if you're riding the bus.

DOLLY: Yes, and no. Actually, while I'm in school. Before I go on to Pittsburgh next year. In case you didn't know, that means I'm a sophomore. *(She raises her eyebrows questioningly.)*

BRUCE: Oh, yes, me, too. A sophomore. That's what I am. A sophomore.

DOLLY: Then you'll be going on to Pittsburgh too?

BRUCE: *(Caught and he knows it.)* I doubt that. Actually, I doubt it very seriously.

DOLLY: Oh, I understand. You want to go to a music school. Oberlin maybe. Or the Cincinnati Conservatory.

BRUCE: It would be nice.

DOLLY: You haven't been accepted yet?

BRUCE: Not yet. There are...I suppose, you could say, some overriding reasons that compel me to – That is –

DOLLY: I'm sorry. I don't mean to pry.

BRUCE: *(Turning to her and smiling)* I don't mind.

DOLLY: You're sure?

BRUCE: I'm sure. I really am. You were telling me where you live –

DOLLY: My aunt. I'm really from Lambertsville. A little burg – Well, not even that.

BRUCE: I know where it is.

DOLLY: You do? I didn't think *anyone* knew where it was. Sometimes I'm not even sure the people who live there know where it is.

BRUCE: *(Kidding)* So now you're in the big city. Johnstown, PA.

DOLLY: From fifty people to fifty thousand. Mom warned me. "Beware of those city slickers," she said. "You give them the slightest chance, they're going to take advantage." *(Dryly)* Nobody's taken advantage. Nobody's even tried to take advantage.

BRUCE: I'm sure, given half a chance, I'd certainly – *(Embarrassed)*

Sorry. That isn't what I meant. That isn't how it should have come out.

DOLLY: *(Half interested; half self-mocking)* **So tell me, young man, would you take advantage?**

BRUCE: *(Swallowing hard)* **I – That is – I mean –**

DOLLY: *(Shaking her head and smiling)* **Sorry. Just my weird sense of humor. You know what though? And I *am* no longer kidding. I have this instinct. About people. It's never failed me. Long as I can remember. I don't mean to embarrass you even further, but you seem like the sort of man...Obviously, you're intelligent. All I mean...is that everybody could use a friend.**

BRUCE: **Look, my stop's coming up soon. Here.** *(He takes a scrap of paper from his side coat pocket and a pen from his shirt.)* **This is my number. Name's Bruce. Bruce McKinney. Will you give me a call? If...if you want to, I mean.**

DOLLY: **That's very nice of you.**

BRUCE: **Well, you see there's this concert. A pianist. Name of Margolin. Geoffrey Margolin. You heard of him?**

DOLLY: **I don't think so.**

BRUCE: **At the Civic Center. Next week. Friday and Saturday evening. If you'd like. I mean, if you don't have any plans. We could. I could. Nah, it wouldn't work. I don't drive.**

DOLLY: **Well, I don't either. It's not such a big deal, is it? All the boys I knew in high school could hardly wait to get their learner's permit. I find it refreshing –**

BRUCE: **We could take the bus...or –** *(Knows he's taking a chance)* **or Mom could drive us. What do you think?**

DOLLY: **That would be nice. That would be very nice.**

BRUCE: *(Hands her the paper.)* **My name; my number. I gotta get off here.** *(He leans across and yanks an imaginary cord to signal the stop.)* **So anyhow, call me – if you want to, I mean.**

DOLLY: *(An honest compliment)* **You're a very refreshing man. I mean that. I sincerely do.** *(Both pantomime being thrown forward and then back as the imaginary bus stops. BRUCE starts down the aisle.)* **My name's Dolly. Dolores, actually. But everyone calls me Dolly. I don't like the name very much.**

BRUCE: *(Turns to her.)* **I think it's a very nice name. Because you are, you know. A real Do – Sorry.** *(He quickly turns and hurries to the front of the bus. The lights fade to black.)*

Scene ii

(The action switches to the living room of BRUCE's house. A piano dominates the set. Otherwise, there need be only two chairs plus a piano stool or bench. Or the piano can be imaginary. During the interlude between scenes, the audience hears BRUCE practicing scales. Suddenly, he switches to a heavy and difficult piano piece. TYLER sits in one of the chairs leafing through a magazine that obviously doesn't interest him. BRUCE, of course, is practicing the piano. This can be pantomimed with taped accompaniment. In the middle of the piece or movement, BRUCE suddenly stops. TYLER looks up, lays down the magazine, and starts to say something. Unaware of this, BRUCE speaks.)

BRUCE: **Damn! Every time I think I have it, I mess up.**

TYLER: **Sounds good to me.**

BRUCE: **Come on, Tyler. It's crap. My playing is crap.**

TYLER: **Yeah, well, I don't think so.**

BRUCE: **What do you know?!**

TYLER: **Right, what do I know? I'm just a stupid –**

BRUCE: **I'm sorry! It sounds like pounding. It shouldn't sound like pounding.**

TYLER: **Man, Bruce, you've been at this now...** *(Glances at his watch)* **four-and-a-half hours.**

BRUCE: **So who's counting?**

TYLER: **I'm counting, that's who. Look, guy, I come to spend the weekend with you and your folks –**

BRUCE: **I'm sorry. I can't help it. Sometimes I think I'll never be able to play the piano!**

TYLER: *What* **are you talking about? This time last year, you couldn't tell a black key from a white one.**

BRUCE: *(Laughing)* **Close, I suppose...**

TYLER: **But no cigar? God, who else in the whole history of the**

world spends as much time at the piano as you do? What are
you trying to pro –

BRUCE: I gotta make up for lost time.

TYLER: Lost time, maybe. But every waking hour of every single
day. Yeah, I know, you told me. Four hours on weekdays and
eight hours on weekends. What are you...nuts?

BRUCE: I don't appreciate –

TYLER: Well, I don't appreciate being invited for the weekend and
then sitting around bored out of my gourd while you play the
damn piano. Let me look at your hands.

BRUCE: What for?

TYLER: To see how many knuckles are left on each finger.

BRUCE: *(Sighing)* I figure I'm almost sixteen, right?

TYLER: Right. Ask me how I know that? I know because I'll be
sixteen too, two weeks later than you. But you know what? You
don't see me sitting in front of some dumb instrument...My
God, do you really practice that much?

BRUCE: I've taken lessons for nine months now, and –

TYLER: And gone through five years of the course of study. Yeah,
you told me.

BRUCE: But don't you see, I'll be a junior next year. And then after
that –

TYLER: Let me guess. Uh...Uh...I give up. No, no, wait. *(Smacks his
forehead.)* It's coming to me. The little half cell in the head is
beginning to work. You'll be a senior. Yeah, that's it. A senior!
See, I'm not so dumb.

BRUCE: Come on, Tyler. You know how important it is.

TYLER: What is this, a comedy routine? OK, I'll bite. How important
is it?

BRUCE: It's not a comedy routine. It's my life.

TYLER: *(Putting the back of his hand against his forehead in a dramatic
Delsartian gesture. His speech is overly dramatic.)* Ah, yes, your
very life. How could I have forgotten. *(In a normal voice)* But
does your life have to be so...aw, man!

BRUCE: Say it. Come on, say it.

TYLER: Never mind.

BRUCE: No, you started to say it. I want you to say it.

TYLER: *(A pose; a clipped British accent)* **Well, all right then, Bruce L. McKinney, old fellow, old chum.** *(Dropping the accent, he emphasizes each word and shouts the last one.)* **Does it have to be so melodramatic?**

BRUCE: I don't believe this. I mean, I really don't. You're my best friend, right?

TYLER: Yeah, and you're my best friend, too. But you know what?

BRUCE: What?

TYLER: I'm glad I moved away. I'm glad we see each other only every couple of months. I'm glad, and do you know why?

BRUCE: Look, Tyler, the piano is important to me. I don't know how to explain it.

TYLER: God, Bruce. The damned thing sat there forever, and you didn't go near it. That's what you told me. Why this...this overpowering...drive, compulsion, whatever to – Hey, is this a female piano?

BRUCE: *(Astounded)* **What?**

TYLER: Female, you know. Opposite of male. In human beings, except in very rare cases, the sex that never attempts to grow a moustache, that doesn't often go out for football, that –

BRUCE: Have you lost them all?

TYLER: What?

BRUCE: Your marbles? Have you gone psycho, nuts, crazy, insane, goofy, looney –

TYLER: Enough! I get your point.

BRUCE: What is this male/female thing? What are you talking about?

TYLER: You spend so much time with the piano, that I thought it must be...well... *(Shrugs)* **like a girlfriend or something.**

BRUCE: I suppose there is, indeed, some basic truth in your implication.

TYLER: Do you have to do that?

BRUCE: To what, exactly, are you referring?

TYLER: Sound like an English teacher.

BRUCE: You speak in your fashion; I shall speak in mine.

TYLER: Oh, man!

BRUCE: *(Chuckling)* **Gotcha!**

TYLER: You did that on purpose?

BRUCE: You're right. It's time I quit. I'm being really rude, huh? Your parents bring you all the way here for the weekend, and all I do is sit at the piano.

TYLER: So what do you want to do? Walk to the corner for a Coke? Hey, I saw this movie advertised. A sequel.

BRUCE: To what?

TYLER: Some old flick?

BRUCE: What old flick?

TYLER: Something called "The Piano."

BRUCE: I saw that...on TV. Long time ago. About how this woman's husband chops off her finger.

TYLER: Yeah, that one.

BRUCE: So what's the new one?

TYLER: "The Piano's Revenge."

BRUCE: What?

TYLER: That's the name of it. This woman has a metal finger and clicks it against the keys. The piano can't stand it. The indignity. The constant click, click, click. The sour notes the woman's students play. The piano comes to life, yanks out one of its strings, one of the thin ones up near the top, and when the woman isn't looking, it attacks her. Stretches the string, this tough length of wire, around her neck and yanks. Now it's not just a finger. It's her head. Her whole head. It falls to the floor. Bang. Rolls down the steps just as her husband's coming home. What's he going to do? He finds this mask. This rubber mask. Frankenstein's monster or maybe the president of the U.S. He grabs it, runs to her head, grabs her brains, and quickly stuffs them –

BRUCE: All right, all right! I admit it. You put one over on me.

TYLER: Anyhow, Bruce, old buddy, old pal, how are we going to spend the rest of the day?

BRUCE: I'd like to...I mean I wish you could meet...

TYLER: *(Recognizes that BRUCE is serious, that he probably wants to say something important.)* **Yeah?**

288

BRUCE: Nah, it's dumb.

TYLER: What is?

BRUCE: I met this girl.

TYLER: Ah-ha! A real one, not a piano girl with black and white keys for teeth. *(Pause)* I'm sorry. I don't mean to kid around. It's like... *(Suddenly laughs.)* Maybe it's like the piano with you. I can't seem to help it. Anyhow, you were saying...

BRUCE: Her name's Dolly, can you believe?

TYLER: You mean like in "Hello, Dolly"? *(Stands, bows, does a dance step or two, looks at the audience and opens his mouth as though he is going to sing. He stops and turns to BRUCE.)* **Or as in the country-western singer who...** *(Simultaneously, he thrusts his two fists against the middle of his chest so his elbows stick out resembling large breasts)* **...has these great, immense –**

BRUCE: Stop!

TYLER: Stop?

BRUCE: I want to talk to you, seriously. You thought I was being melodramatic before! *(Sighs.)* She's perfect. Really perfect, except that...

TYLER: What's the problem?

BRUCE: Let me tell you about her first, OK?

TYLER: Sure.

BRUCE: I was on the bus coming home. It was crowded. I was trying to find a seat, and the bus...lurched, I guess. I started to fall. And as it turns out, I fell into the only empty seat on the bus. Right next to this girl.

TYLER: It was an accident. I'd be embarrassed, too.

BRUCE: You don't understand. We started to talk. You know me, Tyler. How I am around girls.

TYLER: I think so. Like a marble statue with moving eyes. And even the eyes look frozen in fear.

BRUCE: That's the way I've been.

TYLER: Me, too. Don't know why. I'm this comedian, you see. But around girls I can't talk at all, let alone normally.

BRUCE: But I did talk. We talked. Dolly and I. We really hit it off. She's...oh, God, she's beautiful. Beautiful body, beautiful soul.

TYLER: My God, you mean she let you take a peek at...her soul.

BRUCE: *(Exasperated)* Tyler, this is important. All right?

TYLER: I'll try to restrain myself. I really do want to hear about her, Bruce. I do.

BRUCE: I know. I wouldn't tell you if I thought...

TYLER: So tell me.

BRUCE: We really hit it off. She told me I was a...a "very refreshing man."

TYLER: Man? Wow, I am impressed.

BRUCE: Well, that's the problem.

TYLER: What is? You don't mean she wanted to...you know? I mean the "Me woman, you man" bit.

BRUCE: Oh, no, no. Nothing like that. *(Pause)* Did you ever read *Don Quixote*? Ever see *Man of La Mancha*?

TYLER: I read the book. You know how I usually have my nose in a book. *(His voice becomes Tarzan-like.)* At school I act like big macho he-man; want to kill saber-toothed tigers. *(Overplaying the melodrama)* But you know my secret life, my sordid occupation with things...printed on paper.

BRUCE: I saw the play, long ago at Canal Fulton near Canton, Ohio. We were visiting my aunt. She works there. It's a dinner theatre. She's like in charge of the kitchen or something. I saw the play. And...I know. Damn, it's going to sound stupid. But it's like Dolly's my...my...

TYLER: *(Neutral tone)* Dulcinea?

BRUCE: Right. My ideal woman. And I feel like the nut case who's out fighting windmills.

TYLER: Why, for heaven's sake? It sounds like you two –

BRUCE: It's like now that I met her, I would never want to date other girls.

TYLER: You have...gone to a movie or something?

BRUCE: A piano concert.

TYLER: Of course, why didn't I guess!

BRUCE: No, listen, Tyler. It's serious. I...God, I'm fifteen, and I...I really love her.

TYLER: I...guess I can understand that. What is it then? She doesn't feel the same about you?

BRUCE: Oh, yeah. No. I mean, she does. At least I think she does. She says she does.

TYLER: You're losing me.

BRUCE: She's a sophomore –

TYLER: And so are you.

BRUCE: At Junior Pitt.

TYLER: Oh, my God, an older woman. Is that what it is? Let me guess. Your folks say –

BRUCE: No! My folks don't know how old she is.

TYLER: They haven't met her, right?

BRUCE: Mom has. *(TYLER looks puzzled.)* She had to drive us to the concert.

TYLER: Oh, geez, so how did you keep her from finding out? How *could* you keep her from finding out?

BRUCE: We sat in the back seat.

TYLER: So far as I know, you don't own a cop car.

BRUCE: What?!

TYLER: Your mom doesn't drive a limo?

BRUCE: *(Irritated)* No!

TYLER: Then there's no barrier, no grill or soundproof glass.

BRUCE: Oh. *(Shakes his head.)* Much simpler. This was my first...my first real datc, OK? I asked Mom please not to talk to me or to say anything about me.

TYLER: And especially not to embarrass you by talking to Dolly.

BRUCE: Right.

TYLER: I still don't understand. Why are you worried? Afraid your mom will ask questions later or what?

BRUCE: The problem isn't Mom. *(Another sigh)* Dolly thinks I'm a sophomore, too.

TYLER: Oh, the light begins to dawn. You were wearing a suit, right? *(BRUCE nods.)* And your thick glasses. *(BRUCE nods again.)*

TYLER: And that dumb felt hat!

BRUCE: Hey, it's a great hat.

TYLER: For someone fifty years older than you are! I never understood why you always insisted on wearing –

BRUCE: When I was younger, I thought I looked younger.

TYLER: Duh...

BRUCE: Younger than I was. I thought the hat —

TYLER: Uh-huh. So why do you wear it now?

BRUCE: *(Feeling miserable, he shrugs.)* I don't know. You see, I was coming home from my piano lesson, which I told her. Dolly, I mean. And she assumed I was studying at Pitt. I wanted to tell her, but I didn't get the chance...No, that's not true. I did get the chance. I just didn't take it. I...Oh, man. Right away, I knew.

TYLER: Knew what?

BRUCE: She was the one. The one love of my life. And I couldn't bear to lose her.

TYLER: Really got it bad, huh?

BRUCE: It's true.

TYLER: So what are you going to do?

BRUCE: I don't know.

TYLER: Why don't you practice?

BRUCE: What?!

TYLER: The piano. Come on. You didn't put in nearly as much time as you wanted.

BRUCE: What's that got to do with it?

TYLER: It's simpler.

BRUCE: Simpler?

TYLER: The piano. Playing the piano. It's a simple thing, a piano. Much, much simpler than a...nineteen-year-old?

BRUCE: Yeah, nineteen.

TYLER: Than a nineteen-year-old woman is. Just deal with the piano then. Go play the damned piano!

Scene iii

(The lights come up on a park bench. It's near the end of May. School will soon be out for the summer, both at Southmont High School and the University of Pittsburgh. DOLLY and BRUCE enter Stage Right. Although BRUCE seems eager to hold DOLLY's hand, she pointedly avoids any physical contact. They sit at opposite ends

of the bench.)

DOLLY: *(Making a deliberate show of dropping BRUCE's hand)* **I don't understand, Bruce. It's like you have this whole secret life.**

BRUCE: Secret life?

DOLLY: I call and your mother says you can't come to the phone.

BRUCE: My mom?

DOLLY: You're not a sophomore at Junior Pitt, are you, Bruce?

BRUCE: What do you mean?

DOLLY: No more games, Bruce. *(Pause)* **OK, I admit that I've played my share of games, too.**

BRUCE: What do you mean?

DOLLY: Manipulative. Trying to get you to like me. It's just that I've never met another ma – never met another *boy* like you. When I said you were refreshing, I meant it. I really did.

BRUCE: Manipulative? No. I went into this with my eyes wide open.

DOLLY: And full of stars!

BRUCE: What do you mean?

DOLLY: Answer my question, will you? You're not a sophomore.

BRUCE: Yes, I –

DOLLY: For once, please, no games.

BRUCE: OK. No games. I love you.

DOLLY: Love me!

BRUCE: Yes, I love you. I've never loved anyone else in the way that I –

DOLLY: Love me? How many other women – girls – have you met?

BRUCE: Lots! I've known lots of girls. Dozens and dozens.

DOLLY: *(Laughing)* **Dozens and dozens, huh? And of those dozens and dozens, how many have you actually dated?**

BRUCE: Dated?

DOLLY: Yeah, you know, gone out with. Like with me. To concerts, movies, restaurants.

BRUCE: Not many, I admit. What is this? What's going on?

DOLLY: I like you, Bruce. I want to be your friend...

BRUCE: But! I hear a "but" at the end of that sentence.

DOLLY: OK, straight out. I guess I was wrong.

BRUCE: Wrong? What do you mean?

DOLLY: I trusted you.

BRUCE: Trusted me! Dolly, I'd never try anything...you know what I mean.

DOLLY: You'd never try to take advantage, the way we kidded around about on the bus. The day we met. Yeah, I know that. I said you're a gentleman, and you are. You're bright; you have a great future. I've never heard you play the piano, but I can tell. In my whole life I'll never be that dedicated to anything. Don't you know me well enough to realize that?

BRUCE: I don't understand.

DOLLY: Sure, I want to be a psychologist. A damned good one. But we're different, you and me. I'll do a good job, but I won't live that job, that role.

BRUCE: OK, all right. I know I'm...what? I get carried away with the piano. I can't help it. I can't explain it. *(Pause)* Well, maybe. I've – I've always been a misfit. *(Big sigh as he shakes his head)* I have this friend, my best friend, I mean besides you. He's the only person I've told that too. He's a misfit, too.

DOLLY: Stop it, Bruce! I'm not your best friend, not by a long shot.

BRUCE: What do you mean?

DOLLY: I don't want to hurt you. I really don't. In my own way, I suppose, I do love you. I'd never want to do anything...Damn it!

BRUCE: *(Scoots closer and tries to put his arm around her shoulder.)* You love me, and I love you. Isn't that all that's important?

DOLLY: *(Slides away, but at the same time picks up BRUCE's hand and gives it a squeeze. She continues to hold his hand in both of hers.)* Bruce, will you give me an answer? An honest answer, please?

BRUCE: About what?

DOLLY: Will you?

BRUCE: You know I'd do anything for you. I was talking to Tyler, my best friend Tyler. I told him you were like my...my Dulcinea. My ideal.

DOLLY: Ideal? Me? I don't think so. Cervantes' book. Don Quixote de la Mancha.

BRUCE: Exactly.

DOLLY: Do you know the story? Have you read it?

BRUCE: No. I saw the musical. Two or three years ago.

DOLLY: It's romantic rot!

BRUCE: *(Shocked)* What?!

DOLLY: Dulcinea wasn't real. She was an idea this crazy old man had in his head. The woman he fantasized was nothing more than –

BRUCE: Stop! Stop it, Dolly. I love you. My God, don't compare yourself –

DOLLY: I'm not what you want me to be. No one could be what you want me to be.

BRUCE: But you are! You're beautiful...sweet...wonderful...

DOLLY: You romanticized me. I'm an older woman. You're flattered by my attention.

BRUCE: It's not true –

DOLLY: That I'm older?

BRUCE: That I romanticize you.

DOLLY: No one can live up to your sort of expectation! No one, except maybe...God!

BRUCE: Dolly, it's you I love.

DOLLY: For God's sake, Bruce, you're only fifteen!

BRUCE: Sixteen.

DOLLY: Yes, in a couple of days.

BRUCE: You know? How could you –

DOLLY: Does it matter how I found out?

BRUCE: That doesn't mean we have to –

DOLLY: You're right. In itself it doesn't mean much of anything. *(Laughs.)* Yeah, I suppose my friends back home, my family even, would think it weird I've been dating a kid three-and-a-half years younger than I am. But I wouldn't care about that. Surely, you can see enough of the real me to know I wouldn't have hangups about –

BRUCE: Is it that I...misled you? Made you think I attended Pitt?

DOLLY: No, it's not that...exactly.

BRUCE: I never lied. Not outright.

DOLLY: I take your word for it. And I respect your word, Bruce. You're the kind of man – boy – who wouldn't hurt anyone. Not deliberately.

BRUCE: Then what is this all about? *(Pause)* You mean the world to me, Dolly.

DOLLY: Surely not. Your life is ahead of you. You have years to find a woman to love. Right now you should be concentrating on the piano, a love affair that will probably last.

BRUCE: I love you as much as I could love any damned piano.

DOLLY: As much as? *(Laughs.)* At least, I think that was an honest comment. *(Smiles sadly.)* Maybe they stem from the same place inside your heart, your soul. I don't know; I'm not a psychologist yet who can answer that kind of question. I don't know that a real psychologist can. But they're different. You can't equate passion for a person and passion for a thing! A job, an occupation.

BRUCE: I didn't mean it that way. I didn't!

DOLLY: Look at me, Bruce. Look me in the eye and tell me what you did mean.

BRUCE: I – Dolly. You're my one true love.

DOLLY: You're a sophomore in high school! When I was a sophomore in high school, I suppose I romanticized everything, too. Every emotion was so intense.

BRUCE: And it's not now?

DOLLY: You'll always be here in my heart. I promise you. Always.

BRUCE: This sounds as if – as if you want to –

DOLLY: It didn't add up, Bruce. Your not driving, my never seeing you at school, the *private* piano recitals. At most schools I know of, anyone can attend. Anyone can listen in who wants to. So I asked around, not to spy on you, but to surprise you. To root for you. To cheer you on. You've meant a lot to me, Bruce. *(Pause)* I suppose if it were one of my friends, a girl my age dating a fifteen-year-old – *(Pause)* In five or six years, I suppose it wouldn't matter. But at our age – your age and mine – we're worlds apart. Can you see that? Can you understand?

BRUCE: Yes, but –

DOLLY: I admit I thought a lot about it. I really never have met anyone as refreshingly different as you. I mean that in the very best sense. You said you were a misfit –

BRUCE: The piano was always there, always something I could turn to, something I could be good at. You're right. I didn't mean to say I love you with the same kind of passion I love the piano. I love you, the person. I love what I can learn and do and become because of the piano.

DOLLY: You don't need to explain. *(Pause)* What I started to say was that even after I knew there was this difference in our ages, I tried to figure how it could work. I thought of dropping out of school and getting a job. Saving money till you caught up, till you go to college. It wouldn't work.

BRUCE: Why wouldn't it? *(Pause)* No, it wouldn't. I wouldn't want to hold you back, make you "wait" for me. Your goals are as important as mine.

DOLLY: So you see...

BRUCE: But –

DOLLY: What do I see then? I see that though you don't want it to be this way...and honestly, I don't either, it hasn't a chance.

BRUCE: What did you start to ask me?

DOLLY: Ask you?

BRUCE: You said to look you in the eye and give –

DOLLY: Me an honest answer. *(Shakes her head.)* It doesn't matter now.

BRUCE: It matters, Dolly. I'd do anything, anything I could to be with you –

DOLLY: Would you quit school? Give up the piano? Move with me to Pittsburgh next year?

BRUCE: I... Oh, God, Dolly –

DOLLY: You couldn't, could you?

BRUCE: With me it was the piano! With my friend Tyler it was always clowning around. Because we're misfits. That's how we became best friends. Then he moved away. He's shy; so am I, you know that. It took all the courage I had to – to talk to you that day. Tyler's the same. He pretends to be an extrovert, only because he's afraid. Well, I am too. He's a reader, wants to be a writer and maybe a part-time comedian. I want to play the piano. Be really good at it, the best I can possibly be.

DOLLY: Just as it wouldn't be right in your eyes for me to work while you finish high school, I couldn't expect you to quit. *(Laughs.)* Anyhow, what would people think? Besides...

BRUCE: What?

DOLLY: Your folks. They'd never let you do it.

BRUCE: I suppose they wouldn't.

DOLLY: It wouldn't be fair for either of us. *(Pause)* I was going to ask you before if you know what love is. I don't mean that to be cruel. I don't even know if I know what it is to give your whole life over to someone else, place your future in that person's hands. You're a manchild, Bruce! A manchild, right in between. Neither a child, nor a man yet. *(BRUCE starts to interrupt.)* Please, Bruce, let me finish. I don't mean that as a put-down, a way to hurt you. I just mean to state a fact of life. Maybe in other times it was different. Maybe kids of twelve or fourteen were ready for marriage. I don't know if their biological clocks ticked faster. Maybe. Sure, lots of girls my age are married and settled down, so to speak. I'm not ready for that. I've thought it through.

BRUCE: Love isn't enough? Isn't it important that —

DOLLY: Love...In six months or a year, you'll have forgotten all about me.

BRUCE: Never, Dolly. I would never forget you. You're more important to me than —

DOLLY: *(Placing her fingers against his lips)* No more, Bruce. Please don't say anymore. Both of us have a lot of exploring to do. A lot to look forward to.

BRUCE: God, Dolly! I told my friend Tyler...I told him you were the one great love of my life. And I mean it! I really mean that. I'll never date anyone else.

DOLLY: Shhh!

BRUCE: I never will.

DOLLY: Bruce, believe me, I care for you. But you have to go your way, and I have to go mine. It would be nice if several years down the road...You know what I mean?

BRUCE: I guess so.

DOLLY: But it's not likely to happen. Both geography and interests are going to keep us apart.

BRUCE: I'll wait. I'm willing to wait.

DOLLY: I'm not so sure I am. Suppose...just suppose...that in year or two I meet a man who's my age, a man who's finishing school or maybe already finished –

BRUCE: Please don't say it!

DOLLY: But I doubt even that. In my own way, I'm determined. No, I don't have the passion that you do. But I want my bachelor's degree, and my master's and maybe even a Ph.D. No one in my family has even gone to college. Most never finished high school. Can you understand then how important it is –

BRUCE: You've made up your mind?

DOLLY: Ah, Bruce. *(She leans forward and kisses his forehead.)* I don't want to hurt you. I don't.

BRUCE: I'll always love you.

DOLLY: *(Laughs.)* Think of that five years from now and see if it's true. I do hope you'll remember me with fondness though.

BRUCE: Always, Dolly.

DOLLY: Can I ask you something?

BRUCE: Anything.

DOLLY: Did you ever tell your mother how old I am?

BRUCE: *(Shaking his head)* No...but I'd never, ever be asham –

DOLLY: I have an early evening class. I have to go now if I'm going to make it.

BRUCE: Will I see you again?

DOLLY: *(Rising)* I love you, Bruce. *(She pauses for a second and rushes Off-Stage Left. BRUCE gazes after her for a second, his shoulders droop, and he holds his face in his hands. The lights dim to black.)*

Scene iv

(The action occurs in the living room of BRUCE's house, which is arranged as in Scene ii. TYLER is seated in the same chair he occupied previously. BRUCE is seated on the piano bench or stool,

but he's facing TYLER instead of the piano.)

TYLER: What happened?

BRUCE: She broke it off.

TYLER: Broke it off? I thought you two were like peas in a pod, catsup and french fries, a hot dog and mustard –

BRUCE: Tyler!

TYLER: Sorry. *(Pause)* **It's the way I do things. Avoid what's unpleasant. Not face reality.** *(Pause)* **Why, Bruce? Why did you two break up?**

BRUCE: I...I'm not really sure.

TYLER: What?

BRUCE: I'm not! Sure, I mean. We talked too much. Too many things. Too many reasons.

TYLER: There had to be something.

BRUCE: Oh, yeah! Not just something. Everything! Just...God... everything!

TYLER: Remember Mrs. Philbun? Ninth grade English?

BRUCE: What's this got to do with English, for God's sake?

TYLER: She always said to narrow the topic. Don't write about everything. Don't write about the Revolutionary War. Write about George Washington. Don't write about George Washington's whole life. Just pick an incident or a day or –

BRUCE: I think you fail to see the seriousness –

TYLER: I thought she really influenced you.

BRUCE: Who did!

TYLER: Mrs. Philbun.

BRUCE: What?!

TYLER: "Everything." That's too broad.

BRUCE: I thought you were my friend.

TYLER: Good old Tyler, everybody's friend. *(Pause)* **I'm trying to make you feel better.**

BRUCE: Never in my life am I going to feel better.

TYLER: Isn't that a little extreme? Hey, man, you knew her for what? Three months, four months?

BRUCE: Four months, three days, five hours –

TYLER: You're kidding. You actually keep track –

BRUCE: If you ever meet anyone like her...

TYLER: Did you think that maybe our tastes in women are different?

BRUCE: That's not what I meant. Look, if you met someone you fell in love...at first sight.

TYLER: I did that...once.

BRUCE: You never told me.

TYLER: My teddy bear. When I was two years old. Couldn't stand to be separated from that bear for more than five minutes. Screamed my head off when Mom insisted on washing him. Poor old thing. Panda, I called him. He wasn't a panda; I just liked the name. I'd think about him squishing around in the washing machine. Then I'd watch through the little glass door in the dryer. You know how some dryers have little glass doors.

BRUCE: For God's sake, Tyler.

TYLER: Spinning around. Not knowing which end was up. Banging his head, banging his butt. And his poor little arms spread out pleading for me to rescue him from extreme abuse. Poor old thing. Finally got to be too much for him. Fell apart on me. I mean it. Literally fell apart. Do you realize the things they stuff those bears with? *(BRUCE sobs and leaps to his feet.)* Bruce!

BRUCE: *(Stops and turns.)* What?!

TYLER: I'm sorry. *(Pause)* I can't help myself. I can't. Do you think I need to see a psychiatrist?

BRUCE: Is this another one of your so-called jokes?

TYLER: No! I'm giving it to you straight. I live in my own little world. I think you know what it's like to do that. I created the world to block out everything unpleasant. Except...except for when you and I lived close. Except when we saw each other every day.

BRUCE: *(Crossing slowly to his seat)* Everyone always thought I was weird. I don't like football. I don't like baseball.

TYLER: Can I ask you something? Seriously.

BRUCE: *(Vulnerable)* I suppose so.

TYLER: I, uh...don't mean – It's not meant as an insult.

BRUCE: What is it?

TYLER: Do you think maybe this is why you...fell so hard for Dolly?

It was really fast.

BRUCE: How long does it take to know you've met the love of your life?

TYLER: I can't answer that, Bruce. I've never had the experience.

BRUCE: *(Shrugs.)* Maybe there's truth to what you say. Dolly said almost the very same thing.

TYLER: Oh?

BRUCE: That I was idealizing her. Romanticizing. That she wasn't like I thought she was. It's like she thought I was placing her on a throne, a pedestal.

TYLER: Were you?

BRUCE: I don't know. I'm all screwed up over this. Really. Didn't know anyone could feel so miserable...except with a terminal illness or something. *(Sits.)* But I loved her. I do love her. Does it matter if I see her differently from the way she really is?

TYLER: I'm not the one to be giving suggestions on this. *(Smiles.)* But I guess that never stopped me.

BRUCE: What kind of suggestions?

TYLER: Suppose she didn't break it off. Suppose you somehow worked this out. I don't know how, since you're in high school and she's going off to Pittsburgh.

BRUCE: That's what she said. The last part, I mean, about working it out.

TYLER: Can you think of yourself a year from now, two years, three? Would you still feel the same? Maybe you'd start to see the warts and the chin hairs.

BRUCE: Chin hairs!

TYLER: You know what I mean. Nobody's perfect.

BRUCE: Dolly's as close to perfect as anyone I've ever known.

TYLER: Present company excluded, of course.

BRUCE: *(Bitter laugh)* Yeah, sure. Present company excepted.

TYLER: Hey, look, I didn't mean – I was just trying to cheer you up.

BRUCE: Nothing can ever do that. I told you months ago, just after Dolly and I met. In all of my life there'd never be another person like her.

TYLER: Listen to me, Bruce –

BRUCE: No! Let me say this. I want you to understand. No matter how long I live, there will never be another person like Dolly. Nobody who can even approach her perfection.

TYLER: As you see it, you mean.

BRUCE: Whatever, damn it! Does it matter?

TYLER: *(Shrugs.)* I guess not.

BRUCE: I want you to understand something. I made a vow, a solemn promise.

TYLER: What kind of promise?

BRUCE: No matter how long I live, I will avoid close relationships. I cannot stand the hurt. Dolly said I had two passions – her and the piano. That's right, I did. Now I have one.

TYLER: My God, Bruce, do you know what you're saying? You're condemning yourself to some kind of hell here on earth.

BRUCE: Not of my making.

TYLER: Dolly's, you mean.

BRUCE: No, I don't mean Dolly. I mean fate. Me. The way I am. Who would ever love me like Dolly – *(Sobs.)*

TYLER: *(Gets up and goes to him. Awkwardly pats his shoulder.)* Hey, Bruce, that's not right. We're kids. Sixteen. Juniors in high school, for God's sake. We have our whole lives –

BRUCE: The most important thing I'll ever have in my life is gone.

TYLER: I can't believe this.

BRUCE: You think I'm being overly melodramatic!

TYLER: Yeah, Bruce, I do.

BRUCE: Well, I mean it. All I have now is the piano. There never will be anything else.

TYLER: You have...a good friend. Trustworthy, loyal, helpful, friendly, courteous – Oh, man, Bruce, you really can't mean this.

BRUCE: I do.

TYLER: What about your mom and dad? Your sister? Aren't they important?

BRUCE: Don't do this to me, OK?

TYLER: What am I doing, man? Just trying to help you out. Don't they...Don't I...count for anything?

BRUCE: You'll always be my best friend. I'll always think of you that way.

TYLER: What's that supposed to mean, Bruce? Come on, tell me, what's that supposed to mean?

BRUCE: I told you. I have the piano. Oh, yeah, I'll finish school. Go to a good conservatory or wherever, but only so I can concentrate more completely on the only passion that's left. The one real thing that gives my life meaning.

TYLER: You don't know what you're saying. And, hey, what am I, a piece of garbage? We've been best friends –

BRUCE: I know. And I value the friendship. I do promise, as long as I can, I'll keep in touch. I will.

TYLER: It's not like you're going to Mars or another galaxy or something. I don't know what you mean.

BRUCE: I'll try to spell it out for you then. There was Dolly and the piano. Two passions. In order to cope with the loss of one, all I can do is concentrate more completely on the other. There won't be time nor a place for anything else in my life.

TYLER: How can you say that?

BRUCE: May I ask you a favor?

TYLER: Anything. Don't you know that?

BRUCE: Would you...Since you drove here yourself, you can stay as long as you like or go whenever you want.

TYLER: Within reason. I got a summer job. At a bookstore.

BRUCE: Will you...please – I don't want to hurt your feelings. I don't want you to remember me –

TYLER: Remember you. Hey, you're not thinking of...killing yourself or –

BRUCE: No, I promise that, at least.

TYLER: Remember you...

BRUCE: As your best friend. Think of the fun times. The weekends together. Going to summer camp together. Riding our bicycles for whole day trips.

TYLER: I remember. I wouldn't ever –

BRUCE: Please, Tyler. It's the only favor I'll ever ask. Will you leave? Will you...just pack your things and then go?

TYLER: We're never going to see each other again?

BRUCE: I didn't say that. I need to be alone.

TYLER: I think you need company. More than you've ever needed it before in your life.

BRUCE: Please, Tyler, please!

TYLER: Sure, Bruce. OK. No problem. *(BRUCE and TYLER stare at each other as the lights dim to black.)*

Epilogue

NARRATOR: As you surely have seen, Bruce is the important character here. He was my friend. He was the one I cared about. Dolly is the one who precipitated the action. The inclusion of myself is only a device to clarify and define it.

Who knows? I might have liked the real Dolly, had I met her. Or again, maybe not. At that age, a nineteen-year-old woman seemed of a different world. I have little idea what the real Dolly looked like, except superficially – long brown hair, skin like porcelain, emerald green eyes, lips in a perpetual pout, at least according to Bruce.

In a way this story has a happy ending; in a way, it does not. Bruce went on to become the well-known concert pianist that he is – record contracts, concerts in Africa, Asia, Europe. For years we kept in touch, saw each other whenever we could, phoned each other frequently. Then one day the phone rang, and I had the sense that something dreadful was about to happen. Or did I? Sometimes it's difficult to separate fact from fiction.

At any rate, Bruce called to tell me he'd kept his vow. He'd never dated another woman. "Why, for heaven's sakes?" I asked him. "Why! You remember what I told you that day after Dolly left me." "I remember," I told him. "But that was so long ago." "I suppose," he said. "But I was stuck with my vow. Every concert I gave, every new piece of music I played, I dedicated my performance to Dolly. Only she kept me going. Do you understand?"

"No, Bruce, I don't. I don't understand."

"Well...nevertheless," he said, "I wanted to tell you that I've decided to break all associations except those concerned with my playing. I will totally dedicate the rest of my life to my music, which, in turn, is dedicated to Dolly."

That's the last I heard from him. I've seen him, as you most certainly must have – getting out of a limousine, shoving past reporters at various concert halls across the globe. From what I hear, he never talks to anyone, except out of necessity for his music. Perhaps, then, his two passions combined into one and gave us one of the greatest pianists the world is ever likely to know.

(Curtain)

Production Notes and Considerations

Throughout the play, Bruce has two passions, in his eyes pretty much equal, and they mean everything to him. Almost nothing else, even his close and nearly lifelong friendship with Tyler, seems to mean much. He is focused too much on his infatuation with Dolly and his love for the piano to allow anything else to intrude.

When he loses one, he has lost that which gives half his life meaning. Because of this he feels he has no choice but to concentrate on the remaining half to the exclusion of all else.

When performing the play, keep in mind that Dolly is a character who is twice removed from the present. First, the character has been recreated from what Tyler has been told (and even that was long ago). Second, even the memories are more inexact than those we usually carry with us. This is because they are second-hand, having come first from Bruce's perceptions of Dolly, which cannot have been objective due to his feelings for her, filtered through Tyler's memory. Thus she is not a "real" character. She is a composite of memory and imagination. She is nebulous, hazy, not quite human.

The only truly developed character is Bruce, and even he is shown through Tyler's memory. Yet because he is the focus of the play, he is much more well-rounded than Tyler. On the other hand, he cannot be a completely well-rounded individual in that he is so obsessed by the piano and by Dolly and then becomes even more obsessed when Dolly breaks off their relationship. Bruce cares little about any other facet of his life, even going so far as to ask his one friend in life to leave.

In playing the role of Bruce, you need to try to understand a person so caught up in his passions that he excludes almost everything else, and to understand how he transfers one of these obsessions to the other so that it becomes the entire focus of his life.

Tyler is less complicated in a way because he is more a device through which to tell Bruce's story. Yet, since Tyler the Narrator is telling about Tyler the young man, he cannot help but allow the audience to catch glimpses of who and what he is — a shy, introverted kid who constantly cracks jokes as a defense against life.

Once more, the staging can be simple with only various pieces of furniture to mark the various locations. Bruce dresses much "older" than he is, but otherwise the costumes can be casual and fairly contemporary, even though the play takes place at some time in the past. It, of course, would be better to avoid any clothing fads since that would contradict the fact that the play does not take place in the present.

Bored!

Comedy of Manners originated in seventeenth-century France with the playwright Molière, who felt that the purpose of comedy should be to correct social absurdities. The idea is to use wit and humor to point up these absurdities so they will be corrected.

"Bored!" is really a parody of Comedy of Manners in that it exaggerates the idea that the wealthy are too jaded about life to enjoy it. Since they can afford whatever they want, material things have no further meaning. There are no surprises nor struggles. Everything is too easy.

The sketch exists for fun, rather than to correct a social ill. In fact, the message is that while boredom is not a social evil that affects others, it is not good for the person experiencing it.

Further satirized is the idea that although the wealthy may be bored, they still are envied. Paula wants to experience the sort of life Marlene has. Marlene wants something that will interest her. Yet despite wanting to change places, the girls are perceptive enough to see that a permanent switch wouldn't work since there are advantages and disadvantages to each style of living.

The idea of changing places is an old one, seen, for instance, in such tales as Twain's *The Prince and the Pauper*. In "Bored!" the switch in lifestyles satirizes the conviction that "the grass is always greener on the other side of the fence." For a time, it may be, but no lifestyle is completely satisfactory.

CHARACTERS: MARLENE, 15; PAULA, 15. They resemble each other.
SETTING: The action takes place in Marlene's room at home.
AT RISE: MARLENE and PAULA are sitting in MARLENE's room talking.

Scene i

MARLENE: Oh, life is so boring. Once you have everything, there's little need to go on.

PAULA: My heavens, Marlene, you're fifteen years old.

MARLENE: I've seen it all. What's the point of seeing more of the same?

PAULA: You really think you've seen everything?

MARLENE: Everything worth seeing? Of course. Everything worth seeing; everything worth doing; everybody worth knowing.

PAULA: What?!

MARLENE: Rock stars, movie stars. I've met them. None of them interest me any longer. Not a one of them. Everything is boring.

PAULA: You've met –

MARLENE: Everyone. Absolutely everyone. I sometimes see no point in going on.

PAULA: You're not thinking of...I mean –

MARLENE: *(Terribly bored)* Oh, no. Mumsy did tell me that when she and Daddy go to the theatre tonight, they'll stop off and buy me a second BMW. This one platinum-plated. Gold, you know, is so flashy and trite.

PAULA: Trite?

MARLENE: And boring.

PAULA: You're getting a platinum-plated BMW?

MARLENE: Of course. To go with the one that's gold-plated. Everyone has one, you know. Everyone worth –

PAULA: But you're not old enough to drive.

MARLENE: Oh, no, but I do have dear Ronald.

PAULA: Ronald?

MARLENE: My personal chauffeur.

PAULA: I didn't know.

MARLENE: One never mentions these things. It's so boring.

PAULA: When did you start to feel so bored?

MARLENE: Perhaps I was born that way. I mean, when you can have everything you want or need, how can you not be...bored?

PAULA: Is there nothing you enjoy?

MARLENE: Perhaps my new BMW. For a moment or two.

PAULA: I have a suggestion.

MARLENE: *(Bored)* All right, Paula, I might as well hear it. *(To the audience)* I know it will be boring. Everything is.

PAULA: Give everything away.

MARLENE: Are you insane!

PAULA: No, I'm just trying to keep you from being bored.

MARLENE: Well, just how do you mean...give everything away? Would Mumsy and Daddy allow such a thing, even though no one denies that I'm spoiled?

PAULA: Perhaps they wouldn't, but couldn't you...

MARLENE: What, Paula?

PAULA: Not use what you have. Get a job after school. Earn your own spending money.

MARLENE: How boring.

PAULA: Have you tried it?

MARLENE: Certainly not!

PAULA: Why not?

MARLENE: I told you, Paula. It would be boring.

PAULA: Have you ever had a job?

MARLENE: Of course, I've never had a job. Daddy had a job...once. He saw no future in it. He gave it up after a day.

PAULA: A day!

MARLENE: Not quite a day, actually. It was so boring.

PAULA: What sort of job, was it?

MARLENE: Chairman of the board. And he was...bored!

PAULA: The board of what?

MARLENE: I don't know. General Motors, Alcoa...something like that.

PAULA: You've never tried any sort of work?

MARLENE: Are you joking?

PAULA: Maybe you'd enjoy it.

MARLENE: Can one...enjoy a job?

PAULA: Many people do.

MARLENE: Oh, how boring.

PAULA: Will you stop saying that.

MARLENE: What, Paula?

PAULA: That everything is boring.

MARLENE: Oh, but it is.

PAULA: Come on, give it a try.

MARLENE: *(Yawning in boredom)* **Give what a try?**

PAULA: A job.

MARLENE: What sort of job?

PAULA: I don't know. Bagging groceries.

MARLENE: Groceries! For other people, you mean!

PAULA: Yes, of course.

MARLENE: People actually do that for other people?

PAULA: You know they do, Marlene.

MARLENE: Not my sort of people.

PAULA: What...sort of people are your people?

MARLENE: Boring people.

PAULA: All right then.

MARLENE: What?

PAULA: We look quite a bit alike, do we not?

MARLENE: What does that have to do with anything?

PAULA: I have a job bagging groceries.

MARLENE: You?

PAULA: Yes. To earn extra money.

MARLENE: How do you mean..."extra."

PAULA: Marlene, this may come as a shock. But not everyone is
wealthy.

MARLENE: I see. You yourself have just one BMW.

PAULA: This may come even as a worse shock. I don't have even one
BMW. My family doesn't have a BMW. We have a ten-year-old
Chevrolet.

MARLENE: Whatever for?!

312

PAULA: For transportation.

MARLENE: Isn't a BMW better?

PAULA: Not everyone can afford BMWs, Marlene.

MARLENE: "Not afford"? I'm not acquainted with "not afford." What does it mean?

PAULA: It means not having enough money to buy something.

MARLENE: Are there situations like that? Do some actually not have enough money to buy something?

PAULA: Yes, many people.

MARLENE: Hmmm.

PAULA: What are you thinking?

MARLENE: Where would I meet such people?

PAULA: I meet many of them.

MARLENE: Where?

PAULA: At the store where I work.

MARLENE: How do you know that?

PAULA: Often they can't buy all the groceries they want.

MARLENE: You're not serious.

PAULA: Of course, I'm serious.

MARLENE: This, I do not understand. Would you...I mean...

PAULA: Yes?

MARLENE: As a matter of curiosity, would you show me such people?

PAULA: Even better than that, I'll let you become acquainted with some of them.

MARLENE: Acquainted?

PAULA: Do I detect a hint of interest?

MARLENE: Anything not to be bored.

PAULA: I'll take you to the store where I work, and on the way I'll explain how to bag properly.

MARLENE: It might be...interesting.

PAULA: You'll have to do it for the evening.

MARLENE: Evening?

PAULA: I work from six till nine.

MARLENE: And you will show me how.

PAULA: Yes.

MARLENE: Why would you do that?

PAULA: I told you, so you can meet...the customers. And maybe you can keep from being bored.

MARLENE: Do you really think so?

PAULA: As I said, I'll explain. It's simple. And you can take my place.

MARLENE: Your place? *(PAULA nods.) **Ooh**,* it sounds delicious.

PAULA: And I'll take your place.

MARLENE: My place?

PAULA: Yes.

MARLENE: But it's boring.

PAULA: Yes, well...I'll take my chances. *(The lights fade to black and come up a moment later.)*

Scene ii

(The action occurs in MARLENE's room. MARLENE and PAULA are seated as in Scene i.)

MARLENE: Paula!

PAULA: Yes?

MARLENE: You never came back.

PAULA: Oh, didn't I?

MARLENE: What's the matter?

PAULA: I'm bored. I'm so bored.

MARLENE: Bored! I don't understand.

PAULA: Your Daddy and Mumsy gave me the platinum-plated BMW. You're right. Gold is trite. Very trite.

MARLENE: I don't understand.

PAULA: I've met everyone, done everything, and it's boring.

MARLENE: No, it's not.

PAULA: Oh, but I beg to differ.

MARLENE: Paula, you did this deliberately.

PAULA: Oh, let's just not talk about it. I find the subject too... *boooring.*

MARLENE: I liked the job. But I started to miss Mumsy and Daddy.

PAULA: Miss them? I don't understand.

MARLENE: Neither do I. But I want to come back. I want to see

them again.

PAULA: But that would be tedious.

MARLENE: I went to your house.

PAULA: How very fortunate.

MARLENE: This has gone on long enough!

PAULA: Oh, definitely. It has gone beyond the point of boredom. On past dreariness and into monotony.

MARLENE: I have an idea.

PAULA: Is it anything but boring?

MARLENE: I hope it isn't tedious.

PAULA: Tell it to me then before I fall asleep from all this... boredom.

MARLENE: Do you miss your folks?

PAULA: Oh, I suppose so. My mind is too dulled –

MARLENE: Exactly. And you'd like to see your folks and go back to your job.

PAULA: I would? Hmmm. Perhaps I would.

MARLENE: We can change places again. Any time we want.

PAULA: Any time?

MARLENE: When we're bored or not...pampered enough. When we miss our folks.

PAULA: Tell me more.

MARLENE: I'll give you back your job...for a week.

PAULA: A week?

MARLENE: And I'll come back to live with Mumsy and Daddy. By then I should be bored!

PAULA: And I will long to be pampered.

MARLENE: Exactly.

PAULA: How fortunate we are to be friends!

(Curtain)

Production Notes and Considerations

The boredom felt by Marlene and later by Paula is highly exaggerated and unrealistic and is a satire of people who project that they find life monotonous. This is pointed up by extremes — Marlene's father working for less than an entire day, Marlene's not knowing what "can't afford" means, and in Paula's becoming completely jaded in two weeks.

The only requirements of setting are two places for the girls to sit. The acting style, particularly for Marlene in the first scene and for Paula in the second, should be a highly exaggerated parody of boredom. For humorous effect, there should be a distinct change between the acting styles of the two girls from one scene to the other.

The Valedictory Speech

Although "The Valedictory Speech" is a monolog, it is of a particular type that has been called by other names. In vaudeville, for instance, it was sometimes called a comic lecture. In minstrel shows, a similar type of presentation was the stump speech, which used the same sort of humor but dealt with a current topic. In the present, it is an example of standup comedy of the sort presented in a night club or comedy club setting where most often the comedian stands for the entire presentation.

A piece such as "The Valedictory Speech" always has at least most of the following characteristics. It relies largely on nonsense, though some such speeches do make more sense than others. Usually, it is built around a certain theme. "The Valedictory Speech" is unified around the idea of someone's delivering a graduation address. There often is contradiction, which adds to the humor. For instance, there is no possibility that anyone who speaks the way the character does in "The Valedictory Speech" would ever graduate at the head of his or her class. Much of the humor comes from this.

Nearly all monologs of this type rely on malapropisms, that is, substituting words that sound somewhat like the appropriate word but mean something entirely different. An example in "The Valedictory Speech" is using Basket of Robins for Baskin Robbins. This sort of monolog also relies on puns, such as Howe for how.

Pieces such as this almost always are delivered in a dialect. One of the most popular is an exaggerated fake Dutch or German dialog, such as Franklin or Fran Candace use.

CAST: FRANKLIN STEIN, 17-18; or FRAN CANDACE STEIN, 17-18, depending on whether the monolog is delivered by a boy or a girl.
SETTING: The action occurs at high school commencement exercises.
AT RISE: FRANKLIN or FRAN CANDACE is behind a lectern or perhaps a speaker's stand resting on a table.

FRANKLIN STEIN or FRAN CANDACE STEIN: Ladies und gentlemen, good evening, if you care to haf one.

Let me introduce yourself to me, und den I introduce mineself to yous. Yous are dem audience vat come to see dem graduated exorcisms. As you know, dat is vere dem principal exorcises da whole bunch of us young mens und womens from haunting de sacred halls from dis building no more.

Take dis principal, Mr. Conn. *(Glancing over his/her shoulder and then back toward the audience)* **Ghengis, we call him...for short.** *(He/she holds out his hand as if indicating someone between four and five feet tall.)* **Anudder liddle joke 'cause yous know he stand mit seven feets to his full height. I see dat some of yous ain't so smart as me, so I explain vat I mean. From de place he touch da floor to da rug on dat top of his shiny bald dome be five of dem feets. Und den we count da two he has in his shoes und on which he stands. Makes seven feet. Like dey say, he ride tall in da saddle. Of course, to do dat, he haf to saddle da tyrannis rex. But as every vun knows, tyrannis is dead for un long, long time.**

I promised I introduce me to you, though your program say who I am, already. But yust to re-mind you since your old minds are crazy or all used up. Re-mind you? Give you new minds! Dat is funny, nein? *(Pauses and shakes his head.)* **Nein.**

As I was sez, before I vas so rudely interruptering mineself, mine name is Val. Val E. Dictorian. *(Pause)* **Another liddle yoke, you vill forgive me, no?** *(Pause)* **Aw vell, too bad. Maybe den I should tell you mine real name is Franklin [or "Fran Candace] Stein. Sounds Churman, no? I'm really Dutch. But since I being born in dat country of da good old U.S.A, you vonder, "Vere does dis young man [or woman] get dat accent den?"**

Yous vants to learn dat? *(Pause)* I tell you anyhow. Ven Mama und Papa be goin' together, Papa haf not enough money for two. So ven dey go to movie show or to ice cream Basket of Robins or vatnot, each pay for his own self or hers.

You know vat dats called? Yous don' know? Let me give you dem new minds still vun more time 'cause you all be pretty dumb und could use dem. OK? So I tell you vat is called. Dutch treat. So naturally, ven I vas born, I come into dis world mit big Dutch accent. But mein fodder is Churman und mein Mama is Scandanahoovian, und so mein talking is very mixed all up together. Vy, you ask? Don' ask. I ain't gonna tell yous.

Vich brings me to der topic of dis evening, written by me for your knowledgeability und enjoinment. Is how anybody can be vatever dey vant, so long as dey finds dem lucky stones or dems four-leaf clovers or goes to home economicals class. Laugh all yous vant, but is true.

Let me tell you story about some big discoverizations und inventations. So Howe am I going to do dat? I tell you Howe. Elias Howe. *(Pause)* You vant to laugh now, you can laugh. *(He spreads his hands and waits for a beat.)* Vun day Elias vas in school, something like dis school right in front of yourn very nosses und under de feet of your souls. Vell, not eggsactly like dis school. It vas a liddle less like Alcatraz maybe. *(Shrugs.)* I don' know. Maybe.

Anyhow, Elias und dis friend of hims is valkin' down der hall from dis home economicals class dey had. Vy dey takin' home economicals, I don' know. But dat be der vay it happening. So Elias is telling dis friend dis yoke. It go someting like dis.

"You know de summertime goin' to be here soon. Und den dere is going to be lots of bugs. Dem katydids. But dey lie all de time. You know vy? Dey never did! Und anyhow dey ain't all named Katy or nothing like dat. Some of dem be Sally or Pieter. Und den dere are dos ants. Don' worry about dem neither. Mitout dem uncles dey gonna die off real soon. But den we got dem fleas. Und dats vat dey do real quick. Dey flees in a flash. Dats 'cause dem fireflies lights da way for dem. Und dat really burns me up 'cause I like to see dem fireflies flashing. But da fireflies flash da flees flight so dey don' flounder along dere way. Und dat not be good for da fleas 'cause dey don' want to be eaten by no flounder und maybe drown too." Is hokey story, nein? Ja. But vat can yous do? Dis is Elias Howe told it. *(Irritated with self)* Nein. Nein. Wat I mean is...dis is *how* Elias told it.

All da time dis friend be laughing und laughing. Den Elias grabs dis friend's arm so he's be sure to listen. Und he tell him, "But de ting I really don' like am dose flies. I want dem tings to scat. To scoot." Und he look at dis friend und real serious he asks him, "Do you know da best way to shoo dem flies?" Da friend shakes his head und says, "How?" Elias tell him, "Dats being mine name, all right." Da friend rephrase da question. "Vat is dere vay to shoo dem flies?" he ask.

"First ting you catches dem. Den you get dem tiny liddle nails und dat tiny liddle hammer. Den you trow dat fly on it'sn back und grabs it'sn little leg real tight. Und den you hammer on da shoes."

And da friend says, "Elias, you keep me in *stitches*." Und Elias, he start ter tink, but he don' know quite vat about. Is worrisome, dis almost tought. But den da friend change dur subject und ask Elias Howe – how Elias – vatever – did on der home economicals test dey taken dat day. Elias yust shrug und tell dem friend he did not know. "Vat about you?" Und da friend tell Elias, "If you vants me to tell dem truth, I'd says dat in dat dere class I gots der 'A' pretty well sewn up."

Der tought Elias tried *(Tapping his temple)* to tink of before now is coming to da front of his'n brain. He is tinkin' of dem words da friend say. Vords like "stitches" und "sewn." Next dem friend says, "Not dat I vant to needle you or nothing, Elias, but if you put your mind..."

Und den right dere above Elias Howe's head comes on dis light bulb. Und who you tink be walkin' down da hall toward dem dere two boys und see dis bulb. Dat's right. Thomas Alva

Edison. Und he run down dat hall real quick 'cause he know he gots some inventing ter do. Und ven Elias see him runnin' und *bobbin'* up und down. Up und down; up and down, Elias gots no more doubts. He takes off running for da other door, 'cause he gots his'n own inventing ter do yust den too.

Vun more ting. I'ne forgotten to tell you da name of dat friend of Elias's. I vill tell yous. But vait vun minute, vill you please? I vant first to tell you dat dis boy left standin' dere, he look outside und see de rain be comin' down hard. Und since it be cold, dis boy tink dat maybe dis rain is going soon to turn itself inter sleet. Und he haf der key to der whole ting right den. Vat he vas going to do. Der day before dis one, he vas trying to talk to his fodder, which his fodder didn't vant to take der time right den to answer. Und so da fodder tell him to go fly der kite.

Ya, dat is right. Dis vas Benjamin Franklin. Und him bein' un goot und obedient child, dat's vat he plan to do. Like his fodder tell him, "Go fly der kite." But instead he tink to himself. No, it is getting too cold to fly der kite today. Instead, I'm going to go home und invent us a stove. But maybe I invents some spectacles first so I can see yust how to invent dat dere stove. But Howe iss off inventing his own machine mit der tread und needles, und Benjamin Franklin tink...scw vat? Yous get it, or does yous need ter be re-minded vun more time? Nein? *(Shakes his head.)* Anyhow, Franklin be tinkin', Ja, der stove I'n be makin' iss going ter be hotter inventation den dat der sewing machine.

So you see, every vun can succeed in life if he takes a home economicals class or knows somebody else who has. Und so concludes my speeching for dis evening. I vant to leave you mit yust vun tought. Ven you leave here tonight und if it is raining, do not tie your car keys to a kite string. Tank you, ladies und gentlemens. *(He makes a low sweeping bow.)*

Production Notes and Considerations

The comedy is so broad that it comes across as hokey. It takes a certain type of performer, one who is completely uninhibited and unafraid of "bombing," to deliver this type of humor. If you are not the sort of person who feels comfortable with this, there is no reason you have to try to present it. However, if this type of piece appeals to you, you are free to make it as hammy or exaggerated as possible. Since it is low comedy, you can use as many gestures and exaggerated facial expressions and as much movement from place to place as you like, so long as it reinforces the performance rather than detracting from it.

Most of the dialect is indicated in the spelling. However, all "z" sounds, such as in the words is, his, has, and so on, should be pronounced as "s." For example, "his" should be spoken as "hiss" and "yous" as "yuss." Even though you are free to exaggerate, don't stray too far from the idea that this is a parody of a speech given by the valedictorian of a high school graduating class.

Most likely, the character would have notes — and this could be a hokey device in that they could be scrawled on odd-sized pieces of paper he or she keeps dropping and getting confused — and would use a speaker's stand. Other than that, no props or set is required. The piece is designed to be presented on an otherwise empty stage.

APPENDIX

Analyzing the Play

Questions like the following should help you analyze your character.

1. Figure out what the playwright hopes to convey to an audience both with your character and with the comedy as a whole. What, in other words, is the central idea or theme. Then think about the best way of communicating this to an audience.

2. Determine the prevailing mood and how best to convey it. Mood is not the same as the emotions your character feels. For example, a character could be angry, but the play itself could convey a sense of helplessness.

3. Unless you are doing a monolog, you need to get together with your director and fellow actors and agree both on theme and mood. Then work out together the way to emphasize these things for an audience. Try to remain true to the playwright's intentions. It would be both inappropriate and ineffective, for instance, to present "The Eyes Have It" as a realistic play.

4. When analyzing your character, consider:

   a. Present situation. Where does the character live? What country or area? What is the person's financial situation? Social status? How does all this affect what he or she is like?

   b. Origin. Where did the character grow up? Live most of his or her life? Is the culture vastly different from the one you are used to? How might all this affect the way a person thinks, feels, or believes?

   c. Age. If the character's age is different from your own, what can you do to make the person convincing?

   d. Major influences in the person's life. How do they affect beliefs and outlook?

   e. Personality traits. Is the character jealous, greedy, stingy, loving, caring and so on? How do you know this? How does all this affect the way the person comes across in a scene?

   f. Likeable personality. How do you feel about the character? What makes you feel this way?

   g. Relationship with the other characters. How does the character interact with others, and how do they feel about each other? How do you know this? Why is the character friends with one person, enemies with another, lukewarm with a third?

h. Goal to be reached. Every character has something he or she is working toward in each scene. For a minor character, it can be as simple as providing atmosphere. In "The Boy With Nine Lives," for instance, Jepson's assistant is largely to provide atmosphere, as well as a device for getting Ron and his mother to the television studio. The nurse provides atmosphere and authenticity. Sometimes actors' goals vary from scene to scene. At first Ron simply wants to save the kitten's life; then he wants to convince his mother that he hasn't gone back on drugs. Later he wants to avoid being bullied, and so on.

Take into consideration what your character wants and why the goal is important. Then figure out how you might portray the character's needs or wants.

5. Next you should meet with your director and the other actors to agree on everything you've discovered. Sometimes you may need to compromise.

If you are the type of person who normally uses a lot of gestures and movement in everyday life, you probably will use more in presenting your scene. But again consider whether your use of gestures matches that of the other actors in the play. Each person's style of acting should match that of the others, except where it deliberately is different. An example is the acting style of the parents versus the children in "Father Knows Better."

You should be guided by several things in the way you move and in your gestures: 1) the type of person your character is; 2) how you interpret the emotional situation that either calls for more movement, as anger or nervousness might, or less movement as fright could, 3) and how comfortable you are with gestures.

In "Ghoul," for instance, Sobinski certainly would move differently than Timothy.

6. Some people like to memorize the text before working on movement and gestures; others like to memorize everything at the same time. This is up to you and the director. Yet, remember that memorization is an individual thing, so what works well for someone else might not work for you.

a. Be certain that you know the meaning of each word and phrase. Although this is important for every type of scene, you may have to do more investigating of the meanings of words and references in historical pieces.

b. Memorize the ideas and the flow of the scene, along with your cues, so that you have the outline or the ideas firmly in mind before you try to memorize exact words.

c. Work on memorizing the scene the last thing before you go to sleep at night; this helps you retain it.

The analysis sheet that follows can help you because it often is better to write things out so you are sure you have covered everything important. But remember that you do not have to do the sheet in any particular order.

It might be a good idea for you to photocopy this sheet for each play in which you are involved.

Since the plays are comedies, you need to pay special attention to what is or could be funny and figure out how you can point it up. You can do this through timing (including pauses), changing your pitch, through the vocal quality you use, and through an increase or decrease in loudness.

Analysis Sheet

Title of the Play:

Playwright:

Theme or Central Idea:

Secondary Themes:

Overall Mood:

My Character:

 Where From:

 Age:

 Environment (Time and Location of Scene):

 Major Influences:

 Personality Traits:

 Motives and Goals:

Interests:

 A. Jobs:

 B. Hobbies:

 C. Friends:

Relationship With Other Characters:

Brief Description of the Other Characters:

About the Author/Editor

Marsh Cassady is the author of more than fifty books including novels, true crime, biography, collections of plays, short stories and haiku, and books on theatre and storytelling. His plays have been widely performed in the United States (including Off-Broadway) and in Mexico.

A former actor/director and university professor, he has a Ph.D. in theatre, is a member of Actors Equity Association and the Dramatists Guild, and has worked with more than a hundred productions. In addition, Cassady has taught various creative writing courses at UCSD and elsewhere. A former small press publisher, he also has been editor of three magazines. Since the early 1980s he has conducted all-genre writing workshops in San Diego and in Playas de Rosarito, Baja California Norte, Mexico, where he has lived since 1997. While teaching at Montclair State in the 70s, he started a playwriting program that included classes, workshops, and individual projects. He has won regional and national awards in the U.S. in playwriting, fiction, nonfiction, and haiku.

Cassady writes editorials, a column and occasional articles for *The Baja Times*, and his digital art and ceramic sculptures are exhibited in several galleries. He continues to write books in various genres.

Also by Marsh Cassady

Acting Games

The Theatre and You

Great Scenes From Minority Playwrights

Characters in Action

The Art of Storytelling

Spontaneous Performance

An Introduction to: The Art of Theatre

327

Order Form

Meriwether Publishing Ltd.
PO Box 7710
Colorado Springs, CO 80933-7710
Phone: 800-937-5297 Fax: 719-594-9916
Website: www.meriwether.com

Please send me the following books:

_____ **Funny Business #BK-B212**   **$19.95**
by Marsh Cassady
An introduction to comedy

_____ **The Theatre and You #BK-B115**   **$17.95**
by Marsh Cassady
An introductory text on all aspects of theatre

_____ **Great Scenes from Minority Playwrights**   **$16.95**
#BK-B207
by Marsh Cassady
Seventy-four scenes of cultural diversity

_____ **The Art of Storytelling #BK-B139**   **$15.95**
by Marsh Cassady
Creative ideas for preparation and performance

_____ **An Introduction to: The Art of Theatre**   **$24.95**
#BK-B288
by Marsh Cassady
A comprehensive text — past, present and future

_____ **Theatre Games for Young Performers**   **$16.95**
#BK-B188
by Maria C. Novelly
Improvisations and exercises for developing acting skills

_____ **Acting Games #BK-B168**   **$17.95**
by Marsh Cassady
A textbook of theatre games and improvisations

These and other fine Meriwether Publishing books are available at your local bookstore or direct from the publisher. Use the handy order form on this page. Check our website or call for current prices.

Name: _____ e-mail: _____ .

Organization name: _____

Address: _____

City: _____ State: _____

Zip: _____ Phone: _____

❑ **Check Enclosed**

❑ **Visa / MasterCard / Discover #** _____

Signature: _____   *Expiration date:* _____ / _____
          (required for Visa/MasterCard orders)

Colorado residents: Please add 3% sales tax.
Shipping: Include $3.95 for the first book and 75¢ for each additional book ordered.

❑ *Please send me a copy of your complete catalog of books and plays.*